Raspberry Pi
ASSEMBLY LANGUAGE
RISC OS
Beginners
Hands On Guide

Bruce Smith

www.brucesmith.info

Raspberry Pi Assembly Language RISC OS Beginners Hands On Guide

© Bruce Smith
ISBN-13: 978-0-9923916-2-1
First edition: 05 February 2014 [001]

Editor: Alan Ford Edits
Cover: Sumit Shringi, Graphic Designer (Book Cover-Design)
Typeset in 11 on 12pt Garamond by BSB using Serif PagePlus x6

Published by BSB – www.brucesmith.info.

Printed by CreateSpace.

Contents

List Of Programs

About the Author

Bruce Smith purchased his first computer — an Acorn Atom — in 1980. He was immediately hooked, becoming a regular contributor to the mainstream computer press including 'Computing Today' and 'Personal Computer World'. With the arrival of the BBC Micro his magazine work expanded into books and his 1982 title 'Interfacing Projects for the BBC Micro' (published by Addison Wesley) has become regarded as a classic of the time as the first book showing home users how to connect the computer to the outside world. He was one of the first to write about the ARM chip when it was released on the Acorn Archimedes in 1987.

Well over 100 books later Bruce has written about all aspects of computer use. His friendly, lucid style of writing caused one reviewer to write, 'This is the first computer book I have read in bed for pleasure rather than to cure insomnia!' Bruce's books have been translated into many languages and sold across the world.

Bruce also writes about sport and his publishers have included BBC Books, Virgin Books, Rough Guides, Headline and Mainstream Publishing. He has been a regular contributor for BBC local and national radio and has appeared on Channel 4s The Big Breakfast and BBC World Service.

Follow Bruce on Twitter: @brucefsmith

www.brucesmith.info

Preface

This original edition of this book was published under the title *Raspberry Pi Assembly Language Beginners*. The original title seemed to create confusion as to which operating system it dealt with, especially after the launch of *Raspberry Pi Assembly Language* RASPBIAN *Beginners*, which was an introduction to the ARM using GCC on the Raspbian operating system and its various Linux incarnations.

I thought it was a good time to substantially revise and update the original text and take the opportunity to rename the book—since it well over a year old—to make it clear where its sits in Raspberry Pi distro hierarchy. This new release contains several new chapters that deal specifically with features supplied by the Raspberry Pi system-on-chip structure and expansion ports. This includes a look at the Floating Point co-processors and how to program the GPIO port.

It should be acknowledged that there are many ways to archive a particular outcome when programming in assembly language and especially within the RISC OS environment. I am rather 'old school' in my approach to these matters and more of a traditionalist to the original RISC OS concepts.

The revision of this volume goes hand-in-hand with the release of *Raspberry Pi RISC OS System Programming Revealed* which could be considered a companion volume, especially if you wish to delve further into the working and operations of RISC OS. Note that a couple of chapters overlap between the two book, so please check the website at www.brucesmith.info if you are looking for specific information so as to ensure you do not double up.

Bruce Smith, *Sydney, January 2014*

1: Introduction

It didn't surprise me when, early in 2013, it was announced that the Raspberry Pi had sold one million units. And counting... It took me back more years — decades even — than I care to remember when it was announced that the BBC Micro had done the same. Both came out of businesses based in Cambridge in the UK and there were even more links between the two than you might imagine.

Both systems fascinated me and literally millions of other people. The first system took every last penny of my savings at the time, but the Raspberry Pi didn't even drain the cash in my wallet. But while the ticket price for each was vastly different, pretty much everything else about them was so familiar. Not least their ability to run a wide range of software and educational tools and how easy it was to connect external devices and control the outside world. I would suspect that most people who own one Raspberry Pi, actually own several.

For the first time since the BBC Micro there is an affordable and infinitely accessible system that just about anyone can use. Meanwhile, the PC and Mac have dominated the market and other more games-orientated boxes have been available. But none of these have impacted the technical home hobbyist user. The techsperts have had a variety of development boards to experiment and fiddle with, again mostly beyond the scope of the home hobbyist computer market. For the cost of a couple of music albums or new release DVD, the Raspberry Pi has changed all that. I wonder if the Raspberry Pi could be classed as the world's first disposable computer?

Imagination Unlimited

One reason for the birth of the Raspberry Pi was to make it easy for people to take up programming, with the aid of a competitively priced computer system whose use was limited only by the user's imagination. I hope this book will help many of you reading it realise that dream. In fact, it isn't a dream. It is a probability if you continue your way through the pages that follow — a first step on a rewarding and educational pastime. And, who knows, you may become part of a new generation of computer programmers working at the sharp end of what is possible.

This book provides an introductory tutorial in writing assembly language on the Raspberry Pi and specifically using RISC OS. Assembly language generates machine code that can be run directly on your computer. I first learned to program assembly language on the Acorn Atom (the BBC Micro's predecessor) and then on its successor (the Archimedes) the assembly language now used on the Raspberry Pi. If anything that proves that what you learn here should stand you in good step for many years to come. So it is a significant investment.

Start Experimenting

While this is not a book for the complete novice, you certainly do not require any experience with assembly language or machine code to be able to pick it up and start reading and experimenting. Programming experience would be beneficial and any structured language will have provided the groundwork for many of the fundamental concepts required.

This is a *Hands On Guide*, so there are plenty of programs for you to try for yourself. Learning to program is about experimenting, making mistakes and then learning from them. Experimenting by changing values and information is without doubt the best way to understand what is happening and is to be encouraged. All programs are available to download from the companion website. The book is equally applicable to the Model A and Model B and should not be affected by any later releases of the Raspberry Pi itself.

Learn By Example

The programs presented in this book are provided to illustrate concepts being explained with a simple and — where possible — practical application. I will not try to baffle you with long and complex listings; there is no need to. I will leave it to you to take the examples and information and combine them two, three, four and more at a time to create a useful outcome, learning a great deal along the way.

Some degree of 'chicken and egg' syndrome has been unavoidable, but I have tried to keep it to a minimum. Concepts are introduced in an order that goes with knowledge so far acquired. However, sometimes this is not always possible; in such cases I will highlight the fact. In such cases, you need to accept that it works and you will understand the how and why later in the day!

Programming really is fun. I have written a tonne of books on the subject and a good percentage of them have been about home computers — how to program and use them. I have never had a computer lesson in my life. If I can do it, so can anyone. It is also frustrating! There is not a programmer who ever lived, novice or expert, who has not spent an inordinate amount of time trying to solve a programming problem, just to realise later that the issue was right there in front of them all along. I would go so far as to say the real satisfaction comes when you solve problems for yourself.

One word of advice: If you can't solve something, walk away and do something else for a while. It's amazing how often the solution comes to you when you are doing something else.

What Will You Learn?

In a nutshell, you will learn to become a proficient assembly language programmer. By the end of this book, provided you have worked through and applied the example programs and small snippets of programs that are dotted through the text, you will be able to design, write and produce machine code programs to undertake any number of tasks. You will also have the grounding to allow you to delve into the more generic texts relating to the ARM chip and system programming on your Raspberry Pi.

Notation in Use

A standard notation has been adopted throughout this book. Number types and certain operations on numbers are common place in programming books such as this, and it is important to distinguish among them. The short list here is for reference. Their exact meaning will be described as we encounter them within the text of the book.

% or 0b   Denotes that the number that follows it is in binary or base 2. For example: %11110000 or 0b11110000

&   Denotes that the number that follows it is hexadecimal or base 16. For example: &CAFE

< >   Angle brackets or chevrons are used extensively to enclose a word that should not be taken literarily, but read as the object to use with the command. For example, <Register> means a register name, R0 for example, should be used in the angled brackets and not the word 'Register' itself.

Dest   Short for destination.

Operand1   The commentary in the text often talks about Operand1 and its use. The relevant values for Operand1 as defined at that point should be used. For Operand1, this is normally a register.

Operand2   The commentary in the text often talks about Operand2 and its use. The relevant values for Operand2 as defined at that point should be used. For Operand2, this is normally either a register or an immediate value.

Op1   Shorthand format for <Operand1> when space is tight.

Op2   Shorthand format for <Operand2> when space is tight.

( )   Brackets show that the item within is optional and may be omitted if not needed. For example, ADD (S) means that S may or may not be included.

Companion Website & Social Media

Go to **www.brucesmith.info** and follow the directions to the book companion pages. From the site, you can download all the programs and access updates to the book and additional information and features. In addition, links to other support websites and useful downloads can be found, along with details of forthcoming Bruce Smith Books publications covering the Raspberry Pi.

Like Bruce Smith at **www.facebook.com/authorbrucesmith** to receive updates on what Bruce is and has been up to and to ask questions. Follow Bruce on Twitter and to ask questions **@brucesfsmith** or via the Contacts page on the website. Check out an occasional blog **Alan Turing Rocks** which can be found on via the website.

Acknowledgements

Thanks to **Mike Ginns** for the concepts of several programs listed here. Some listings originate from his book *Archimedes Assembly Language* which was first published by Dabs Press in 1988. (A key to how old the ARM actually is!) Also I am grateful to **Brian Scallan** for his feedback on the original text.

Special thanks also to **Andrew Gregson** for his input, feedback and additional text concerning the chapters on GCC and C.

2: Starting Out

Assembly language gives you access to the native language of the Raspberry Pi – machine code. This is the tongue of the ARM chip which is the heart and brain of your computer system. ARM stands for Advanced RISC Machine, and it ultimately controls everything that takes place on your Raspberry Pi.

Microprocessors such as the ARM control the use and flow of data. The processor is also often called the CPU – Central Processing Unit – and data the CPU processes are digested as a continuous, almost never ending stream of 1s and 0s. The order of these 1s and 0s has meaning to the ARM, and a particular sequence of them will be translated into a series of actions. Just like Morse Code where a series of dots and dashes in the correct order has meaning if you know how each letter is represented.

Numbers with Meaning

A machine code program is a sequence of numbers which are a form of code and represent actions the microprocessor chip must take. In their basic form these numbers are endless strings of 1s and 0s. For example:

```
11010111011011100101010100001011
01010001011100100110100011111010
01010100011001111111001010010100
10011000011101010100011001010001
```

It would be almost impossible — or at the very least extremely time-consuming — to interpret what these numbers mean. Assembly language helps to overcome these issues.

Assembly language is a form of shorthand that allows machine code programs to be written using an English style lexicon. An assembler is a program which translates the assembly language program into the machine code, thereby taking away what would otherwise be a laborious process. The assembly language program is often just a text file and this is read by the assembler before being converted into its binary (1s and 0s) equivalent. The assembly language program is called the input or source file, and the machine code program the object file. The assembler translates (or compiles) the source file into an object file.

Assembly language is written using mnemonics. A mnemonic is a device that aids learning or acts as a reminder. This relies upon associations among easy-to-remember letter sequences that can be related back to the information to be remembered. You've probably encountered these at some point as acronyms. For example, to remember the colours of the rainbow you could take the phrase:

'Richard Of York Gave Battle In Vain'

And use the first letter of each word. Or use the fictitious name:

'Roy G. Biv'

A mnemonic language has developed around SMS messages sent on mobile phones. These enable text messages to be shorter and more compact. For example, 'L8R' for later', 'GR8' for Great and '2mrw' for 'tomorrow'.

ARM Instructions

The ARM chip has a specific set of machine code instructions that it understands. These operation codes or 'opcodes' and their use are really what this book is about. The ARM is just one type of microprocessor; there are many different types and each has its own unique set of instructions.

You cannot take a machine code program written for ARM and run it successfully on a different microprocessor. It simply would not work as expected, if at all. That said, the concepts introduced here can be applied with a broad brush to most other microprocessors available and are pretty consistent in application. If you learn to program in one, you are well on your way to programming others. Essentially you just need to learn a new set of mnemonics, and most likely many will be similar to the ones you are about to learn.

Microprocessors move and manipulate data, so not surprisingly many of the machine code commands deal with this control, and most instruction sets (the collective term for these mnemonics), include commands to add and subtract numbers. The assembly language mnemonics used to represent these tasks are typically in the form:

```
ADD
SUB
```

These examples are pretty straightforward as are many other ARM mnemonics, However, they can also appear complex when combined in a single line sequence. By breaking them down into their component parts their action can be determined without any real difficulty.

An assembly language mnemonic is normally three characters in length, but there are occasions when it may be longer. Like anything new, this may take a bit of 'getting used to', but if you work through the examples given in this book, and apply them in your own examples you should not have too much trouble.

MOV is the mnemonic for the MOVe command. It takes information from one place and moves it to another place. How hard was that?

The Transformation Process

Once you have developed your assembly language program you have to convert it into machine code. This is done using an application called an assembler. For example, when the assembler encounters the MOV mnemonic it will generate the correct number that represents the instruction. It stores the assembled machine code as a sequential file in memory and then allows you to run or execute it. In the process of assembling the program, the assembler also checks its syntax to ensure it is correct. If it spots an error, it will identify it to you and allow you to correct it. You can then try and assemble the program again. Note that this syntax check will only ensure that you have used the assembler instructions correctly. It cannot check their logic so if you have written something that has used instructions correctly, but not in the way that achieves what you wanted, it will assemble without error but will produce an unwanted result.

There are various ways to write an assembly language program. The first ARM chips were designed by Acorn and so not surprisingly appeared on a range of Acorn-based computers running RISC OS. This included the Archimedes and RISC PC. These machines ran BBC BASIC, which was innovative in that it allowed you to write assembly language programs as an extension of BBC BASIC. This method is still available to you today and it is the system we will us in this book not least because it is an effective 'user-friendly' method to employ that includes great error checking and verbose feed-back to you, which you will find infinitely helpful when, and you will, make mistakes. That said, towards the end of this book we'll spend a few chapters looking at how the GCC Compiler can be used to the same end.

Why Machine Code?

This is an easy question to answer. Essentially everything your Raspberry Pi does is done using machine code. By programming in machine code you are working at the most fundamental level of the Raspberry Pi operation.

If you are using a language such as BBC BASIC or Python then ultimately all its operations have to be converted into machine code every time you run the program. This takes a finite amount of time – in human terms lightning fast – but still time. This conversion or interpretation process does therefore slow the operation of the software down. In fact, even the most efficient languages can be over 30 times slower than their machine code equivalent, and that's on a good day!

If you program in machine code, your programs will run much faster as there is no conversion being undertaken. There is a conversion process when you run the assembler, but once you have created the machine code you can execute this directly — it is a one-off process. You do not have to run the assembler every time. Once you are happy with your program you can save the machine code and use it directly. You can also keep the assembly language source program and use it again, or perhaps make changes at some later point.

Language Levels

Languages such as BBC BASIC or Python are called high-level languages. High level languages are often easier to write as they have a more English-like syntax and also include commands that do a complex sequence of actions using one command that would otherwise take a long list of machine code instructions to perform. Machine code is a low level language as it is working amongst the 'nuts and bolts' of the computer: it spells out every technical step and detail and as a result is harder to understand.

This is the advantage of a high level language as opposed to a low-level one. That said, as you become more proficient in assembly language, there is nothing stopping you from building libraries of routines to do a specific task and just adding them to your programs as you write them. As you dig deeper into the world of the ARM, you will find that such libraries already exist out there in cyberspace.

By writing in assembler you can also transport your assembly language programs onto other computers or systems that use the ARM chip. You simply load the assembly language file into an assembler at the new destination, assemble it and run the machine code program.

Provided you take full advantage of the ARM chip's facilities you can even transfer and run the machine code directly. This has exciting possibilities when you consider that just about every Smart Phone and Tablet device available these days utilises ARM chips!

Into Orbit

Just to underline the power of the ARM chip and indeed smart phones in general, a whole new generation of satellites called CubeSats, are being placed into orbit around the Earth. They are small (about 10cms square) and have very specific tasks. The Surrey Space Centre in the south of England has designed several CubeSats that are powered by Android phones. At around $100,000 each, these satellites are a fraction of the cost of previous machines. At the same time, the computing power of a single smart phone is perhaps tens of thousands of times more than could be found in the computers on all the Apollo moon missions put together! This is all at your disposal on your Raspberry Pi.

Figure 2a. A Cubesat under construction.

The world is not all rosy! There are differences in the CPU releases. As with software, the ARM chip has gone through continual development and has had new version issues. But the base instruction set remains the same so 'porting' is not as hard as it might seem. It only becomes an issue if you are using more advanced features of the microprocessor. For this introductory guide, these changes are not relevant. Everything in these pages is applicable to your Raspberry Pi.

RISC and Instruction Sets

The R in ARM stands for RISC. This is an acronym for Reduced Instruction Set Computing. All CPUs operate using machine code and each of these machine code instructions or opcodes has a specific task. Together these instructions form the instruction set.

The philosophy behind RISC has been to create a small, highly-optimised set of instructions. This has several advantages — fewer instructions to learn for one — but obviously greater variation in their use. A lot of this will become apparent as we progress, and as you start to look at the instruction sets of other microprocessors.

Assembler Structure

Programming in any language, just like speaking in any language, requires us to follow a set of rules. These rules are defined by the structure and syntax of the language we are using. To program effectively, we need to know the syntax of the language, and the rules that structure the language.

The simplest way to design a program is simply to create a simple list of things you want it to do. It starts at the beginning and executes linearly until it gets to the end. In other words, each command is executed in turn until there are no more commands left. This works, but is very inefficient.

Program languages today are structured and allow you to build them as a set of independently executable procedures or subroutines. These subroutines are then called from a main program as and when they are required. The main program, therefore, controls the flow of control and also executes anything that may not be available as a subroutine. Programs are smaller and more manageable when they are created using subroutines. In a linear program concept, we would have probably had to repeat large sections of code several times to have achieved its goal.

Figure 2a illustrates some pseudo-program language to show how such a structured program might look.

```
main
      DO getkeyboardinput
      DO displayresult
      DO getkeyboardinput
      DO displayresult
END

.getkeyboardinput
      ; Instructions to read input from keyboard
RETURN

.displayresult
      ; print the result on the screen
RETURN
```

Figure 2a. Pseudo code illustrating a structured approach to programming.

In the example, program commands are listed in capitals – uppercase letters. Sections of subroutine code are given names – in lowercase – and are identified with a full-stop at their start. The entire flow of the program is contained in the six lines starting with '.main' and finishing with 'END'. Admittedly it is short, but it is clear to read, and you can understand just with a glance, what is happening. Each subroutine name is meaningful.

In this example, the main program just calls subroutines. In a perfect world, this would always be our aim because it also makes it easier to test individual subroutines separately before they are included in the main program. This helps to ensure our program works as we put it together.

Error Of Your Ways

One big challenge you face when learning any new program is locating errors. This process is known as debugging. I guarantee (and I have proven this many times) you will first write a program that does not work as expected. You will look at it until the cows come home and not see the error of your ways. You will insist you are right and the computer is the issue. Then like a bolt out of the blue, you will see the error right there staring at you — and this does not always happen when you are sitting in front of the keyboard.

By building a subroutine and then testing it separately, ensuring that it works, you will know when you come to use it as part of your larger program that your hair is safe for another day (by the way, mine is all gone...).

The Raspberry Pi ARM Chip

The ARM chip in the Raspberry Pi is (to give it its full title) a Broadcom BCM2835 system on chip multimedia processor. The system on chip (SOC) means that it contains just about everything needed to run your Raspberry Pi.

The BCM2835 uses an ARM11 design, which is built around the ARMv6 instruction set architecture. The more recent ARMv7 (and possibly subsequent versions as they arrive) are not compatible with the Raspberry Pi's ARMv6 and so software developed for the later version will not run on v6 unless it is modified first. We'll come back to the SOC towards the end of this book.

3: BASIC Environment

All the full program examples in these early chapters are written using BBC BASIC. The overriding reason for this is because BBC BASIC makes it easy and relatively straightforward to write, assemble and execute machine code. It will immediately flag up any errors you make, allow you to correct them, and try again. It also includes many additional tools that will help you as you develop your assembly language skills. (We will see how to use other assembly tools in due course and in particular the GCC Compiler and assembler.)

To use BBC BASIC you will need to install and run RISC OS. This is a tried-and-tested window based operating system (WIMP-Windows, Icons, Menus, Pointers).

From a machine code programmer's point of view, RISC OS provides an amazing library of ready-to-use machine code routines. It shouldn't be overlooked that there is also an extensive range of applications available for use with RISC OS, many of them free.

Emulating Pi

Because BBC BASIC is popular it is available on many other computers, sometimes running under an emulator. For example, it is possible to run BBC BASIC on a PC or a Mac and have access to the BBC BASIC Assembler. There are emulators to run RISC OS And to simulate the ARM chip. This means you can write and test files on PCs and Macs and transfer them onto your Raspberry Pi, and vice versa.

BBC BASIC and the Assembler are so inexorably intertwined that they share the same variables and workspace. Thus it is possible to initialise variables to useful values in BASIC and then use them in the assembly language program. For example, to create a constant we might use:

```
character=64
```

Thereafter we could employ the variable 'character' throughout the assembler program. This has the virtue that we need only alter this one variable and reassemble our software to update all its occurrences.

Your RISC OS World

From this point on, I will assume that you have RISC OS running. If you have used any form of windows environment before you should have no issues with RISC OS. Windows, Linux and Mac users will find it easy to adapt. RISC OS is also good at helping you with short prompts and messages if you try to do something it is not expecting.

The first thing you need to do is to get BBC BASIC running. There are a couple of ways you can do this. On some versions of RISC OS you will see a BASIC icon in the toolbar (to the left). Clicking on this will open BBC BASIC in its own window; however, you will not have access to any of the other items on the desktop through the mouse and pointer. The better solution is to run BBC BASIC inside its own task window. This way you can still use the rest of the desktop and all the other functions of RISC OS.

There are two ways to open this window. One is from the keyboard, by pressing the <CTRL> and F12 keys simultaneously (<CTRL>-F12). Alternatively, you can also access a task window by middle clicking over the Raspberry Pi icon in the task bar (bottom right hand corner) and selecting 'Task Window'. I will use the term 'middle click' here, but it is whatever button on your mouse you need to press to display a menu.

When the task window opens it will display an asterisk as a prompt. Select the window (move the pointer over it and click the mouse button) and type:

    BASIC

after the *. Then press the <RETURN> key. You will be presented with the BBC BASIC startup response screen. An underscore will be blinking. The '>' is the prompt, and it is immediately after this where you type your programs and commands. If you press the F12 key *without* <CTRL>, a task window will open under the Desktop. To exit this simply press the <RETURN> key at the '*' prompt.

RISC OS uses the middle button of a mouse to display context sensitive menus. On a PC-style mouse, this is often mapped at the scroll wheel in the middle.

Try entering this short program just to make sure everything is working:

```
10 FOR A%=1 TO 10
20    PRINT "TEST"+STR$(A%)
30 NEXT
```

If you type:

    LIST

At the '>' prompt, the program will be listed with each line printed to the screen in number order. Type:

RUN

You should now see the program go through its paces.

Keyboard Drivers

A couple of things to note: BBC BASIC is case sensitive so all commands must be in CAPS. Also, if your keyboard isn't configured correctly you may find that when you press the " key you get an @. If this is the case you might like to change the keyboard driver you are using. If you don't then there may be no way to generate the hash, '#', character that you will certainly need. Typing '#' may give you a pound character on the screen. These are more suited to a wallet than a keyboard.

In RISC OS changing the keyboard driver is simple. Type the following at the prompt:

*COUNTRY USA

or:

*KEYBOARD USA

Now if you try those keys the response should be correct. (If you want to stay with your normal keyboard driver, you may find that the '#' key can be reached using the '\' key on a normal PC keyboard. If not, then it is just a matter of trying them all until you find the key that produces a hash!)

Line numbers in BBC BASIC are mandatory (unless you are using an Editor to write your program - see later). You can turn on automatic line numbering by using the command AUTO at the prompt. You can exit by pressing the <ESCAPE> key. You can start automatic line numbering from any whole number that you wish:

AUTO 250

This will start line numbering at 250, which is great if you have entered part of a program already.

You will need to be able to save your programs. You can do this on your SD Card (there is a sub folder called 'Public" which is a good place for them) or onto a USB drive if you wish. The discs and storage devices that are available to you will be displayed in the left hand side of the Task Bar.

The SAVE command is used to save files:

SAVE "TestLoop"

BBC BASIC programs are saved as tokenised files. This means they are encoded to save space and also to make them execute quicker. You can clear memory of any 'loaded' program by typing NEW and you can load a program in with the LOAD command:

```
LOAD "TestLoop"
```

The LOAD operation replaces any existing program with the one from the disc if you haven't already used the NEW command. Besides loading a program, you can add a program to the end of the current one using APPEND. The appended program is renumbered to ensure that its line numbers start after those of the initial program.

By default the SD Card directory is set as the root directory '$'. If you do not change this then files will be saved to and searched for at that location.

Editing Programs

The BASIC line interpreter is fine for short programs but for longer files it is better to use an editor. StrongED is a popular choice amongst seasoned RISC OS users as it provides many excellent features. StrongED is supplied as part of the official RICS OS Pi release and, if not found on the desktop, will be in the Apps directory.

The editor that has been consistently supplied with all versions of RISC OS distribution is called (simply) Edit. Whilst this does not have the bells and whistles of StrongED it does the job and if you are a beginner I would suggest that you master it first before moving onto one of the other file editors like StrongED.

Edit is easy to use and five minutes of experimentation with a sample file will make you an expert! Edit can be found in the Apps directory which itself is located on the Task Bar on the lower left hand side of the screen. Click the folder and you will find !Edit in the window that opens. Double click on the icon and Edit will install on the right hand side of the toolbar. Place the pointer over the Edit icon and press the middle button to see a list of options.

(From now on when this text refers to 'click Menu' it means depress the menu button, the middle button as described above, and hold it down to display a context sensitive list of items.)

To start writing a new program, click Menu on the Edit icon and from Create choose BASIC. You can now type your program directly into the Edit window. Although in this BASIC line numbers are mandatory as I have explained, when using Edit there is no need to physically type them in because Edit will insert them for you when you save the file!

Click the menu button over the Edit window and select the Save option. You can enter a filename here and then click OK. Edit will save in the currently selected directory or, you can drag the file icon presented with the Save option to the window of your choice. Edit remembers this destination and will use it for future loads and saves. Of course, the window must be a portal to a device where it can be saved, like an SD Card or USB drive.

You load a BASIC program file in the same way, by using the Load option from the Edit menu. Alternatively you can drag the file icon into the Edit window. Unlike the BASIC line interpreter, if you drag and drop the file into an Edit window it will not overwrite any existing file; instead it will add it at the point where you dropped it. So make sure you drop the icon in a new window or onto the Edit icon on the task bar itself, which will open the file in a new Edit window. Dropping a file into an open window which already contains a file can have some weird effects on line numbers, so beware!

Edit Options

There are a couple of menu options worth looking at in the BASIC options submenu.

'Strip line number' creates an Edit file with no line numbers: Selecting this will toggle its actions (on being denoted by a tick to the left of the item). If your program contains a reference to a line number, for example GOTO 560, then an error message will be displayed asking whether you want to leave the number in or remove it. This option is on by default.

'Line number increment' sets the number increment among successive lines in the program. This sets the increment step for line numbers, 10 by default.

If you are saving a BASIC file from Edit which does not have line numbers in place Edit will add them, starting at 10 and incrementing by 10 per line. One point to bear in mind: If line numbers are used, Edit will not sort them into an ascending sequence and the resulting BASIC program may behave very strangely when you load it. As part of the conversion process Edit will also notify you if it finds common errors such as mismatched quotes or brackets. Once you have the BBC BASIC program loaded you can make changes directly.

You can use:

RENUMBER

at the BASIC prompt to renumber your program if desired. This might be useful if you make additions at the command line. If you have Edit running, you can send a BASIC program to the printer by dragging its file icon onto the printer driver icon.

4: The Assembler

Here is a listing that provides a wrapper for just about any assembler program you wish to write. It does absolutely nothing as there are no assembler mnemonic instructions included, but it is the framework you will need — the point here is to show the various components of a BBC BASIC Assembler program.

Program 4a: An assembly language framework.

```
 10 REM >Prog4a
 20 REM RPi ROAL
 30 DIM code% (100)
 40 FOR pass =0 TO 3 STEP 3
 50 P%=code%
 60 [
 70 OPT pass
 80 .start
 90 ; do nothing
100 ]
110 NEXT pass
120 END
```

Type it in, or download it from the website and LOAD it. Let's look at the program line by line.

10 REM >Program4a

This is a normal remark statement and is ignored by the program. What is interesting here is the use of the '>' before the program name. If you enter a program in this way in BBC BASIC and then just type SAVE, it will use the text after the '>' in the first REM statement as the file name. All programs are named by chapter in this book. If you have the program file from the website, then this program is identified by its name in the REM statement.

30 DIM code% (100)

The machine code the assembler generates will need to be stored in memory somewhere. This line reserves 100 bytes of memory, the start address of which is pointed to by the variable 'code%'. DIM is short for 'dimension' and it reserves the amount of space defined. By reserving this space, it is protected and cannot be overwritten by anything else the program might do. The amount of space you will need to set aside will depend on the size of your program and you will get a feel for this in due course. Suffice to say for now that it is best to reserve too much space than not enough. This may not be a problem for short programs, but with long programs if you do not reserve enough space you could overwrite information or corrupt your program. As we are assembling nothing this time then 100 bytes are more than enough!

40 FOR pass =0 TO 3 STEP 3

BBC BASIC uses a two-pass approach. This means it actually assembles your program twice. This is to ensure it can resolve any 'forward references' that you may make in the program. BBC BASIC programs are executed sequentially, line-by-line and in order. Any action that the program refers to that is not defined until a later line number would cause an error to occur. In this sample program, this feature, together with line 70, suppresses the error until the second pass, by which time all definitions will be known as the assembler, which has made one pass through the program already. For this sample program there are no such forward references — you could delete lines 40, 70 and 110 and it would have no effect. However, good habits are worth the effort and, for almost every instance you will encounter these three lines, or their equivalent, should always be included. The variable 'pass' is set to 0 on the first run and 3 on the second run. There are only two passes as the increment is 3 (STEP 3). On the first pass the variable 'pass' is set to 0, which suppresses errors, and on the second, 'pass' is set to 3, where the errors are reported.

50 P%=code%

The integer variable P% is special. It directs where each line of machine code is being stored in memory. So in this instance it is being pointed to 'code%' which is the start of the reserved space. This will become clearer when we run and assemble the program.

60 [

Square brackets '[' and ']' are used to mark the start and end of the assembly language program. When BBC BASIC encounters the '[' it invokes the assembler.

70 OPT pass

OPT is a special function which controls how the program is assembled. It must always be followed by a value. The value determines how the assembler creates the machine code. Here, the OPT value is provided by the variable 'pass'.

Because the assembly language is stored within a FOR...NEXT loop, OPT is set to 0 on the first pass and 3 on the second. We'll look at just what OPT can do when we re-visit the BBC BASIC Assembler later in this book. Broadly speaking, when OPT 0 is executed it turns off error reporting. When OPT 3 is encountered it turns on all error reporting.

80 .start

Anything preceded by a full-stop is deemed to be a label. This is a placeholder — a point you have marked in the program. In this case, the label is called 'start'. When the assembler identifies a label, it creates a variable of that name and stores its address within it. By defining labels in an assembly language program we can mark different areas which can be used as reference points. In the machine code itself the variable is not saved; instead it is the location marked by the variable that is used. Labels are often the items referred to in forward references.

90 ; do nothing

The ';' is used to indicate a comment follows and anything after it is ignored. This is also used to create empty lines to break the program up and make it more readable. It is the assembler version of BBC BASICs REM statement.

100]

The ']' tells the assembler to return to BBC BASIC.

110 NEXT pass

This invokes the second pass of the assembler.

120 END

This signifies the end of the program. It is optional.

The Assembler Listing

To assemble this program, just type RUN at the prompt. What you see should look something similar to that shown in Figure 4a. It may not be identical but the elements should be the same.

```
008FAC
008FAC
008FAC                    opt PASS
008FAC                    .start
008FAC                    ; do nothing
```

Figure 4a. The assembled output of Program 4a.

The left hand column shows the address in memory where the program is assembled. This may be totally different on your set-up; if so, don't be concerned. The label 'start', which in this case was assembled at 008FAC, can be seen along with the comments in the listing.

Add the following line to the program. You can do this just by typing it in as is at the BBC BASIC prompt:

```
115 PRINT "PROGRAM ASSEMBLED AT: &" ~code%
```

RUN the program again. Compare the assembly listing generated with your original. Note how the start address has changed. This is because the program is longer now because of the additional line. Thus, the first available space that can be used by DIM has also moved. One advantage of assembling into reserved space like this is that you don't have to worry about a change in program size as BBC BASIC does it all for you.

Let's add a few more lines to the program and something that assembles machine code that does something. The listing should now look like this. Lines 81, 82, 83 and 116 are new:

Program 4b: Print an asterisk to the screen.

```
10 REM >Prog4b
20 REM RPi ROAL
30 DIM code% (100)
40 FOR pass =0 TO 3 STEP 3
50 P%=code%
60 [
70 OPT pass
80 .start
81 MOV R0, #ASC("*")
82 SWI 0
83 MOV R15, R14
90 ; do nothing
100 ]
110 NEXT pass
115 PRINT "PROGRAM ASSEMBLED AT: &:" ~code%
116 PRINT "PROGRAM SIZE IS: &"; P%-start; " Bytes long"
120 END
```

RUN this to assemble the machine code which will look similar to that shown in Figure 4b (again the addresses may be different):

```
0009008
0009008
0009008                                          OPT pass
0009008                      .start
0009008    EAA0002A                              MOV R0, #ASC ("*")
000900C    EF000000                              SWI 0
0009010    E1A0F00E                              MOV R15, R14
0009014                      ; do nothing
Program Assembled at:  &009008
Program Size:          12 Bytes long
```

Figure 4b. The assembler listing with additional instructions.

The numbers in the second column are machine code. They are in a particular format called hexadecimal or base 16. As I have explained, the ARM chip executes machine code as a series of 1s and 0s. A compact way of expressing these often lengthy strings of bits (binary digits) is by using hexadecimal notation. If you look at the fifth line in the listing above, the first column gives the machine code &EAA0002A, if this was given in binary it would be a line of 1s and 0s that would total 32 in all. Imagine what that would do to your eyes! We'll examine this hex-binary relationship in due course.

Look at the three new lines of assembler. MOV and SWI are assembler mnemonics. Line 81 illustrates the versatility of the assembler and what makes it so easy to use. In the line:

MOV R0, #ASC ("*")

We used the BBC BASIC function ASC to look up the keyboard value for an asterisk. The assembler inserted the correct value, and if you look at the assembly listing, this is the &2A at the end of the numbers in the second column. Without this ability we would have had to look up the numeric value for '*' ourselves and would have had to use the literal value, thus:

MOV R0, #&2A

This integration with BBC BASIC can be as simple or complex as required. If it is a legitimate function, it will assemble correctly. Something like this is acceptable:

MOV R0, #INT (SIN (DEG 60) *100)

It looks complex but it will assemble! If you run the program, it will print a 'J' and by the end of this book you will be able to work out why!

Executing and Saving Machine Code Programs

By running the program above we have converted the assembler into machine code. To execute the machine code itself, use BBC BASIC's CALL statement at the command prompt thus:

```
CALL start
```

Here 'start' is the variable label which signifies where the machine code begins. When you CALL the program, you will see an asterisk printed on the screen. This machine code could also have been executed by typing:

```
CALL code%
```

or:

```
CALL &9008
```

In this last case use the value printed out on the screen by the 'Program Assembled at:' statement, as it may be different for you.

Once the machine code is assembled and is tested, you can save the actual code to disc. To do this you need to know the start addresses and length of the machine code. These should have been printed out by lines 115 and 116 of the program. The command *SAVE has this format:

```
*SAVE<filename><startaddr>+<length>
```

The address-related information is assumed to be entered as hexadecimal, and this is the format shown in the assembly listing. For the example above, the *SAVE command would look something like this:

```
*SAVE asterisk 9008+12
```

The *SAVE command does not know it is saving machine code; it simply saves an area of memory. The address of the last byte of memory saved is given by adding the length to the start.

Once you have the machine code file saved, you have something you can execute directly from a file. This can be performed using the *RUN command thus:

```
*RUN <filename>
```

To execute the asterisk program, enter the following at the command prompt:

```
*RUN asterisk
```

The program will load into the address where it was originally assembled and will then run. The result will be the asterisk as before. However, note that you have not been dropped back to the '>' prompt, but you are at the OS * prompt instead. To get to BASIC just type:

```
BASIC
```

and press <RETURN>.

If you are running machine code you can omit the RUN portion and just use the filename thus:

```
*asterisk
```

Here's a thought to ponder: If you extended your BBC BASIC program by a few lines, so that it extended into the space where the original machine code was loaded, and then you executed the machine code again using the *SAVEd version with *RUN what do you think might happen? The file will load in and run where it was originally created. Anything there will be overwritten and if it was part of a BBC BASIC program it would most likely corrupt the program. The point to remember is that when you are using machine code that is loaded in as an executable file it is you who has the responsibility for managing the contents of the Raspberry Pi memory. In general though, the worst thing that can happen is that the computer will hang or freeze. This must be remedied by cycling the power, which is usually merely annoying and time consuming.

A good tip is to always save your source program before executing the machine code, so that you have the original file to load back in if anything goes amiss. This is also why I like to avoid commands that call the machine code in the BBC BASIC listing itself, until it is tested. Once you run it you are committed.

If you are wondering how long an assembly language can be the answer is that it is probably governed by the amount of memory you have available to use. Remember this isn't just about how big the BBC BASIC program is — you have to leave space for the machine code to be assembled.

USR Calls

Another way of calling machine code programs is to use USR. This is similar to CALL; however, it allows you to pass a result back from your machine code. It takes the format:

```
<variable>=USR <address>
```

As you can see the address, which may be a variable, is used to identify where the machine code is located. A variable into which a value will be returned is specified at the left of the command. For example:

```
Result=USR start
Value=USR &9300
```

We'll look at how we return these values back in due course when we have a few examples to try, but for completeness here, we'll just say it is passed through the ARM register R0.

Any code called with USR should still always end with:

```
MOV R15, R14
```

Otherwise the program will not exit correctly.

Dumping Code

If you want to have a look at your machine code you can use *DUMP. This command takes the filename specified and then displays its contents on the screen in hexadecimal and ASCII. If you have the 'asterisk' file to hand try dumping it to the screen using:

```
*DUMP asterisk
```

You may need to resize the window to see it all, but what you should get is something like that shown in Figure 4c. Each line shows the address, hexadecimal value and ASCII value of each byte, with unprintable codes represented by full stops.

```
Address : 30 31 32 33 34 35 36 37 38 39 4A 4B
00009030: 21 00 A0 E3 00 00 00 EF 0E F0 A0 E1
```

Figure 4c. *DUMPed output of Program 4b.

Compare the *DUMP listing with the assembly listing and see what you notice; the numbers listed correspond with the opcodes assembled in the earlier listing.

A Comment On Comments!

Not everyone will agree, but I think it is imperative that you comment your assembly language programs extensively. The program code that you write today will be fresh in your mind, but if you need to upgrade or adapt it at a later date, you may be struggling to remember exactly what each segment does. To my mind commenting — that is good commenting — is an essential part of writing assembly language programs. Indeed, all types of programs. All assemblers allow you to place comments in your source file. Comments do not make the final machine code file any longer or any slower in execution. The only overhead is that they affect the size of your source program.

So comments are a good thing but don't comment for comments sake. If every line of your assembly language program had a comment it would become ungainly and takes away from the important comments. For example, look at this simple line and comment relative to the ADD operation:

```
ADD R0, R1, R2   ;   R0=R1+R2
```

The comment here is really pointless from a program documentation perspective as it merely repeats what the program line does in a slightly different way. What would be relevant here is detailing the significance of the values stored at locations R1 and R2. This might be a better comment then:

```
ADD R0, R1, R2   ; Balance of act1 + act2
```

If you break your assembly program into segments using the format shown in Chapter 1, then for a lot of the time a pertinent comment or two at the start of the section is often also enough. Some things to keep in mind as guidelines:

- Comment all key points in your program.

- Use plain English; don't invent shorthand that someone (even you, later!) may not understand.

- If it is worth commenting, then comment properly.

- Make comments neat, readable and consistent.

- Comment all definitions

If you keep these key points in mind you shouldn't go wrong, and I mention them at the start so you'll hopefully take the point and get into good habits that will last a programming lifetime.

If you are planning to write a lot of machine code, you might want to consider documenting your files externally, creating a database or perhaps a work book where you keep their details.

5: Bits of a RISC Machine

There are 10 types of people in the world — those that understand binary notation and those that don't.

If that statement leaves you confused then don't worry. After reading this section of the book you'll 'get' the joke. If you have already had a smile at it then you're well on your way to racing through this section. What I will say at the onset though is that a thorough understanding of the way binary notation is presented and how it can be manipulated is absolutely fundamental to effective, efficient machine code programming.

When you create machine code programs you are working at the most basic level of the computer. There is nothing below it. In the opening chapters we touched on binary and hexadecimal numbers. Hex numbers are actually a compact way of writing numbers which in binary would be long strings of 1s and 0s. Because of its design as a reduced instruction set computer, the Raspberry Pi can do many different things using a base set of instructions, and does so by getting the absolute maximum meaning out of every single one of these 1s and 0s. To understand fully how a RISC machine works we need to understand how binary and hex are constructed and how they are utilised by the ARM chip.

To recap from the opening chapters: The instructions the ARM CPU operates with consist of sequences of numbers. Each number represents either an instruction (opcode) or data (operand) for the machine code to execute or manipulate. Internally these numbers are represented as binary numbers. A binary number is simply a number constructed of 1s or 0s. Binary is important as internally these 1s and 0s are represented as 'on' or 'off' conditions (electronically usually +5V or 0V) within the microprocessor, and as an assembly language programmer we will often want to know the condition of individual binary digits or bits.

Opcodes and operands are built by combining sets of eight bits, which are collectively termed a byte. Convention dictates the bits in these bytes are numbered as illustrated in Figure 5a.

7	6	5	4	3	2	1	0

Figure 5a. Numbering of the bits in a byte.

The number of the bit increases from right to left, but this is not as odd as it may first seem.

Consider the decimal number 2934, we read this as two thousand, nine hundred and thirty four. The highest numerical value, two thousand is on the left, while the lowest, four, is on the right. We can see from this that the position of the digit in the number is very important as it will affect its weight.

The second row of Figure 5b introduces a new numerical representation. Each base value is suffixed with a small number or power, which corresponds to its overall position in the number. Thus, 10^3 is 10 x 10 x 10 = 1000. The number in our example consists of two thousands plus nine hundreds plus three tens and four units.

Value	1000s	100s	10s	1s
Representation	10^3	10^2	10^1	10^0
Digit	2	9	3	4

Figure 5b. Decimal weights of ordinary numbers.

In binary representation, the weight of each bit is calculated by raising the base value, two, to the bit position (see table below). For example, bit number 7 (b7) has a notational representation of 2^7 which expands to: 2 x 2 x 2 x 2 x 2 x 2 x 2= 128. The weight or value of each bit is shown in Figure 5c.

Bit Number	b7	b6	b5	b4	b3	b2	b1	b0
Representation	2^7	2^6	2^5	2^4	2^3	2^2	2^1	2^0
Weight	128	64	32	16	8	4	2	1

Figure 5c. The binary weights of numbers.

Binary to Decimal

As it is possible to calculate the weight of individual bits, it is a simple matter to convert binary numbers into decimal. The two rules for conversion are:

1. If the bit is set, add its weight

2. If the bit is clear, ignore its weight

Let's try an example and convert the binary number 10101010 into its equivalent decimal value.

Bit	Weight	Value
1	128	128
0	64	0
1	32	32
0	16	0
1	8	8
0	4	0
1	2	2
0	1	0

Figure 5d. Converting binary numbers to decimal numbers.

In Figure 5d, we add the value column to get 170. Therefore, 10101010 binary is 170 decimal (128+0+32+0+8+0+2+0). Similarly, the binary value 11101110 represents 238 in decimal as shown in Figure 5e.

Bit	Weight	Value
1	128	128
1	64	64
1	32	32
0	16	0
1	8	8
1	4	4
1	2	2
0	1	0

Figure 5e. Converting binary numbers to decimal numbers.

Decimal to Binary

To convert a decimal number into a binary number, the procedure is reversed — each binary weight is, in turn, subtracted. If the subtraction is possible, a 1 is placed into the binary column, and the remainder carried down to the next row. If the subtraction is not possible, a 0 is placed in the binary column, and the number moved down to the next row. For example, the decimal number 141 is converted into binary as shown in Figure 5f.

Decimal	Weight	Remainder	Binary
141	128	13	1
13	64	13	0
13	32	13	0
13	16	13	0
13	8	5	1
5	4	1	1
1	2	1	0
1	1	0	1

Figure 5f. Converting a decimal number to its binary equivalent.

Therefore, 141 decimal is 10001101 binary.

Binary to Hex

Although binary notation is probably as close as we can come to representing the way numbers are stored within the Raspberry Pi they are rather unwieldy to deal with. And row after row of 1s and 0s simply get lost as your eyes start to rebel and make funny patterns. When dealing with binary numbers we more commonly use an alternative form to represent them – hexadecimal or 'hex' for short. Hexadecimal numbers are numbers to the base of 16. This at first sight may seem singularly awkward; however, it really isn't and presents many advantages.

Base 16 requires sixteen different characters to represent all possible digits in a hex number. To produce them, the numbers 0 to 9 are retained and then we use the letters A, B, C, D, E, F to represent values from 10 to 15. The binary and decimal values for each hex number are shown in Figure 4g. If you have followed the previous section on binary numbers something interesting may stand out when you look at Figure 5g:

Notice how four bits of a binary number can be represented in one hex number. Thus, a full byte (8 binary bits) can be depicted with just two hex characters. Using decimal notation a byte would require three characters. Hex is a very compact and easy way of representing binary.

Decimal	Hex	Binary
0	0	0000
1	1	0001
2	2	0010
3	3	0011
4	4	0100
5	5	0101
6	6	0110
7	7	0111
8	8	1000
9	9	1001
10	A	1010
11	B	1011
12	C	1100
13	D	1101
14	E	1110
15	F	1111

Figure 5g. Decimal, hexadecimal and binary numbers.

To convert a binary number into hex, the byte must be separated into two sets of four bits, termed nibbles, and the corresponding hex value of each nibble extracted from the table above:

Convert 01101001 to hex:

```
0110 = 6
1001 = 9
```

The answer is 69.

Because it is not always apparent whether a number is hex or decimal (69 could be decimal), hex numbers are usually preceded by a unique symbol such as '&' (which is the notation used in this book):

```
&69
```

By reversing the process hex numbers can be converted into binary.

Hex to Decimal and Back

To transform a hex number into decimal, the decimal weight of each digit should be summed,

Convert &31A to decimal:

3 has a value of $3 \times 16^2 = 3 \times 16 * 16 = 768$

1 has a value of $1 \times 16^1 = 1 \times 16 = 16$

A has a value of $1 \times 16^0 = 10 \times 1 = 10$

Add these together to give 794 decimal.

Converting decimal to hex is a bit more involved and requires the number to be repeatedly divided by 16 until a value less than 16 is obtained. This hex value is noted, and the remainder carried forward for further division. This process is continued until the remainder itself is less than 16.

Example: convert 4072 to hex:

4072/16/16 −15= F   Remainder: 4072-(15*16*16)=232

232/16   =14 = E   Remainder: 232-(14*16)=8

Remainder =8 = 8

Therefore, 4072 decimal is &FE8.

Both of these conversions are a little long winded, and you can probably see why it is so much easier to work in hex and forget about decimal equivalents. In truth, this is what you will get used to doing. Although it may seem alien at present, it will become second nature as you develop your assembly language expertise. (Besides, if you want to convert hex to decimal, you can use the Pi!)

Binary Arithmetic

It is easy to add and subtract binary numbers. In fact, if you can count to two you will have no problems whatsoever. Although it is not vital to be able to add and subtract 1s and 0s 'by hand', this chapter introduces several concepts which are important, and will help you in your understanding of the next chapters and ultimately in programming the ARM.

Addition

There are just four simple straightforward rules when it comes to adding binary numbers. They are:

0+0=0   [nought plus nought equals nought]

1+0=1   [one plus nought equals one]

0+1=1   [nought plus one equals one]

1+1=0(1)   [one plus one equals nought, carry one]

Note in the last rule, *one plus one equals nought, carry one*. The '1' in brackets is called a carry bit, and its function is to denote an overflow from one column to another, remember, 10 binary is 2 decimal (and thus the opening funny!). The binary carry bit is like the carry that may occur when adding two decimal numbers together whose result is greater than 9. For example, adding together 9+1 we obtain a result of 10 (ten), this was obtained by placing a zero in the units column and carrying the 'overflow' across to the next column to give: 9+1=10. Similarly, in binary addition when the result is greater than 1, we take the carry bit across to add to the next column (the twos column). Let's try to apply these principles to add the two 4-bit binary numbers, 0101 and 0100.

```
      0101      &5

+     0100      &4

=     1001      &9
```

Going from right to left we have:

```
    1+0          =1
    0+0          =0
    1+1          =0(1)
    0+0+(1)      =1
```

In the example, a carry bit was generated in the third column, and this is carried to the fourth column where it is added to two noughts. Adding 8-bit numbers is accomplished in a similar manner:

```
    01010101    &55

+   01110010    &72

=   11000111    &C7
```

If the eighth bit, also called the most significant bit, creates a carry then this can be carried over into a second byte. However, within the CPU of most chips there is another way to handle this using something called a *Carry flag*.

Subtraction

So far we have dealt exclusively with positive numbers, however, in the subtraction of binary numbers we need to be able to represent negative numbers as well. In binary subtraction though, a slightly different technique from everyday subtraction is used, in fact we don't really perform a subtraction at all – we add the negative value of the number to be subtracted. For example, instead of executing 4-3 (four minus three) we actually execute 4 + (-3) (four, plus minus three).

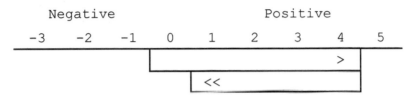

Figure 5h. Subtracting numbers.

We can use the scale in Figure 5h to perform the example 4+(-3). The starting point is zero. First move to point 4 (four points in a positive direction) signified by the '>' and add to this -3 (move three points in a negative direction). We are now positioned at point 1 which is indicated by '<<'. Try using this method to subtract 8 from 12, to get the principle clear in your mind.

To do this in binary we must first have a way of representing a negative number. We use a system known as signed binary. In signed binary, bit 7 is used to denote the sign of the number. Traditionally a '0' in bit 7 denotes a positive number and a '1' a negative number.

Sign Bit	Bits 0-6 give value						
1	0	0	0	0	0	0	1

Figure 5i. Signed binary representation of -1

Figure 45 shows how a signed binary number is constructed. Here, bits 0-6 give the value, in this case '1'. The sign bit is set so denoting a negative value, so the value represented in signed binary is -1.

Sign Bit	Bits 0-6 give value						
0	1	1	1	1	1	1	1

Figure 5j. Signed binary representation of 127.

The value 01111111 would represent 127 in signed binary. Bits 0-6 give 127, and the sign bit is clear. This is illustrated in Figure 5j.

Twos Complement Numbers

Just adjusting the value of bit 7 in this way is not an accurate way of representing negative numbers. Adding -1+1 should equal 0, but ordinary addition gives the result of 2 or -2 unless the operation takes special notice of the sign bit and performs a subtraction instead. Twos complement representation provides a means to encode negative numbers in ordinary binary, such that addition still works, without having to take the additional sign adjusting step.

So to convert a number into its negative counterpart, we must obtain its twos complement value. This is done by inverting each bit and then adding one. To represent -3 in binary, first write the binary for 3:

          00000011

Now invert each bit by flipping its value so that 0s become 1s and 1s become 0s. This is known as its ones complement value:

          11111100

Now add 1:

          11111100
    +   00000001
    =   11111101

Thus, the twos complement value of 3 = 1111101. Now apply this to the original sum 4+(-3):

          00000100   4
          11111101   -3
    = (1) 00000001   1

We can see that the result is 1 as we would expect, but we have also generated a carry due to an overflow from bit 7 (this is the value in brackets above). This carry bit can be ignored for our purposes at present, though it does have a certain importance as we shall see later on when performing subtraction in assembly language.

Here's another example that performs 32-16, or: 32+(-16).

32 in binary is:

          00100000

16 in binary is:

        00010000

The twos complement of 16 is:

        11110000

Now add 32 and -16 together:

        00100000   32

    +   11110000   -16

    =(1) 00010000   16

Ignoring the carry, we have the result, 16.

We can see from these examples that, using the rules of binary addition, it is possible to add or subtract signed numbers. If the carry is ignored, the result including the sign is correct. Thus, it is also possible to add two negative values together and still obtain a correct (negative) result. Using twos complement signed binary let's perform -2+-2

2 in binary is:

        00000010

The twos complement value of 2 is:

        11111110

We can add this value twice to perform the addition:

        11111110   -2

    +   11111110   -2

    =(1) 11111100   -4

Ignoring the carry, the result is -4. You might like to confirm this by obtaining the twos complement value of -4 in the usual manner.

Understanding twos complement isn't strictly necessary for most applications, but it can come in handy as you can discover the value of every bit in a number whether it is positive or negative.

When Twos Don't Add Up

There are a couple of occasions when twos complement doesn't add up and interestingly they are based around representing 0 and -0.

The first is when dealing with 0 (zero). Working with 8-bits for simplicity, the twos complement of 00000000 is 10000000. When you drop the most significant bit, you get 00000000, which is what you started with. This works as it means that you can't really have -0 and also that you can only have one value of 0 in twos complement.

The second situation arises with 10000000 because it can have no negative value. The inverse of 10000000 is 01111111, and now add one to obtain its twos complement and you get 10000000, which is what you started with.

Because the most significant bit in 10000000 is 1, the value is negative. When you invert it and add 1, you get 10000000 which is the binary representation of 128 so the original value must, therefore represent -128.

This anomaly is the reason why integer and long value variables in many forms of BASIC are asymmetrical. In 8-bits, the values range from -128 to +127 and in 32-bits values range from -2,147,483,648 to +2,147,483,647.

6: ARM Arrangements

The ARM has a very specific and special design. This is known as its architecture because it refers to how it is constructed and how it looks from the user's point of view. Having an understanding of this architecture is an important aspect of learning to program the chip. You need to appreciate how it all fits together and how the various elements interact. In fact, the purpose of much of the machine code we will be creating is to gain access and manipulate the various parts in the ARM itself.

Because of its design as a reduced instruction set computer it can do many different things using a small set of instructions. The way it operates is determined by the mode. This means that once you have understood the basic layout of the ARM chip you only then have to understand what its different operational modes are. That said, for almost all situations that you encounter when learning to program the ARM you will be operating in User Mode.

Word Lengths

In the binary examples we looked at in the previous chapters we have used single byte values. Indeed all the early popular computers worked at this level with machine code. The design of these circuit boards reflected this in that they had the eight data lines. In broad terms, these lines were directly related to the bits in the CPU byte. Thus, the CPU could move data around the board by toggling the logical condition on each line by making it a 1 or 0. It did this by changing the voltage on the line between 5V and 0V.

An ARM chip is more sophisticated and is able to operate much faster by manipulating larger amounts of information. It does this by being designed as a 32-bit CPU. This equates to four bytes of information. So instead of manipulating eight lines of information there are 32 lines. Collectively these four bytes are called a word. The ARM word length is said to be four bytes. However, it is more than capable of working with single byte lengths, and it does this just as effectively. Keep in mind that other computer systems may define their word length as something different, but on the Raspberry Pi a word is four bytes or 32-bits in length.

The most significant bit (msb) in an ARM word is located at bit 31 (b31), and the carry bit in an operation is generated if there is an overflow out of bit 31. If a carry occurred from bit 7 it would be carried into bit 8, or from the first byte in the second byte.

Byte and Word Accessed Memory

The early ARM chips only used 26-bits of the 32-bits for addressing memory. This placed certain restrictions on the processor — and of course, the amount of memory it could directly address — so later ARM chips had full 32-bit addressing. The lowest address in this range is accessed by placing 0s on all the lines, and the highest by placing 1s on all the lines. The first is addressed as &00000000 and the highest as &FFFFFFFF (or &3FFFFFFF on old 26-bit address bus ARMs).

Figure 6a illustrates schematically how memory is arranged as word blocks composed of four bytes a piece.

	bit31			bit 00
(Word 0)	b03	b02	b01	b00
(Word 1)	b07	b06	b05	b04
(Word 2)	b0B	b0A	b09	b08
(Word 3)	b0F	b0E	b0D	b0C

Figure 6a. Memory word blocks on the ARM.

The ARM 'sees' memory in these word blocks, but can also address the individual bytes within each word. From an operation point of view, all memory is arranged as word- aligned blocks. As illustrated in Figure 5a above the word-aligned blocks corresponded with Word 00, Word 01, Word 02 and Word 03. Note how Word 00 has the byte numbers b00, b01, b02 and b03 within it. Word 01 has bytes b04, b05, b06 and b07 in it, and so on. Word blocks are aligned in this fashion and cannot be changed. You cannot have a word-aligned block that consists of the bytes, b02, b03, b04 and b05. (Note that 'b' here relates to byte and not bit, as used in some previous examples.)

Addresses in memory are given in hexadecimal numbers. A memory address that corresponds to the start of a word is called a word boundary and is said to be word-aligned. A memory address is word-aligned if it is directly divisible by 4. The following addresses are all word-aligned:

&00009030

&00009034

```
&00009038
&0000903C
```

Word-aligned addresses are especially significant to the ARM as they are fundamental to the way the ARM chip fetches and executes machine code.

For example, the address &00009032 is not word-aligned. You cannot store an ARM machine code instruction on a non-word-aligned address.

The BBC BASIC Assembler provides a few tools to help ensure word boundaries are correctly managed. At the very least trying to assemble something that is not correctly addressed will generate an error message to that effect.

Registers

The ARM has several internal areas where it stores, tracks and processes information. This speeds things up and makes operations quicker as there is no external memory access required. These internal areas are called registers. In User Mode (the standard operating configuration) there are 16 registers available and each is capable of holding a word (four bytes) of information. You can think of these registers as single word locations within the ARM. Figure 5b shows how this comes together and includes an extra register — the Status Register.

As you can see from this *programmer's model*, registers R0-R12 are available for use at any time. R13-R15 have defined uses, however R13 and R14 are only used occasionally and are manipulated by just a few instructions. As the programmer will be controlling these operations we can also use them if required. Only R15 should not be used. I don't say cannot because it can be used, but you should be very clear what you are doing with it, and the complications it can bring if you do. ARM instructions can access R0 to R14 directly while most instructions can access R15.

As each register is one word wide, this means that each register is capable of holding an address location in a single register. In other words, a register can hold a number which points to a location anywhere in the memory map of the Raspberry Pi. A key function of registers is to hold such addresses.

The BBC BASIC Assembler allows us to use the labels listed above to refer to these registers, for example, R0 and R10. In addition, when you call your machine code from BBC BASIC the values of the integer variables A% through to H% are passed into the registers R0 to R7 respectively. Conveniently, these integer variables are all one word wide.

For example if your program included:

```
A%=&FF
B%=&FF0000FF
```

When you CALL the machine code from BASIC, these two values would be loaded in registers R0 and R1 respectively. This technique is used in a few demonstration programs in later chapters of this book, so look out for it. Note that the values of the registers is *not* passed back into the variables when the machine code operation ends. If you want to do that you need to use the USR command (introduced in Chapter 4).

The LDR and STM instructions are used to LoaD a Register and STore to Memory in a variety of ways. Here are a couple of examples:

```
LDR R1,[R5] ; Load R1 with contents of loc in R5
STR R1,[R6] ; Store R1 content at location in R6
```

In both of these examples, one register is expected to have a memory address in it. The registers are enclosed in square brackets in these examples, and this tells the assembler that they contain addresses. This type of specification is called an addressing mode and the ARM instructions have several addressing modes. We'll examine these in later chapters.

R0	Available
R1	Available
R2	Available
R3	Available
R4	Available
R5	Available
R6	Available
R7	Available
R8	Available
R9	Available
R10	Available
R11	Available
R12	Available
R13	Stack Pointer
R14	Link Register
R15	Program Counter
Current Program Status Register	

Figure 6b. The ARM User Mode register bank.

R15 - Program Counter

The Program Counter R15 is important. If you don't treat it with respect, your whole program can crash. Its function is simple — to keep track of where your program is in its execution of machine code. In fact, the PC holds the address of the instruction to be fetched next. We will look at this register in more detail later in the book, a Chapter is dedicated to it.

The BBC BASIC Assembler allows you to use PC as well as R15 when referring to the Program Counter. For example:

```
MOV PC, R0 ; Move R0 into R15, Program Counter
```

The PC in the instruction will resolve correctly as if you had used R15.

Current Program Status Register

The CPSR — or just plain Status Register — is used to store significant information about the current program and the results of operations it is carrying out and has carried out. Specific bits within the register are used to denote pre-assigned conditions and whether they have occurred or not. So how does the information get flagged inside the one register? It does this by manipulating the values of individual bits within the register. Figure 6c illustrates how this is configured.

31	30	29	28	27...8	7	6	5	4	3	2	1	0
N	Z	C	V		I	F	T	MODE				

Figure 6c. The Status Register configuration.

The four most significant bits hold what are known as flags, called as such as they are designed to flag a certain condition when it happens. These flags are:

N = Negative flag

Z = Zero flag

C = Carry flag

V = Overflow flag

When an instruction executes, if it has been requested to, the ARM updates the Status Register. If the condition under test occurred then a 1 is placed in the relative flag bit: it is set. If the condition has not occurred then the flag bit is cleared: a 0 is placed in it.

Bits and Flags

If you followed the previous sections on binary arithmetic, then some of the concepts here will be familiar to you. We have discussed negative numbers, and the Negative flag is used to signify a potential negative number. The Carry flag represents the carry bit — we discussed this in 8-bit operations, but the addition of 32-bit numbers works the same. The Zero flag is straightforward; it's set if the result is zero. Finally, the Overflow flag is new, but simply sets if the operation caused a carry from bit 30 into the top bit at bit 31. If this occurred using signed numbers, it could indicate a negative result, even if a negative number was not generated. (Remember, bits start numbering at zero so, the 32nd bit is, in fact, numbered bit 31, or b31.)

For example, if the result of an operation gave 0, the Zero flag would be set. This is the Z bit in Figure 5c. If an addition instruction generated a carry bit then the Carry flag would be set to 1. If a carry was not generated then the Carry flag would be clear (C=0).

Assembly language has mnemonics that allow us to test these Status Register flags and take action based on their condition. Here are a couple of examples:

```
BEQ zeroset    ;jump to zeroset if Z=1
BNE zeroclear ;jump to zeroclear if Z=0
```

BEQ is Branch if EQual and this instruction will cause a 'jump' to a named label if the Zero flag is set. BNE is Branch if Not Equal and this instruction will cause a jump to the named label if the Zero flag is clear.

There are instructions to test the other flags in a like manner. The BNE instruction is often used to make sections of program repeat or loop a predetermined number of times until counter decrements to 0 at which point the Zero flag will be set.

In Figure 6c, the I and F bits are called interrupt disable bits and we'll discuss these in Chapter 25. The T bit is to do with processor states. At this point we'll assume that it is always set to 0 to signify ARM state (we will come back to this in Chapter 30). The final five bits are used to signify the processor mode — we will be largely using User Mode (but this will be touched on again in Chapter 25 as well).

Interestingly there is no one single instruction that you can use to gain access to the Status Register. You can only manipulate its contents at bit level by carrying out an associated action. Things like flags and program counters will become second nature to you as you begin to master assembly language.

Setting Flags

There are two instructions that have a direct effect on the Status Register flags. They are CMP (CoMPare) and CPN (ComPare Negative). Of these the first is the more common in use and it takes the form:

```
CMP <Operand1> <Operand2>
```

CMP performs a notational subtraction, taking Operand2 away from Operand1. The physical result of the subtraction is ignored, but it updates the Status Register flags according to the outcome of the subtraction, which will be positive, zero or negative (there can never be a carry). If the result of the subtraction was 0 the Zero flag would be set.

Operand1 is always a register, but Operand2 can be a register or a specific or immediate value. For example:

```
CMP R0, R1     ; Compare R0 with R1. R0 minus R1
CMP R0, #1     ; Compare R0 with 1.  R0 minus 1
```

The CMP instruction is often used in combination with the BEQ instruction, to create a branch or jump to a new part of the program:

```
CMP R0, R1
BEQ zeroflagset
```

Here control will be transferred to the part of the program marked by the label 'zeroflagset' if the comparison between R0 and R1 is zero. If the branch does not take place then it would show that the result of the CMP was not zero – there would be no need to perform a BNE function. The code following could handle that situation.

CMP and CPN are the only instructions that directly affect the condition of the Status Register. By default, the rest of the ARM instruction set does not update the Status Register. For example, if R0 and R1 both contained 1 and we performed:

```
SUB R0, R0, R1
```

The result would be 0. But none of the flags in the Status Register would be altered in any way. They would retain the status they had before the instruction was performed.

S Suffix

However, the ARM does provide a method of allowing an operation such as SUB to update the Status Register. This is done by using the Set suffix. All we have to do is append an 'S' to the end of the mnemonic we want to use to modify the flags:

```
SUBS R0, R0, R1
```

This subtracts the contents of R1 from R0, leaving the result in R0 and at the same time updating the flags in the Status Register.

This S suffix effectively allows you as the programmer to use one less set of instructions. Without it we might use:

```
SUB R0, R0, R1
CMP R0, #0
BEQ iszero
```

But with it we can remove the CMP line thus:

```
SUBS R0, R0, R1
BEQ iszero
```

The BBC BASIC Assembler recognises the use of the S suffix. It is also tolerant of spaces between the instruction and the S, so these two examples will assemble perfectly:

```
SUBS R0, R0, R1
SUB  S R0, R0, R1
```

The Set suffix is one of many that exist, and we'll have a look at more of these in Chapter 10.

R14: The Link Register

The BEQ and BNE instructions illustrated above are examples of conditional branch instructions. These are absolute in that they offer a definitive change of direction — branch if equal or branch if negative. There is a second style of branch instructions known as Branch and Branch with Link (BL). The BL implements a subroutine operation; effectively it jumps to somewhere else in the program and allows you to come back to the point right after the BL instruction in the program.

When the BL instruction has executed, this return address (the address of the next instruction) is loaded into R14, the Link Register (LR). When the subroutine has completed, the Link Register is copied into the Program Counter, R15, and the program continues operating where it left off before the call was made.

One way of copying the Link Register into the Program Counter would be thus:

```
MOV R15, R14
```

The following is also accepted by the assembler:

```
MOV PC, LR
```

If you are familiar with any form of BASIC you can think of BEQ and BNE as being the equivalent of GOTO commands and BL as being a GOSUB command.

R13: Stack Pointer

The Stack Pointer contains an address that points to an area of memory which we can use to save information. This area of memory is called a stack and it has some special properties that we will look at in Chapter 17. It is worth noting at this point that you can have as many stacks as you like, and you are not limited to just one.

7: Data Processing

In this chapter we'll look at some of the data processing instructions. This is the largest group of instructions, 18 in all, which manipulate information. They can be divided further into sub-groups as follows:

ADD, ADC, SUB, SBC, RSB, RSC

MOV, MVN, CMP, CPN

AND, ORR, EOR

BIC, TST, TEQ

MUL, MLA

The AND, ORR, EOR, BIC, TST and TEQ instructions are examined in the next chapter.

Each of these instructions expect information to be supplied to them in the following configuration:

```
<Instruction> <Dest>, <Operand1>, <Operand2>
```

Let's look at each field in more detail.

<Instruction>
This is the assembly language mnemonic to be assembled. It can be used in its raw form as listed above, or with the additions of suffixes, such as S.

<Dest>
This is the destination where the result is to be stored, and the destination is always an ARM Register, in the range R0-R15.

<Operand 1>
This is the first item of information to be manipulated and, again, will always be an ARM Register in the range R0-R15. Operand1 may be the same as the Destination register.

<Operand 2>
Operand2 has more flexibility than Operand1 in that it can be specified in three different ways. As with Operand1, it may be an ARM Register in the range R0-R15. It may also be a specified value or constant — a number for example. For a constant, the exact number to be used is quoted in the assembler listing.

The hash —'#' —, is used to signify an immediate constant. Operand2 may also be what is called a shifted operand and we will look at this instance in Chapter 11 when we have looked at the arithmetic shifting of numbers.

Here are some examples of data processing instructions in use:

```
ADD R0, R1, R2   ; R0=R1+R2
ADDS R2, R3, #1 ; R2=R3+1 and set flags
MOV R7, #128     ; R7=128
```

Some instructions do not require both operands. For instance, the MOV instruction does not use Operand1; it only requires Operand2. The reason for Operand2 rather than Operand1 is that it is able to use a Register definition or a constant value (or shifted, as we shall see).

Arithmetic Instructions

In this section we'll look at the ADD and SUB commands in a little more detail, and we'll also start looking at what is happening in the registers themselves, including the Status Register and its flags

Addition

There are two instructions that handle addition. They are ADD and ADC. The latter is ADd with Carry. They both take a similar form:

```
ADD (<suffix>) <dest>, <Operand1>, <Operand2>
ADC (<suffix>) <dest>, <Operand1>, <Operand2>
```

Here's some code that uses the ADDS instruction. This program clears R0, places 1 in R1 and sets all 32-bits of R2. THIS is the largest number we can store in a four-byte register. So what will happen if we were to run this program?

```
MOV R0, #0
MOV R1, #1
MOV R2, #&FFFFFFFF
ADDS R0, R1, R2
```

On completion if we looked at the registers they would show:

```
R1:   &00000001
R2:   &FFFFFFFF
R0:   &00000000
```

Nothing seems to have happened! The values have all been loaded, but no addition seems to have taken place as R0 still has 0 in it. In fact it has, but by adding the 1, we created a carry bit (remember the binary additions we did in the earlier chapters?). So if we were to look at the Status Register we would see:

```
NZCV
0110
```

If we had run this program using only ADD and not ADDS then the Carry flag would not have been updated and would merely reflect the condition they were in when they were last updated via an appropriate instruction. Of course, the Carry flag may have been set by a previous instruction, so we might have received a correct answer, but only by good fortune. The good fortune method is not an efficient way to program in any language. It pays to double check.

Integer to Register Transfer

Program 7a will take two numbers requested at the keyboard, place them into integer variables A% and B% and after CALLing machine code will add R0 and to return the result in R0. Remember that BBC BASIC places the contents of A% and B% into R0 and R1 respectively. The program uses the USR function to return the result back to BBC BASIC's variable 'start'. How could you test to see if there was a Carry and signal the fact?

Program 7a. Passing information into a machine code program.

```
 10 REM >Prog7a
 20 REM RPi ROAL
 30 REM Pass values from BASIC into MC
 40 :
 50 DIM code% (100)
 60 A%=0 : B%=0
 70 FOR pass=0 TO 3 STEP 3
 80 P%=code%
 90 [
100 OPT pass
110 .start
120 ADDS R0, R0, R1
130 MOV R15,R14
140 ]
150 NEXT pass
160 REPEAT
170   INPUT "NUMBER 1: " A%
180   INPUT "NUMBER 2: " B%
190   PRINT "RESULT IS: "; USR(start)
200 UNTIL FALSE
```

The code segment below adds two 64-bit numbers. This relates to two words, so two registers are needed to hold the number with one holding the low four-bytes and the other the high four-bytes. Because we have a potential carry situation from low-word to high-word when we add the two it is imperative we take the Carry flag into consideration. For this we need to use the ADC instruction.

The code assumes that the first number is in R2 & R3 and the second is in R4 & R5. The result is placed in R0 & R1. By convention, the lower register always holds the lower-half of the number

```
MOV R2, #&FFFFFFFF      ; low half number 1
MOV R3, #&1             ; high half of number 1
MOV R4, #&FFFFFFFF      ; low half of number 2
MOV R5, #&FF            ; high half of number 2
ADDS R0, R2, R4         ; add low half and set flags
ADCS R1, R3, R5         ; add high half with carry
```

On completion, registers R0 and R1 will contain &FFFFFFFE and &101 respectively. So the result was:

&101FFFFFFFE

In the first ADDS instruction, the addition would have caused the Carry flag to be set, and this was picked up in the ADCS operation. If we substitute the ADCS with another ADDS the result is:

&100FFFFFFFE

In decimal terms the result is starker, out by 4,294,967,296!

You may be wondering why the ADCS instruction was not used in both parts of the addition. Generally if you set out doing any addition you would want to ensure the Carry flag is clear before starting. If not and you used ADCS and it was set from a previous operation you would get an erroneous result. Use of ADDS ensures that the carry is ignored but gets updated at the end of the addition.

How would you modify this segment to add two three-word values? The temptation might be to repeat the ADDS and ADCS sequence. This would be wrong. You should continue using the ADCS instruction until all the words have been added. You only use ADDS on the first word to define the Carry condition in the first instance. From then on it is ADCS.

If you are writing a program that does not produce the correct result and the values it is returning are wildly out, it is always worth checking that you have used the correct sequence of addition instructions. Chances are that is where the 'bug' sits.

If the three word numbers were held in R4, R5, R6 and R7, R8, R9 we could sum the result in R1, R2, R3 as follows:

```
ADDS R1, R4, R7 ; Add low words & check for carry
ADCS R2, R5, R8 ; Add middle words with carry
ADCS R3, R6, R9 ; Add high words with carry
```

It should go without saying that you need to check to see if the Carry flag is set as it is the most significant bit in your result.

Subtraction

While there are two instructions that deal with addition, there are four for subtraction.

```
SUB (<suffix>) <dest>, <Operand1>, <Operand2>
SBC (<suffix>) <dest>, <Operand1>, <Operand2>
RSB (<suffix>) <dest>, <Operand1>, <Operand2>
RSC (<suffix>) <dest>, <Operand1>, <Operand2>
```

You can see that there are complementary instructions to addition: a straightforward subtraction that ignores the flags and then one that takes into account the Carry flag (SBC). The second set of subtraction instructions works in an identical fashion, but uses the operands in the reverse order. For example:

```
SUB R0, R1, R2
```

subtracts the contents of R2 from R1 and puts the result in R0. However,

```
RSB R0, R1, R2
```

subtracts the contents of R1 from R2 and puts the result in R0. As with the previous examples the S suffix can be used with the instructions:

```
SUBS R0, R1, R2
```

If R0=0, R1=&FF and R2=&FE, the SUBS instruction is performing &FF-&FE which is 255-254. The result should be 1, and this is indeed so. However on investigation the Status Register would show that the Carry flag has been set. Why?

If we change SUBS to RSB so that:

```
RSBS R0, R1, R2
```

Then by loading the same values into the registers the result in R0 is &FFFFFFFF and the Carry flag is clear! In subtraction, the Carry flag is used the 'wrong' way round so that if a borrow is required the flag is unset or clear. It acts like a NOT Carry flag! This is useful when dealing with numbers over 32-bits and ensures the correct result. The result in this last instance also sets the Negative flag as &FFFFFFFF represents a negative value in signed numbers. The above example illustrates this perfectly and is because of the use of twos complement numbers.

When a section of code is not giving you the result you expect it always makes good sense to check the condition of the Status Register flags. They may not behave as you expect.

The two rules here to remember then are:

- If a borrow is generated, then the Carry flag is clear, C=0
- If a borrow is not generated, then the Carry flag is set, C=1

When we perform a multi-word subtraction, borrowing from one word means we need to subtract an extra one from the next word. However, as we have seen, a borrow results in the Carry flag being zero, not one as we would have liked. To compensate for this, the ARM actually inverts the Carry flag before using it in the SBC operation. This system can be extended to subtract operands which require any number of words to represent them — simply repeat the SBC instruction as many times as required.

You may be wondering why the ARM instruction set has reverse subtract instructions. Again, this ties in with the overall philosophy of speed. By being able to specify which operand is subtracted from which, we effectively remove the necessity of having to go through a data swapping process to get the operands in the right order.

Multiplication

The ARM has a couple of instructions that will perform 32-bit multiplication. The first of these, MUL provides a direct multiplication and takes the form:

```
MUL (<suffix>) <dest>, <Operand1>, <Operand2>
```

MUL is a bit different to instructions such as ADD and SUB in that it has certain restrictions on how its operands can be specified. The rules are:

Dest: Must be a register and cannot be the same as Operand1. R15 may not be used as the destination of a result.

Operand1: Must be a register and cannot be the destination register.

Operand2: Must be a register, and cannot be an immediate constant or shifted operation.

In summary, you can only use registers with MUL, cannot use R15 as the destination, and the destination register cannot be used as an operand. Here's an example:

```
MUL S R0,R4,R5   ; R0=R4*R5 and set status
```

Program 7b demonstrates MUL in action. Two numbers are placed in R1 and R2 and the multiplied result into R0.

Program 7b below demonstrates MUL in action. Two numbers are requested and passed to the routine which returns and prints the result. The variables A% and B% are used to seed the numbers entered in response to the prompts to R0 and R1 respectively. The MOV R0, R2 instruction is needed to shift the result from R2 into R0 as the USR function returns the result in line 180.

Program 7b. 32-bit multiplication.

```
 10 REM >Prog7b
 20 REM RPi ROAL
 30 REM Multiply two numbers
 40 :
 50 DIM multiply 256
 60 FOR pass=0 TO 3 STEP 3
 70 P%=multiply
 80 [
 90 OPT pass
100 .start
110 MUL R2, R0, R1
120 MOV R0, R2
130 MOV R15, R14
140 ]
145 NEXT
150 REPEAT
160   PRINT
170   INPUT "Operand 1: " A%
180   INPUT "Operand 2 :" B%
190   PRINT "Result is : "; USR(multiply)
200 UNTIL FALSE
```

MLA is MuLtiply with Accumulate. It differs from MUL in that it allows you to add the results of a multiplication to a total. In other words, you can accumulate values. The format of the command is:

    MLA (<suffix>) <dest>, <Op1>, <Op2>, <sum>

The rules stipulated at the start of this section still apply here. There is an extra operand, <sum>, which must be specified as a register. For example:

    MLA R0, R1, R2, R3 @ R0=(R1 * R2) + R3

The register specified by <sum> may be the same as the <destination> register, in which case the result of the multiplication will be accumulated in the destination register, thus:

```
MLA R0, R1, R2, R0 ; R0=(R1 * R2) + R0
```

For an example, referring to Program7b, add the following line:

```
105 MOV R2, #5
```

And change line 110 to read:

```
110 MLA R2, R0, R1, R2
```

Now run the program. The result returned will always be five more than the product of the two values you enter. This is because the value five was seeded into R2 at the start (line 105).

The ARM does not provide a division instruction, so dividing two numbers either requires a little bit of ingenuity or must be done using a long-hand subtraction method. This along with some other multiplication instruction examples are provided in Chapter 13.

Move Instructions

There are two data move related instructions. MOV and MVN are used to load data into a register from another register or to load register with a specific value. The instructions do not have an Operand1 and take the form:

```
MOV (<suffix>) <dest>, <Operand2>
MVN (<suffix>) <dest>, <Operand2>
```

Here are a couple of examples:

```
MOV R0, R1              ; Copy contents of R1 to R0
MOV R5, #&FF            ; Place 255 in R5
```

If you look at the comment in the first example above, although the instruction is MOVe it is important to realise that the contents of the source register are unchanged. A copy is being made. Also, unless the S Flag is used the Status Register is not changed either. This instruction:

```
MOVS R0, #0
```

would load zero into R0 and set the Zero flag at the same time.

MVN is MoVe Negative. The value being moved is negated in the process. This means that 1s become 0s and 0s become 1s. This is to allow negative intermediate numbers to be moved into registers. You may need to pop back to Chapter 4 and revisit the section of twos complement numbers for a quick refresher on negative numbers in binary. Under the twos complement scheme the number 'n' is represented as:

```
(NOT n) + 1
```

To make MVN use a value of:

```
-n
```

we in fact specify:

```
n-1
```

So, to move -10 into a register we must place 9 into it, as:

```
(NOT 9)+1
```

At bit level this is (and we'll look at logical operations in the next chapter):

```
9:          0000 1001
NOT 9:      1111 0110
Add 1       0000 0001
Result      1111 0111
```

Here are some examples of the instruction:

```
MVN R0, #9  ; Move -10 into R0
MVN R0, #0  ; Move -1 into R0
MVN R1, R2  ; Move (Not  R2) into R1
```

We will learn in Chapter 11 that there are restrictions on the value of contents being loaded into registers as immediate values. Put simply, there are some numbers you just can't use directly, and it is not because they are too big, for instance. This can also be an issue when dealing with addresses in memory. We'll examine why, and how to circumvent the problem in due course.

Compare Instructions

We encountered these instructions when we looked at the Status Register and flags in the previous chapter. They are two comparison instructions and they have the format:

```
CMP <Operand1>, <Operand2> ; Set flags of <Op1>-<Op2>
CMN <Operand1>, <Operand2> ; Set flags of <Op1>+<Op2>
```

These instructions do not move information or change the contents of any of the registers. What they do is update the Status Register flags. Since the purpose of CMP and CMN is to affect directly the Status Register flags there is no reason to use the S suffix. CMP works by subtracting Operand2 from Operand1 and discarding the result.

```
CMP R3, #0
```

The example above would only set the Zero flag if R3 itself contained 0, otherwise the Zero flag would be clear.

        CMP R3, #128

Here, the Zero flag would be set if R3 contained 128. If R3 held anything less than 128 the Negative flag would be set. What would cause the Overflow flag to be set? If you are ever in any doubt what the result would be, then simply check it out longhand by doing the binary arithmetic!

CMN is the negative version of compare. This is good if you want to control a loop that has to decrement past zero. In such case you could use:

        CMN R0, #0 ; Compare R0 with -1

The idea is the same behind the reason of the MVN instruction. It allows comparisons to be made with small negative immediate constants which could not be represented otherwise.

An important point to be wary of is that, in MVN, the logical NOT of Operand2 is taken. In CMN it is the negative of the operand that is used. Thus to compare R0 with minus 3 we would write:

        CMN R0, #3

The ARM will automatically form the negative of Operand2 and then make the comparison.

As with CMP, the purpose of CMN is to affect the Status Register flags and the S suffix is not applicable.

8: RISC OS Ins and Outs

When we use computers and Operating Systems such as RISC OS we take an awful lot for granted. We type commands at the keyboard, the commands get actioned and we get feedback from the action of the command by way of what is displayed on the screen. There's a lot going on.

Consider a couple of what would seem relatively simple tasks, typing a command at the keyboard and then getting a response on the screen. These are things we do every time we interact with the RISC OS command line (the Command Line Interpreter – or CLI). The question is then, how do we get input from the keyboard and write information to the screen in our machine code programs?

In the strictest sense you do it yourself. But this involves a good deal of knowledge about the various hardware components of the Raspberry Pi, because to write a message to the screen for instance, we have to know exactly where the hardware that drives the screen is located within the computer's memory and, in turn how to write the information to it. Equally, to read input from the keyboard we need to understand how the keyboard is mapped and how to read that matrix to identify which keys are being pressed.

Reading and writing to the hardware to do this is often termed *bare metal programming*, because you are 'talking' to the computer hardware directly. Whilst this in itself is potentially exciting, it is rather an advanced topic and not necessarily the domain of a beginner's book such as this. Equally though, unless you are specifically bare metal programming as an exercise there is absolutely no need for you to do it. Instead we can access RISC OS's own routines to do these and several other bare metal style tasks! If fact we did this in Program 4b which printed as asterisk to the screen using SWI 0.

SWI Commands

The SWI instruction allows you as the programmer to gain access to pre-defined routines or libraries of them. SWI stands for SoftWare Interrupt because when it is encountered it causes the flow of your program to be stopped and handed over to the appropriate RISC OS routine. Once the SWI instruction has been completed, control is handed back to the calling program. The SWI command is also often referred to as SVR or Supervisor call as this is a mode of operation that is invoked in the ARM chip when it is called (quite advanced so no more on this until Chapter 25).

To use these SWI calls effectively then, we need to know what they do, what information has to be passed and in what registers. Information may be passed back by the SWI call and in such cases we need to know what information and in what registers.

Names and Numbers

Each SWI is defined by both a name and a number. Both are unique to that SWI and the SWI can be called by either of them. From a readability point of view the name method is preferred. This only affects the size of the source file (more characters to store and save) and not the assembled machine code (the assembler converts the name into a number).

As the SWI works at machine level, information is passed to the routine using a variety of the ARM registers. The more complex the SWI the more information that will need to be passed, and any information returned by the call will be passed back in the registers. In defining SWI calls it is therefore normal to define entry and exit conditions. When a SWI is called, the RISC OS Kernel locates the position of the code it relates to and jumps to the routine. This routine will carry out the required function and if necessary will interact with the Raspberry Pi hardware directly.

As we have already seen one of the easiest things to do with a SWI call is to print a character to the screen and this is something RISC OS does every time you interact with the Raspberry Pi. This would be a little harder and much more long winded to do in machine code without the help of RISC OS and the associated SWI.

The action to be carried out by the SWI is determined by the value supplied with the SWI instruction. Usually register R0 is involved, together with other registers depending on the complexity of the call. Sometimes R0 is used to point to a block of memory which contains information, although other registers may be used for this purpose as well.

OS_Write C

The instruction:

```
SWI "OS_WriteC"
```

will print the contents of ARM Register R0 to the screen. So, if you wanted to print the letter 'A' to the screen you would first load R0 with the ASCII value for 'A' and then call the SWI. You might do that like this:

```
MOV R0,#ASC("A") ; Load R0 with 'A'
SWI  "OS_WriteC" ; and output it
```

Once the SWI instruction has been completed control is handed back to the calling program. The number allocated to OS_WriteC is &00 and this can be used instead of the name, with the same effect. This is a little less clear but certainly just as effective. So,

```
SWI  "OS_WriteC"
```

achieves the same result as:

```
SWI  0
```

OS_WriteC stands for Operating System Write Character. The various SWI names are known to the BBC BASIC Assembler and can therefore be used in your programs. Using the assigned system label makes the program much more readable but the disadvantage is that it makes them more complex to enter, especially as they are case-dependent. So using:

```
OS_WRITEC
```

would generate an error at assembly time. The exact command — including upper case or lower case letters as required — must be used. The named version must also be within double quotes. If you misspell the SWI name an error will be generated.

There is nothing to stop you defining your own set of names at the start of your program, for example:

```
WRITEOS=0
```

and then:

```
SWI WRITEOS
```

This would work fine — it's up to you. But beware — some of the SWI names are long. In such cases you may wish to define your own shorter version of the constant and document it at that point. Also, calls such as:

```
SWI 0
```

are used so frequently that you will know what they are, and it is just as easy to use the number value directly. (This is probably not the perfectionist's view, but the point is to do what suits your programming methods best.)

There are many more SWI calls that can be used to write characters and strings of characters to the screen. Indeed there are SWI calls that can be used to read information from the keyboard. We'll look at these when we have introduced a few more concepts and machine code structures.

SWI calls can be called directly from BBC BASIC by using the SYS command. The previous code can be performed directly from the BBC BASIC command prompt by typing:

```
SYS "OS_WriteC",65
```

This is a quick and easy way to experiment with the OS operations and learn how they act. The SWI names are held by RISC OS. Program10a below reads the details of the first 256 SWI functions and prints their names out.

Program 8a. Printing out a list of SWI calls.

```
 10 REM >Prog8a
 20 REM RPi ROAL
 30 REM Print details of first 256 SWI calls
 40 :
 50 DIM buffer% 127
 60 VDU 14
 70 FOR swi%=0 TO 255
 80 SYS "OS_SWINumberToString", swi%,buffer%,127
 90 SYS "OS_Write0",buffer%:PRINT
100 NEXT
110 VDU 15
120 END
```

This uses OS_SWINumberToString to print out the names of the first 256 SWIs. OS_SWINumberToString returns each SWI name at the location called 'buffer%' and this name is printed using OS_Write0 (detailed later in the book - but effectively;y printing a null terminated string of ASCII characters.). Both the BBC BASIC command 'SYS' and the BBC BASIC Assembler perform this conversion automatically whenever they encounter a SWI name enclosed in inverted commas.

When you call a SWI instruction from your machine code it invokes the SVR (Supervisor) mode of operation. This claims and uses some of the ARM registers (often to return and pass results from the operation). This is discussed in more detail when we will also look at more of the SWI commands and their operation.

The PRMs

RISC OS comes with well over 4,000 pages of documentation in the form of the Programmers' Reference Manuals—the PRMs. These are a fantastic reference source and contain an incredible amount of information, and much of it dealing with SWI calls.. They take the form of seven pdf files and you will find them in the Documents.Books.PRMs directory (folder) on the SD card.

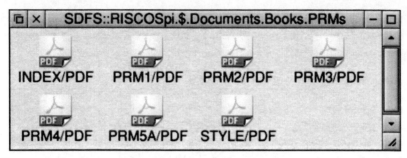

Figure 8a: The PRMs can be found in the Documents.Books.PRMs folder.

The PRMs were first released by Acorn in 1992-95 and were based on RISC OS 3 (including 3.5 and 3.6). This is still the case and while RISC OS has been released in multiple versions and upgrades since then, the fundamental information in the PRMs is still sound. It is true that some things have changed and new RISC OS releases have added more functionality and, in some cases, changed the way things work. Some of this is documented and some of it is not, but the various RISC OS forums are well supported and these changes are invariably discussed. This is certainly the case with the RISC OS Pi. This is an ongoing project and I have no doubt that RISC OS Pi will become the most popular and best supported version available.

Things that relate directly to hardware should be considered carefully as the Raspberry Pi has a very different hardware configuration to the original Archimedes. This includes video and sound related operations, as already discussed. Commands may sometimes work, but on the other hand they may only work to a degree or even not at all. Always bear this in mind and head to the RISC OS Forums to see if you can find more information, or simply to raise the question yourself.

Each PRM takes a similar format and following an introduction and then explanation of any detailed technical information, you can expect to find details of all associated SWI and OS-related calls. When you find something in the PRM index you can click on the page number and the embedded link will take you directly to the referenced PRM and page directly.

Printed versions of the PRMs do exist, but their sheer size makes them expensive. On the other hand, printing the PDFs out is time-consuming and equally expensive, so finding your way around the PDFs and extracting any information you require is probably the best method of using them.

For an introduction to the RISC OS then you might wish to consider the sister volume to the book, *Raspberry Pi RISC OS System Programming Revealed* – you can find more details in the Appendices or on the website.

9: Logical Operations

In computer terms, logic can be defined as the non-arithmetic operations performed that involve yes/no decisions. The ARM has three different logical operators, being AND, OR and EOR. In each case, the logical operation is performed between the corresponding bits of two separate numbers. As such there can only ever be two possibilities: yes or no, that is on or off. In binary these are represented as 1 and 0. These instructions are useful when it comes to identifying or forcing the state of individual bits in sets of data.

Each operation has the four distinct set of rules.

Logical AND

The four rules for AND are:

0 AND 0 = 0   [Nought and nought is nought]

1 AND 0 = 0   [One and nought is nought]

0 AND 1 = 0   [Nought and one is nought]

1 AND 1 = 1   [One and one are one]

The AND operation will only generate a 1 if both of the corresponding bits being tested are 1. If a 0 exists in either of the corresponding bits being ANDed, the resulting bit will always be 0.

Example:

```
        1010
        0011
AND=    0010
```

In the result only bit 1 is set; the other bits are all clear because in each case one of the corresponding bits being tested contains a 0. It is important to remember in these logical operations that there is no carry bit. The tests are done on the individual bits, and we are not adding or subtracting numbers here.

The main use of the AND operation is to 'mask' or 'preserve' bits. To preserve the low nibble (bits 0 to 3) of a byte and completely clear the high nibble (bits

4 to 7) so that the byte is set to all zeros we use the AND operator, masking the original with the value 00001111. If the byte we wished to preserve was the low nibble of say, 10101100, we would logically AND it thus:

```
       10101100
       00001111
 AND=  00001100
```

Here, the top four bits are cleared and the lower four bits have had their condition preserved.

Logical OR

The four rules for OR are:

0 OR 0 = 0 [Nought or nought is nought]

1 OR 0 = 1 [One or nought is one]

0 OR 1 = 1 [Nought or one is one]

1 OR 1 = 1 [One or one are one]

Here the OR operation will result in a 1 if either or both the bits contain a 1. A 0 will only occur if neither of the bits contains a 1.

Example:

```
       1010
       0011
 OR=   1011
```

Here, only bit 2 of the result is clear, the other bits are all set as each pair of tested bits contains at least one 1.

One common use of the OR operation is to ensure that a certain bit (or bits) is set — this is sometimes called 'forcing bits'. For example, if you wish to force bit 0 and bit 7 you would need to OR the byte with 10000001.

```
       00110110
       10000001
 OR=   10110111
```

The initial bits are preserved, but bit 0 and bit 7 are 'forced' to 1. These two bits were originally clear.

Logical EOR

Like AND and OR, the Exclusive OR operation has the four rules:

0 EOR 0 = 0   [Nought eor nought is nought]

1 EOR 0 = 1   [One eor nought is one]

0 EOR 1 = 1   [Nought eor one is one]

1 EOR 1 = 0   [One eor one is nought]

This operation sets the bit if it is Exclusive to the OR operation. If both bits being tested are identical, 0 and 0 or 1 and 1 then the result is 0. A 1 will only result if both bits being tested are not alike.

```
        0101
        1110
EOR=  1011
```

This instruction is often used to complement, or invert, a number. This is done by EORing the other byte with 11111111.

```
        00110110
        11111111
EOR=  11001001
```

Compare the result with the first byte — they are completely opposite: 1s where 0s were and 0s where 1s were.

The MVN instruction introduced in the last chapter effectively performs an EOR on Operand2 to obtain its result.

Logical Instructions

The process remains the same no matter how wide the data is. The examples above are one byte wide. The operation is the same in four bytes (or as many bytes as you need). The operation takes place on the directly associated bits, and no Status Register flags are involved or taken into account, and there is no Carry involved at any point.

AND, ORR and EOR are the instructions used to perform the three main logical operations. The form is the same as previous commands:

```
AND (<suffix>) <dest>, <Operand1>, <Operand2>
ORR (<suffix>) <dest>, <Operand1>, <Operand2>
EOR (<suffix>) <dest>, <Operand1>, <Operand2>
```

In these cases Operand1 is a register, while Operand2 can be a register or immediate value. The operations themselves do not set the Status Register flags but can be forced to do so with the suffix.

Here are a few examples of these instructions in use:

```
AND R0, R0, #1      ; preserve state of b0 in R0
ORR R1, R1, #2      ; ensure bit 1 in R1 is set
EOR R2, R2, #255    ; invert bits in low byte R2
```

Here's a short segment of code to look at:

```
MOV R0, #129
AND R0, R0, #1
ORR R0, R0, #2
EOR R0, R0, #255
```

The result is &FC and here's how we arrived at it (dealing with just the low byte of the word):

```
Load 129          10000001
AND with 1        00000001
Result            00000001
OR with 2         00000010
Result            00000011
EOR with 255      11111111
Result            11111100
```

Here are some practical examples of the ORR and EOR commands in use, with a typical application of each of them.

ORR to Convert Character Case

Program 9a illustrates how the ORR instruction converts a character from upper case to lower case. For example, it will take 'A' and convert it to 'a'. The ASCII value of the letter 'A' is &41 (65) and the ASCII character for 'a' is &61 (97). By comparing the hex numbers, we can see that the difference between 'A' and 'a' is *20.

ASCII	Value	Binary
A	&41	0100 0001
a	&61	0110 0001
Difference	&20	0010 0000

Figure 9a. Binary difference between ASCII 'A' and 'a'.

As both these characters mark the start of their section of the alphabet, it follows that the difference between an uppercase and lowercase value would always be the same. Figure 8a shows how this pans out in 8 bits of binary.

I hope you can see that we can achieve this difference by using the ORR instruction with the binary value 0010 0000 or &20 (32).

Program 9a does this directly in line 110. The program starts by reading a character in from the keyboard and after manipulating it, prints it out with SWI 0. Note that no check is made here to ensure the character entered is in the range A-Z. How would you adjust the program to convert a lower case character into an uppercase one?

Program 9a. Converting character case.

```
 10   REM >Prog9a
 20   REM RPi ROAL
 30   REM Use of ORR to convert Char case
 40   DIM code% (100)
 50   FOR pass=0 TO 3 STEP 3
 60   P%=code%
 70   [
 80   OPT pass
 90   .start
100   SWI 4 ; Read keyboard
110   ORR R0, R0, #%100000
120   SWI 0 ; Write to screen
130   MOV R15, R14
140   ]
150   NEXT pass
160   PRINT
170   PRINT "Enter character to be converted to lower case: "
180   CALL start
```

Note how we can include a binary value directly as an immediate constant in the assembly language by preceding it with '%' (line110). The SWI 4 operator (line 120) is used to read the keyboard for a key press and places the ASCII value of the key pressed in R0. SWI 4 is the OS_ReadC calls.

Note that no check is made here to ensure that the character entered is in the range A-Z. How would you adjust the program to convert a lower case character into an uppercase one?

Toggling Characters with EOR

Program 9b provides a typical use of EOR to toggle a character. Here it toggles from A to Z a predefined number of times and prints the character onto the screen as it does so.

For our purposes the ASCII value of the letter 'A' is &41 (65) and the ASCII character for 'Z' is &5A (90). By comparing the hex numbers we can see that the difference between A and Z is &1B (27). Figure 89 shows how the binary for it plans out. (Difference here meaning the 'gap' between ASCII 'A' and ASCII 'Z' and not the subtracted difference.)

ASCII	Value	Binary
A	&41	0100 0001
Z	&5A	0101 1010
Difference	&1B	0001 1011

Figure 9b. Binary difference between ASCII 'A' and 'Z'.

This value is used to EOR with in line 130. The loop is controlled by the value loaded into R1 in line 100. Line 150 subtracts one from the loop each time until the Zero flag is set and the BNE in line 160 is not executed. The SWI 0 in line 140 prints the character to the screen that is held in R0.

Program 9b. Using EOR to toggle character case

```
 10 REM >Prog9b
 20 REM RPi ROAL
 30 REM Use EOR to toggle char case
 40 DIM code% (100)
 50 FOR pass=0 TO 3 STEP 3
 60 P%=code%
 70 [
 80 OPT pass
 90 .start
100 MOV R1, #20
110 MOV R0, #ASC("A")
120 .loop
```

```
130 EOR R0, R0, #27
140 SWI 0
150 SUBS R1, R1, #1
160 BNE loop
170 MOV R15, R14
180 ]
190 NEXT pass
200 PRINT
210 CALL start
```

Bit Clear with BIC

The BIC instruction sets or clears individual bits in registers or memory locations. Its format is:

```
BIC (<suffix>) <dest>, <Operand1>, <Operand2>
```

The Bit Clear instruction forces individual bits in a value to zero.

```
BIC R0, R0, #%1111   ; clear low 4 bits of R0.
```

If R0 held &FFFFFFFF then the example above would clear the lowest four bits to leave &FFFFFFF0.

```
R0:         11111111 11111111 11111111 11111111
BIC #&0F    00000000 00000000 00000000 00001111
Result is:  11111111 11111111 11111111 11110000
```

The BIC command performs an AND NOT operation on Operand1 with Operand2.

Flag Tests

There are two instru2ctions whose sole purpose is to test the status of bits within a word. Like CMP there is no destination for the result, which is reflected directly in the Status Register (therefore the S suffix is not required). The two instructions are TeSt BiTs (TST) and Test EQuivalence (TEQ). The formats are:

```
TST  <Operand1>, <Operand2>
TEQ  <Operand1>, <Operand2>
```

TST is a test bits instruction, and Operand2 contains a mask to test on Operand1. It performs the equivalent of a logical AND with the outcome updating the Zero flag:

```
TST R0, #128 ; Test if b7 of R0 is set.
```

TEQ is test equivalence and uses an EOR process. It is a handy way of seeing if particular bits in registers are set.

```
TEQ R0, #128 ; Test if b7 of R0 is set.
```

You can use suffixes with both the TST and TEQ instructions so that you can test for other conditions as well as that of the Zero flag (detailed in the next chapter).

Program 9c uses the TST instruction to convert a number entered at the keyboard into a binary number, which is displayed on the screen. The number to be printed is placed in R6. There are a few things of interest in this program which we have not encountered yet and they will be explained in detail in the following chapters. Note how the program is broken into clearly named sections.

Program 9c. Printing a number as a binary string.

```
  10 REM >Prog9c
  20 REM RPi ROAL
  30 REM PRINT WORD AS BINARY
  40 :
  50 number=0
  60 mask=1
  70 preserve=5
  80 :
  90 DIM code% (100)
 100 FOR pass=0 TO 3 STEP 3
 110 P%=code%
 120 [
 130 OPT pass
 140 .start
 150 MOV mask,#1 << 31
 160 :
 170 .bits
 180 TST number,mask
 190 BEQ print1
 200 :
 210 MOV preserve, number
 220 MOV R0, #ASC("1")
 230 SWI 0
 240 MOV number, preserve
 250 BAL noprint1
 260 :
 270 .print1
```

```
280 MOV preserve, number
290 MOV R0, #ASC("0")
300 SWI 0
310 MOV number, preserve
320 :
330 .noprint1
340 MOVS mask, mask, LSR #1
350 BNE bits
360 :
370 SWI "OS_NewLine"
380 MOV R15, R14
390 ]
400 NEXT pass
410 :
420 REPEAT
430 INPUT "ENTER A DECIMAL NUMBER :" ; A%
440 PRINT "BINARY EQUIVALENT IS : ";
450 CALL start
460 UNTIL FALSE
```

There are a few things of interest in this program. First, the use of variables to name registers. Lines 50, 60 and 70 define values 0, 1 and 5 to 'number', 'mask' and 'preserve'. These numbers represent registers, and we are going to use these variable names in place of R0, R1 and R5. Look at line 150, here we use 'mask' instead of R1. The BBC BASIC Assembler realises this and accommodates us!

Another new format appears in line 150. We have not yet examined the concept of shifts and rotates – this is done in Chapter 11, so you may wish to come back to the following few paragraphs after reading that. However, we have used '<<' to signify a logical shift left (LSL). This places 1 in R1 and then shuffles it right across so that only the most significant bit in the register is set. This is because we cannot load the value we require directly into the register due to constraints that are imposed on use of immediate values (more on this shortly).

So the line:

```
150 MOV mask,#1 << 31
```

does this:

```
MOV mask #1: 00000000 00000000 00000000 00000001
<<31        10000000 00000000 00000000 00000000

            <<  shift left by 31 places    <<
```

81

We now enter the 'bits' loop.

```
170 .bits
180 TST number,mask
```

R0 is number and will have the value we wish to print in binary passed into it from A% (line 430). We know that the most significant bit of the mask is set (b31) and TST tests to see if it is in 'number' too. If it is then the BEQ of line 190 will occur and a 1 will be printed. If not a 0 will be printed. Note in each case we preserve the value in R0 as this is our number to be tested and we need to use R0 to print the 1 or 0. So, 'number' is restored in both cases.

In line 340 we use a logical shift right to shift the mask bit along one place to the right, making sure we update the Status Register flags with the use of the S suffix. The program continues to loop, and print 1s and 0s as required, until all 32-bits have been tested.

This program is a great visual aid to see how bit patterns develop. When you run it, work your way up through the numbers from '1' to see the output. You should recognise the binary very clearly now.

There is an alternative listing of this program in Chapter 10 (Program10c), that uses a more efficient process to print 0 or 1 values to the screen so that we do not have to keep saving and restoring the register holding 'number'.

10: Conditional Execution

The concept of the suffix was introduced in an earlier chapter to illustrate how S can be appended onto instructions to force the Status Register flags to be updated. For example:

```
ADDS R0, R1, R2  ; R0=R1+R2 & set flags
```

Without the S, using the instruction in its basic form, ADD has no effect on the Status flags. S is just one of many suffixes that exist and can be used in a similar way to expand the functionality of just about every operation in the ARM's instruction set.

Almost all ARM instructions can have a suffix applied to them that will only allow the command to be executed if the condition under test is true. If the condition is not met, then the instruction will be ignored. The suffix CS denotes Carry Set, so the instruction it is appended to will only be executed if the Carry flag is set at the time the ARM reaches the instruction. In programming terms, it gives you the ability to make every instruction a conditional operation.

The list of condition codes is extensive and is given in Figure 10a overleaf.

The BBC BASIC Assembler understands these conditional codes, and you can append them for use in your programs by adding the letters onto the end of the mnemonic. You can leave spaces between the mnemonic and the condition code as well if this aids readability. These two examples are both acceptable:

```
MOVCS R0, R1
MOV CS R0, R1
```

In these examples:

```
MOV CS R0, R1
```

the contents of R1 will only be moved into R0 if the Carry flag is set. Likewise:

```
MOV CC  R0,R1
```

will only move the contents of R1 into R0 if the Carry flag is clear.

Some suffixes alter more than one flag and in such instances these operations might require certain combinations of flags to be at a combination of set or clear. Thus, we can conveniently group the condition codes into two sets: those that are performed on the result of a single Status Register flag and those that are executed based on the result in two or more flags.

Suffix	Meaning
EQ	Equal
NE	Not Equal
VS	Overflow Set
VC	Overflow Clear
AL	Always
NV	Never
HI	Higher
LS	Lower than or Same
PL	Plus clear
MI	Minus set
CS	Carry Set
CC	Carry Clear
GE	Greater than or Equal
LT	Less Than
GT	Greater Than
LE	Less than or Equal

Figure 10a. ARM assembly language condition codes.

Condition codes act on the status of the flags; they do not set the Status Register flags in the first instance. You will need to use a compare instruction or an associated S suffix instruction to do that. A good understanding of binary and arithmetic operations will aid your understanding of how instructions are affected by these condition flags.

There are examples of the use of conditional execution throughout the programs in this book. Indeed, Chapter 10 also includes a perfect illustration of how the use of conditional codes can greatly reduce the size of your program.

Single Flag Condition Codes

Falling into this group are the suffixes:

```
EQ, NE, VS, VC, MI, PL, CC, AL, NV
```

These conditional flags are provided in complementary pairs. In the first set below, EQ and NE, they both act on the condition of the Zero flag — one when it is set, and the other when it is clear. If you are testing one condition and it is false then you do not have to test for the alternative condition as, by definition, it has to be true as it can only be one of two states.

EQ: Equal Z=1

Instructions that use the EQ suffix will only be executed if the Zero flag is set. This will be the case if the previous operation resulted in zero. Subtracting two numbers of the same value will result in zero and accordingly set the Zero flag. A compare operation would set the Zero flag if the two values being compared were the same. If the result of any operation is not zero then the Zero flag is clear (Z=0).

Example:

```
MOVS  R0, R1     ; Move R1 into R0 and set flags
MOVEQ R0, #1     ; If 0, load R0 with 1
```

Here, the Zero flag will be set if 0 is moved into R0 from R1. If this is the case then the next instruction will be executed, and 1 will be written into R0. The instruction will not be executed if the Zero flag is clear, thereby proving that the value in R0 was non-zero.

NE: Not Equal Z=0

Instructions that use the NE suffix will only be executed if the Zero flag is clear. This will be the case if the previous operation did not result in zero. Subtracting two unlike numbers will clear the Zero flag. A compare operation would set the Zero flag if the two values being compared were the same. If the result of any operation is not zero then the Zero flag is clear (Z=0).

Example:

```
CMP   R5, R6     ;  Compare R6 with R5 & set flags
ADDNE R5, R5, R6 ;  If not zero R5+R6 and put in R5
```

Here, the CMP instruction is used to compare contents of R5 and R6. If they are not the same (so that the Zero flag will be clear, Z=0) then R5 and R6 are summed and the result placed in R5.

VS: Overflow Set V=1

Instructions that use the VS suffix will only be executed if the Overflow flag is set. This flag is set as a result of an arithmetic operation producing a result which cannot be represented in the 32-bit destination register, creating a potential overflow situation. In cases like this, data placed in the destination register may not have value and thus require corrective action by the programmer. Examples of this can be found in Chapter 5.

VC: Overflow Clear V=0

Instructions that use the VC suffix will only be executed if the Overflow flag is clear. This flag is set as a result of an arithmetic operation producing a result which cannot be represented in the 32-bit destination register. That is, an overflow situation. If the flag is clear then no such overflow has occurred. This condition tests for the no overflow condition.

MI: Minus Set N=1

Instructions that use the MI suffix will only be executed if the Negative flag is set. This flag is set as a result of an arithmetic operation producing a result which is less than zero. This would occur if a large number is subtracted from a smaller one. Logical operations may also set the Negative flag if they cause bit 31 of the destination register to be set.

Example:

```
SUBS R1, R1, #1      ; Subtract 1 from R1 & set flags
ADDMI R0,R0, #15     ; If negative add &0F to R0
```

Here, the SUB instruction takes 1 from the contents of R1, and the S suffix is used to update the flags as the result is stored into R1. The ADD in the next line only takes place if the N flag is set and if so 15 is added to R0.

PL: Plus Clear N=0

Instructions that use the PL suffix will only be executed if the Negative flag is clear. This flag is cleared if the result of an arithmetic operation is positive, one that is greater than or equal to zero. Note that the EQ suffix will test for zero only, the PL instruction tests for a plus or non-negative result. It is important to note the subtle difference here.

Example:

```
SUBS  R1, R1, #1        ; Sub 1 from R1 & set flags
ADDMI R0, R0, #15       ; If neg add &0F to R0
ADDPL R0, R0, #255      ; If pos add &FF to R0
```

This example illustrates how compilations of conditional instructions act on alternative results. This builds on the MI example above: if the result was a positive number then 255 is added to the contents of R0 and stored there. As you can see, only one of these instructions can take place and both act on the result of the SUBS instruction. Because neither of the following ADD instructions has used the S suffix, the status flags will not have changed since the CMP instruction.

CS: Carry Set C=1

Instructions that use the CS suffix will only be executed if the Carry flag is set. This flag is set if an arithmetic operation creates a result bigger than 32-bits.

The Carry flag can be thought of as the 33rd bit. The Carry flag can also be set by using an ARM shift operation which is examined in Chapter 11.

Example:

```
ADDS R0,R0,#255 ; Add &FF to R0 and save in R0
ADDCS R1,R1,#15 ; Carry set add &0F to R1 save in R1
```

CC: Carry Clear C=0

Instructions that use the CC suffix will only be executed if the Carry flag is clear. This flag is clear if an arithmetic operation creates a result that fits inside 32-bits. The Carry flag is also affected by using any ARM shift operation which are examined in Chapter 11

Example:

```
ADDS R0,R0,#255   ; Add &FF to R0 and save in R0.
ADDCS R1,R1,#15   ; If Carry=1 add &0F to R1 save in R1
ADDCC R1,R1,#128  ; If Carry=0 add &F0 to R1 save in R1
```

As with the PL example, this has a definitive action that is controlled by the status of the Carry flag.

AL: Always

Instructions that use the AL suffix are always executed and do not rely on the setting of any of the Status Register flags. Given that instructions will always execute if there are no conditional suffixes, the AL suffix is the default setting for all appropriate instructions.

Example:

```
ADDAL, R0,R1,R2   ;  Add R1 and R2 and save in R0
ADD R0,R1,R2      ;  Add R1 and R2 and save in R0
```

These two instructions have exactly the same result.

A common use of the AL suffix is with the Branch instruction to provide a three letter mnemonic and greater clarity:

```
B start    ; Branch to start
BAL start  ; Branch to start
```

NV: Never

Instructions that use the NV suffix are never executed and do not rely on the setting of any of the status flags. This suffix is included for completeness. It can be used as a way of making space within a program as the instruction will be assembled. This space might be used to store data or modify the program itself at some point, and in more advanced cases, allow for pipelining effects (Chapter 14).

Example:

```
ADDNV R0, R1, R2 ; Never perform the addition.
```

Multiple Flag Condition Code

Falling into this group are six suffixes:

```
HI, LS, GE, LT, GT, LE.
```

These condition codes are executed based on the condition of two or more Status Register flags. They are most often used after a CMP or CPN instruction. This set of condition codes is further divided into two groups: those that operate on unsigned numbers (HI and LS) and those that operate on signed numbers (GE, LT, GT and LE).

HI: Higher (Unsigned) C=1 AND Z=0

Instructions that use the HI suffix will only be executed if the Carry flag is set and the Zero flag is clear. This happens in a comparison if Operand1 is greater than Operand2.

Example:

```
CMP R10, R5      ; Compare Registers R10 and R5
MOVHI R10,#0     ; If R10 > R5 then set R10 to zero.
```

It is important to remember that this condition assumes the two values being compared are unsigned and that negative values are not being used in a twos complement format.

LS: Lower Than or Same (Unsigned) C=0 OR Z-1

Instructions that use the LS suffix will only be executed if the Carry flag is clear and the Zero flag is set. This happens in a comparison if Operand1 is less than Operand2. Again it is important to remember that the condition assumes that the two numbers being compared are unsigned.

Example:

```
CMP    R10, R5      ; Compare Registers R10 and R5
ADDLS R10,R10,#1    ; If R10<=R5 add 1 & save in R10
```

GE: Greater or Equal (Signed) N=1,V=1 OR N=0, V=0

This instruction will execute if both the Negative flag and Overflow flag are set or clear. In other words, the flags must be in the same condition. This happens when two values are being compared: Operand1 was greater than or equal to, Operand2.

Example:

```
CMP R5, R6        ; Compare contents of R5 and R6
ADDGE R5,R5,#255 ; If R5 >= R6 then add &FF to R5
```

It is important to remember that this condition assumes the two values being compared are signed quantities.

LT: Less Than (Signed) N=1,V=0 OR N=0, V=1

This instruction will execute if the Negative and Overflow flags are different. This happens if Operand1 is less than Operand2. Again the condition assumes that the two values being compared are signed quantities.

Example:

```
CMP R5, #255     ; Compare contents of R5 with &FF
SUBLT R5,R5,R6 ; If R5<&FF subtract R6 from R5
                 save result in R5
```

GT: Greater Than (Signed)   N=1,V=1 OR N=0, V=0 AND Z=0

This instruction will execute if the result is a positive number and not zero. Here, Operand1 is greater than Operand2 and the assumption is that signed numbers are used. So both Negative flag, and Overflow flag must be set or the Negative, Zero and Overflow flags must all be clear.

Example:

```
CMP R5, R6        ; Compare R5 with R6
ADDGT  R0,R1,R2 ; If R5>R6 add R1+R2 & put in R0
```

LE: Less Than or Equal To (Signed)N=1,V=0 OR N=0, V=1 OR Z=1

This instruction will execute if the result between two values, Operand1 is less than or equal to Operand2. The assumption is that signed numbers are used. To achieve this both Negative flag and Overflow flag must be different, or the Zero flag must be set.

Example:

```
CMP R5, #10          ;    Does R5 contain &0A?
SUBLE  R0,R1,R2      ;    If R5<=&0A subtract R2 from R1
                          and put result in R0
```

Mixing the S Suffix

The S suffix can be mixed with conditional suffixes. This ensures that the result of whatever action taking place will also update the Status Register flags. We saw in a couple of earlier examples how preserving the status of flags after an action means that it is possible to act on the outcome of a conditional execution for both results. This assumes that the Status Register flags are not updated. If you want the Status Register flags to be updated by the conditional operation then the S suffix should be added after the conditions suffix thus:

```
ADDCSS R0, R1, R2        ; Add R2 to R1 if Carry=1.
                           Update Status flags as well.
```

It is important to place the S suffix after the condition code otherwise the assembler will miss it if it is placed before. Trying to assemble:

```
ADDSCS R0, R1, R2
```

gives an error.

11: Shifts and Rotates

The ARM has an internal mechanism called the barrel shifter. This device moves the bits in a word left or right. Most microprocessors have standalone instructions that allow you to perform this directly. However, the ARM only allows these movements as part of other instructions. It is a significant process because moving bits left or right can be a simple way of multiplying or dividing numbers quickly.

There are three types of shifts that can be performed. They are logical, arithmetic and rotate. Rotate is the only one that does not have an arithmetic function — it is included purely to move bits. Figure 11a details the six types of bit moves available for use.

Mnemonic	Meaning
LSL	Logical Shift Left
LSR	Logical Shift Right
ASL	Arithmetic Shift Left
ASR	Arithmetic Shift Right
ROR	Rotate Right
RRX	Rotate Right with eXtend

Figure 11a. Shift instructions available for use.

Although the barrel shifter is in operation during shifts and rotates, practically, its operation is transparent to the user.

Logical Shifts

Logically shifting a number left or right by one position has the effect of doubling it or halving it. By increasing the number of logical shifts you can multiply and divide numbers accordingly.

Figure 11b shows how a single Logical Shift Left (LSL) moves the bits on a full word of data. In an LSL the most significant bit (b31) drops out and into the Carry flag and the hole made by b0 shifting along into b1 is filled with a 0.

LSL	C	Word						b3	b2	b1	b0
Before	x	b31	b32	b29	b28	b27	...	b3	b2	b1	b0
After	b31	b30	b29	b28	b27	b26	<<	b2	b1	b0	0

Figure 11b. Logically shifting bits left.

Consider the single byte binary value 00010001. In decimal this is 17. If we perform a logical shift on this number by one place to the left (LSL #1) we get: 00100010 which is 34. We have effectively doubled, or multiplied the number, by two. This assumes that we drop off the top digit and insert a 0 at the least significant bit. This is illustrated in Figure 11c.

	b7	b6	b5	b4	b3	b2	b1	b0		
Before	0	0	0	1	0	0	0	1		#17
After	0	0	1	0	0	0	1	0	<0	#34

Figure 11c. Doubling a number with a single LSL.

This is a single byte example. The ARM uses four bytes, so the whole word is shifted to the left in this fashion. The bit that was in b7 gets moved across into the next byte and into what is effectively b8, and so on. The bit that gets shifted out at the very top, bit 31, gets moved into the Carry flag. The Carry flag can be tested to see if there is an overflow in the number multiplication.

As mentioned, the ARM does not have any standalone shift instructions, but it does implement them as an add-on to Operand2 to use within instructions and they affect the whole 32-bytes of the register specified. Using the example illustrated above, we might code it thus:

```
MOV R1, #17
MOVS R0, R1, LSL#1
```

Note the structure of the syntax for this. Operand1 is the destination for the result (R0), and the LSL is performed on Operand2 (R1). Here, the logical shift is given as an immediate value, but it could also have been specified in a register, which makes it available for alteration. A value from 0 to 31 can be used in a shift command. Using:

```
LSL #5
```

would multiply a value by two, five times =32 (2 x 2 x 2 x 2 x 2). It would perform LSL five times. Here, the new spaces would be filled with 0s and the Carry flag would reflect the value of the last bit 'falling out' from b31. All the other bits moved out are 'lost'. This means that the multiplication only remains true provided we do not lose any significant bits through the Carry flag. Therefore for large numbers care must be taken that significance is retained.

In other words the result must fit inside 32-bits. This multiplication rule breaks down if we were using twos complement numbers.

Logical Shift Right

Figure 11d shows how a Logical Shift Right (LSR) affects the bits in a word of data. The most significant bit (b31) goes right with a 0 taking its place. The least significant bit, b0 drops into the Carry flag.

LSR	C	Word									
Before	x	b31	b30	b29	b28	b27	...	b3	b2	b1	b0
After	b0	0	b31	b30	b29	b28	>>	b4	b3	b2	b1

Figure 11d. Logically shifting bits right.

The effect of LSR is to divide the number by two. Figure 11e shows this using our previous example. We start with 34 and perform an LSR #1 to arrive back at our original value of 17. Here a 0 is drawn in at the top end (b31) and any value falling out on the right (b0) is taken into the Carry flag. As with LSL the Carry flag is used to capture what is falling out so it can be tested if required.

	b7	b6	b5	b4	b3	b2	b1	b0		
Before	0	0	1	0	0	0	1	0		#34
After	0	0	0	1	0	0	0	1	>0	#17

Figure 11e. Dividing a number by two with a single LSR.

Arithmetic Shift Right

In an arithmetical shift the sign bit is preserved. Here b31 is saved; everything else is shifted one place to the right with b0 dropping into the Carry flag. These examples are shifted by one place only, but the principle is the same for multiple shifts with b31, the sign bit being preserved, and the last bit moved out of b0 is dropped into the Carry flag. This is illustrated in Figure 11f:

ASR	C	Word									
Before	x	b31	b30	b29	b28	b27	...	b3	b2	b1	b0
After	b0	b31	b31	b30	b29	b28	>>	b4	b3	b2	b1

Figure 11f. Arithmetic shift right preserving sign bit.

The advantage of ASR is that the shift takes into account the sign of the data and so a twos complement number may be represented. It extends the original sign of the number from b31 to b30 and ensures the division is performed correctly for both positive and negative numbers.

```
MOV R1, #255
MOV R2, #1
MOVS R0, R1, ASR R2
```

When we execute the segment above it would leave a value of &7F (128) in R0 with R1 and R2 unchanged, but the Carry flag set.

The conditional tests can also be used as with a normal MOV instruction. This following line would only be executed if the Carry flag is set:

```
MOV CS S R0, R1, ASR R2
```

An arithmetic shift left (ASL) is identical in operation to LSL, and there is no difference between them in the result. As a matter of course, you should always use LSL instead of ASL as some assemblers may not compile it and issue an error message. Others may just give a warning.

Rotations

There are two instructions that allow you to rotate bits to the right and in conjunction with the Carry flag. Rotate Right (ROR) moves the bits out from the low end and feeds them straight back in the high end. The last bit rotated out is also copied into the Carry flag as well as being rotated around. Figure 11g illustrates how the bits move. The Rotate instructions have no arithmetic action of significance and are included to shift bit patterns.

ROR>	C	Word									
Before	x	b31	b30	b29	b28	b27	...	b3	b2	b1	b0
After	b0	b0	b31	b30	b29	b28	>>	b4	b3	b2	b1

Figure 11g. The Rotate Right instruction.

The following segment:

```
MOV R1, #&F000000F
MOVS R0, R1, ROR #4
```

would give a result of &FF000000 with the Negative and Carry flags set. The ROR #4 shuffles the bits four places to the right.

The top bytes, &F000 move to the right by four giving &0F00; The low bytes &000F move to the right by four to give &0000; The &F, which has dropped out of the lower byte, is rotated to the top four bits of the high byte to give &FF00. Of course, the bits in the middle would all be shuffled along as well, but as they are 0s this is not noticeable. Finally, a copy is made of the last bit out, which was originally in the position bit 4, and placed in the Carry flag.

Extended Rotate

There is also an extended version or Rotate Right called RRX:

```
MOV R0, R1, RRX
```

This shift operation is unique in that you cannot specify the number of movements it makes as you are only allowed one. RRX always and only rotates data right by one position.

RRX>	C	Word									
Before	x	b31	b30	b29	b28	b27	...	b3	b2	b1	b0
After	b0	x	b31	b30	b29	b28	>>	b4	b3	b2	b1

Figure 11h. Rotate Right With Extend.

The Carry flag value is dropped into b31, and the value in b0 is moved into the Carry flag. Figure 11h shows how the bits are moved.

All bits are preserved albeit in a different order. RRX uses the Carry flag as a 32nd bit and so everything is preserved.

Uses of Shifts and Rotates

The shift and rotate commands can be used with any of the following data processing instructions:

```
ADC, ADD, AND,
BIC,
CMN, CMP,
EOR,
MOV, MVN,
ORR,
RSB,
SBC, SUB,
TEQ, TST
```

They can also be used to manipulate the index value of LDR and STR operations as described in Chapter 14. This also illustrates some handy uses for this group of modifiers.

Immediate Constant Range

We have seen the use of immediate constants in instructions:

```
SUB R0, R1, #3
```

Here the immediate constant (#3) is specified as Operand2. However, there is a limit to the size of the number that can be specified in this constant, and more particularly, some numbers just can't be used — 257, for example.

The reason for this is in the way ARM instructions are encoded. There are only 12-bits available for storing an immediate value as the operand. The encoding of ARM instructions is beyond the scope of this book. However, accepting that 12-bits are available, this is how the ARM uses these bits: The 12-bit field is split into two, one part of 8-bits and one of 4-bits. The 8-bit field is used to represent a numeric constant and the 4-bit field one of 16 different positions (each themselves then shifted by two) which the 8-bit value may be rotated to through an even number of positions.

Figure 11i summarises this scheme showing the position of the 8-bit value afforded within the 32-bits as defined by the position bits, 0-15. The '+' is used in the diagram to represent 0s, in the hope it makes it easier to read. The ROR column shows the value to be used in the shift.

Bit31 bit0	Psn	ROR
++++++++++++++++++++++++++76543210	0	0
10++++++++++++++++++++++++++765432	1	2
3210++++++++++++++++++++++++++7654	2	4
543210++++++++++++++++++++++++++76	3	6
76543210++++++++++++++++++++++++++	4	8
++76543210++++++++++++++++++++++++	5	10
++++76543210++++++++++++++++++++++	6	12
++++++76543210++++++++++++++++++++	7	14
++++++++76543210++++++++++++++++++	8	16
++++++++++76543210++++++++++++++++	9	18
++++++++++++76543210++++++++++++++	10	20
++++++++++++++76543210++++++++++++	11	22
++++++++++++++++76543210++++++++++	12	24
++++++++++++++++++76543210++++++++	13	26
++++++++++++++++++++76543210++++++	14	28
++++++++++++++++++++++76543210++++	15	30

Figure 11i. Immediate operands calculation.

A couple of examples should make this clearer. Suppose we wanted to use 173 as immediate constant. In binary this is:

```
00000000 00000000 00000000 10101101
```

This value can be presented in 8-bits, so no shift is required and the position bits will be set to 0.

Let's now examine the number 19,968. In binary across 32-bits this is:

```
00000000 00000000 01001110 00000000
```

If we compare this to the patterns in Figure 11i, we can see this has the value placed at position 12. To create this number as an immediate operand we would use 78 (01001110) and rotate it right by 24.

This provides us with the second way that an immediate operand can be specified as a shifted operand, and this takes the format shown in the following line:

```
Instruction (<Suffix>)  <Op1>, <Op2>, <Op3> <Shift>
```

Here's an example:

```
MOV R1, #78
MOV R0, R1, ROR #24
```

Here, R1 is loaded with 78, then rotated right 24 places and the result placed in R0. The result generated would be 19,968. Of course, we can use all these values directly as immediate constants as the assembler will resolve them directly for us, so we can use:

```
MOV R0, #19968
```

and the assembler works it out. It is the values that cannot be calculated in this way through Figure 11i that are the issue.

Although 257 cannot be used as an immediate constant, it can be seeded by storing it in a register and then using the register to specify the value.

```
ADD R0, R1, #257
```

would cause an error, along the lines of:

```
Invalid constant
```

but the following would achieve the same result:

```
MOV R2, #256      ; Load R2 with 256
ADD R2, R2, #1    ; Add one to make 257
ADD R0, R1, R2    ; Add 257 to R1 and save in R0.
```

12: Branch and Compare

This chapter has a more detailed look at the use of the compare instructions and the most economical ways of using them.

Branch Instructions

The branch instruction allows the execution of a program to be transferred to somewhere else in the machine code, and continued from there. The two common variants have the format:

```
B (<suffix>) <label>
BL (<suffix>) <label>
```

In effect, combined with conditional flags, there is a branch for every occasion. Although it is perfectly possible to use the B instruction on its own, it is preferable to use the ALways suffix so as not to lose the 'B' in a bigger program:

```
BAL start
```

But this is also perfectly acceptable:

```
B start
```

The <label> is a marked position in the assembly language program. There is a physical limit to the distance a branch can occur. This is plus or minus 32 Mb, as this is the largest address that can be represented in the space allocated for the label position. An absolute address is not stored; what is stored is the offset from the current position. When the ARM encounters the Branch instruction it treats the value following as a positive (forward) or negative (backward) adjustment to the PC from the current position.

Chapter 14 looks at Register 15 in more detail and also discusses how branches are calculated.

The Link Register

The Branch with Link instruction, BL, allows you to pass control to another part of your program – a subroutine – and then return on completion. BL works like the normal branch instruction in that it takes its destination as an address, normally specified by a label in an assembly language program.

However, before it branches it copies the contents of the Program Counter (R15) into the Link Register (R14).

```
BLEQ subroutine ; Branch & save PC if Z flag set
```

Once the subroutine has completed, the contents of the Link Register can be transferred into the Program Counter to return control to the calling segment of code:

```
MOV R15, R14
```

This is arguably the least elegant instruction implementation on the ARM chip. It is effective and does the job; however, many other CPUs have specific subroutine call and return instructions. .

A MOV instruction is used to move the return address from R14 back into the Program Counter. This will have no effect on the Status Register flags, and therefore, flags are preserved from whatever was going on before the return.

It is important to remember that each time a BL instruction is executed the contents of R15 are copied into R14. This means that if the program is already in a subroutine and another is called, the original link address will be overwritten with the new link address.

If your program is going to nest BL calls inside one another, the Link Register must be preserved on each occasion. The Link Register can then be re-seeded with the return address each time the subroutine is completed. In such cases, housekeeping is important. Re-seeding the wrong address back into the Program Counter will most likely crash your program.

A common way to store these nested addresses is to utilise the stack as a store. This is described in Chapter 17.

Using Compare Instructions

Your machine code will regularly need to check the result of an operation and then, depending on that result, take a course of action. There are a range of instructions that allow you to do this and a couple also that jump, or 'branch' to another part of the program. These comparisons instructions{instructions} directly affect the Status Register flags at which point you can act on what you find. The following segment will count from 1 to 50 and uses compare and branch instructions to control the loop to do so:

```
    MOV R0,#1               ;Initialise count
.loop
    ADD R0,R0,#1            ; Increment count
    CMP R0,#50             ; Compare with limit
    BLE loop
```

This program continues to add 1 to the value in R0, which was initially set at 1. R0 is compared to 50, and a BLE occurs if Less than or Equal to is the result. So the loop continues until R0=50. Then the loop continues until R0=51, because R0 would have been incremented to 51 in the instruction before the CMP, which is the point when the BLE instruction fails to loop back to 'loop'.

This segment of code is perfectly acceptable, but we can reduce its length, by making the loop count down thus:

```
        MOV R0,#50              ; Initialise count
.loop
        SUBS R0,R0,#1           ; Decrement count
        BNE loop                ; Loop if not Zero
```

Here, we use the SUBS to decrement and set the flags and can therefore, get away with excluding the CMP instruction. If you are just counting a sequence of iterations and do not need the count value for anything then it is better and more efficient programming practice to count down. This means fewer instructions and therefore a faster execution.

Compare Forward Thinking

Because the only effect of the comparison instructions is to test the condition of Status Register flags, by thinking about what you require, you can actually get away without using them. Let's look at an example. The program below is a loop that will cycle until R0 and R1 are the same. If R0 is greater than R1 it will subtract R1 from R0 and place the result in R0. If on the other hand R0 is less than R1, it will subtract R0 from R1 and place the result in R1. When they are the same, the program will finish.

```
        MOV R0, #100            ; arbitrary values in R0 & R1
        MOV R1, #20
.loop
        CMP R0, R1              ; Are they the same: Z=1?
        BEQ stop                ; if so stop
        BLT less                ; if R0 < than R1 go to less
        SUB R0,R0,R1            ; otherwise sub R1 from R0
        BAL loop                ; branch always back to start
.less
        SUB  R1,R1,R0           ; subtract R0 from R1
        BAL loop                ; branch always to the start
.stop
```

While this code is perfectly acceptable and does the job, we can reduce it by taking full advantage of conditional execution of instructions:

```
        MOV R0, #100           ; arbitrary values in R0 & R1
        MOV R1, #20
.loop
        CMP R0, R1             ; Are they the same: Z=1?
        SUBGT R0,R0,R1         ; sub R1 from R0 if Great Than
        SUBLT R1,R1,R0         ; else sub R0 from R1 as Less
        BNE loop               ; branch is not equal
```

As we are testing for greater than and less than conditions we can make direct use of the GT and LT suffixes respectively and tag them onto the end of the SUB subtraction instruction.

Combining SWIs and Suffixes Effectively

In Chapter 9, we saw how to use the TST instruction to print out a binary number. There, Program 9c used the section of code below to do this printing:

```
190 BEQ print1
200 :
210 MOV preserve, number
220 MOV R0, #ASC("1")
230 SWI 0
240 MOV number, preserve
250 BAL noprint1
260 :
270 .print1
280 MOV preserve, number
290 MOV R0, #ASC("0")
300 SWI 0
310 MOV number, preserve
320 :
330 .noprint1
```

On the face of things, this is a perfectly acceptable way to achieve the result of printing either a 1 or 0 to the screen dependent on the result of a test. Indeed it is, but that is without a full understanding of the ARM instruction set. These dozen or so lines can be replaced by just two! This is how you would do it:

```
        SWI EQ 256+ASC("0")
        SWI NE 256+ASC("1")
```

The first line is executed if the Zero flag is set and the second line is executed if the Zero flag is clear. One or the other will execute, but not both!

RISC OS provides the SWI 256 (VDU) call, which is not a single instruction but a block of 256 of them. They can be called to output a specific character and they provide a quicker way of doing so, rather than loading the ASCII value into R0 and calling SWI 0. The example above also shows how they can be used in combination WITH conditional tests. Essentially the ASCII value of the character to be printed is added to 256 to give the correct SWI number. It is elegant, and the entire binary print listing is given below as Program 12a This program also makes use of the LSL instruction to process the value:

Program 12a. Using conditional suffixes effectively

```
 10 REM >Prog12a
 20 REM RPi ROAL
 30 REM Print Word as Binary using SWI 256+
 40 :
 50 number=0
 60 mask=1
 70 DIM code% (100)
 80 FOR pass=0 TO 3 STEP 3
 90 P%=code%
100 [
110 OPT pass
120 .start
130 MOV mask,#1 << 31
140 .bits
150 TST number,mask
160 SWIEQ 256+ASC"0"
170 SWINE 256+ASC"1"
180 MOVS mask, mask, LSR #1
190 BNE bits
200 SWI "OS_NewLine"
210 MOV R15, R14
220 ]
230 NEXT pass
240 REPEAT
250 INPUT A%
260 CALL start
270 UNTIL FALSE
```

13: Smarter Numbers

In Chapter 6 we introduced the two basic multiplication instructions MUL and MLA. These were the original multiplication instructions wired into the ARM. Since version 3 of the ARM additional instructions have been added to deal with signed and unsigned numbers up to 64-bits long, many of these new to the ARMv6 chip in the Raspberry Pi. We'll look at some of the more useful ones here. Several have very specific uses and are aimed at more complex tasks such as digital processing.

Long Multiplication

The SMULL and UMULL instructions offer signed and unsigned multiplication using two registers containing 32-bit operands to produce a 64-bit result, which is split across two destination registers. The format of the instruction is:

```
SMULL (<suffix>) <destlLo>, <destHi>, <Op1>, <Op2>
UMULL (<suffix>) <destlLo>, <destHi>, <Op1>, <Op2>
```

For signed multiplication the values passed through Operand1 and Operand2 are assumed to be in twos complement form. You cannot use the PC in these instructions and the SP should be avoided as it is not supported in some later ARM chips, although it can be used on the Raspberry Pi. It should go without saying that the two destination registers should be different.

The following example will produce the full 64-bits of a product of two unsigned 32-bit numbers, which assumes that the two unsigned numbers are in R1 and R2, and on exit R3 and R4 hold the result with the low word of the product in R3 and R4 the high word.

```
UMULL R3, R4, R1, R1
```

To give you an idea of how code-saving these newer instructions are, the segment presented in Figure 13a. will perform the same operation using just the original MUL instruction. As with the above example the routine assumes that the two unsigned numbers are in R1 and R2 and on exit R3 and R4 hold the result, with the low word of the product in R3 and R4 the high word. On exit, both R1 and R2 are non-defined.

```
MOVS R4,R1,LSR #16        ; R4 is ms 16 bits of R1
BIC R1,R1,R4,LSL #16      ; R1 is ls 16 bits
MOV R5,R2,LSR #16         ; R5 is ms 16 bits of R2
BIC R2,R2,R5,LSL #16      ; R2 is ls 16 bits
MUL R3,R1,R2              ; Low partial product
MUL R2,R4,R2              ; 1st middle partial product
MUL R1,R5,R1              ; 2nd middle partial product
MULNE R4,R5,R4            ; High partial product - NE
ADDS R1,R1,R2             ; Add mid partial products
ADDCS R4,R4, #&10000      ; Add carry to high partial
                         ; product
ADDS R3,R3,R1,LSL #16     ; Add middle partial product
ADC R4,R4,R1,LSR #16      ; sum into lo and hi words
```

Figure 13a. Long multiplication - the hard way.

The ADDS following the MULNE test is used in preference to MLA here as we need to preserve the Carry flag for the ADDCS that follows.

If you do not follow this example, try writing it out longhand, or come back to this when you have read the chapter on Debugging so that you can step through it .

Long Accumulation

SMLAL and UMALA are the signed and unsigned equivalents of MLA. As with the previous instructions the signed or unsigned values acting at Operand1 and Operand2 are multiplied together, but in this instance the result is added to any value already in destLo and destHi.

    SMLALS R1, R2, R5,R6

There are also a couple of interesting variants of the command which are only applicable with signed multiplication.

SMLAXY permits multiplication with accumulates using 16-bit operands with a 32-bit accumulator. This is interesting and the full syntax is:

    SMLA<x><y> (<suffix>)><dest>, <Op1>, <Op2>, <Op3>

Here <x> and <y> can be either B or T which stand for Bottom and Top, referring to the bottom or top two bytes of Operand1 and Operand2 respectively. Operand3 contains the value to be added to the result of the multiplication of the byes identified in Operand1 and Operand2.

For example:

```
SMLABTCC R0, R1, R2, R3
```

Here if the Carry is clear (CC) then the low half-word of R1 will be multiplied with the top half-word of R2. The result will be added to the value in R3 and the result stored in R0.

The SMLAWy instruction (Signed Multiply Wide) is very similar but in this circumstance either the top two or bottom two bits of Operand2 are utilised to multiply with Operand1. The upper 32-bits of the result (which may be 48-bits long) are placed in the destination register. This is therefore a 16-bit by 32-bit multiplication with accumulation. The full syntax is:

```
SMLAW<y> <dest>, <Operand1>, <Operand2>, <Operand3>
```

For example:

```
SMLAB R0, R5, R6, R7
```

Here the bottom half-word of R6 is multiplied with the full word in R5 and the value in R7 is added to the result, which is dropped into R0.

SMUAD and SMUSD work on 16-bit values and offer Signed Multiply with Addition and Signed Multiply with Subtraction, with the twist of allowing optional exchange of operand halves. The syntax for the commands is:

```
SMUAD<X> (<suffix>) <dest>, <Operand1>, <Operand2>
SMUSD<X> (<suffix>) <dest>, <Operand1>, <Operand2>
```

If 'X' is included in the instruction then the most and least significant half-words of Operand2 are exchanged. If 'X' is omitted then no exchange takes place. The instruction then multiplies the contents of the two lower half-words of Operand1 and Operand2 and saves the result, and then multiplies the contents of the two upper half-words of the operands and saves the result.

For SMUAD (Dual Signed 16-Bit Multiply with Addition) the two partial products are then added and the result placed in the destination register. For SMUSD (Dual Signed 16-Bit Multiply with Subtraction) the second partial product (the upper half-word) is subtracted from the first partial product.

Examples:

```
SMUADXEQ    R5, R6, R7
SMUDS       R5, R7, R9
```

Division and Remainder

The ARM does not provide a division instruction, so the following segment shows how you can perform one using two 32-bit values. It assumes that the dividend is in R1, and the divisor is in R2. On exit R3 holds the quotient, R1 the remainder and R2 the original divisor. No check is made to see if the divisor is zero, which will fail — but this is a simple check to add to your own function.

```
MOV R4,R2              ; Put the divisor in R4.
CMP R4,R1,LSR #1       ; Then double it until 2 x R4 > divisor.
Div1:
MOVLS R4,R4,LSL #1
CMP R4,R1,LSR #1
BLS Div1
MOV R3,#0              ; Initialise the quotient

Div2:
CMP R1,R4              ; Can we subtract R4?
SUBCS R1,R1,R4         ; If we can, do so
ADC R3,R3,R3           ; Double quotient & add new bit
MOV R4,R4,LSR #1       ; Halve R4
CMP R4,R2              ; Loop until we've gone
BHS Div2              ; past the original divisor
```

Figure 13b. Dividing two 32-bit values.

Smarter Simple Multiplication

We had a look at simple multiplication in an earlier chapter. Now armed with the knowledge of shifts and bit operators, we can look at easier ways to achieve multiplication results. In the examples that follow R0 is used as the main register, However, any register may be used.

If you want to multiply by a factor of 2 then you should use LSL directly:

```
MOV R0, R0, LSL #n
```

Where 'n' is the constant. Replacing n above by, say 4, would produce:

```
R0 x 2 x 2 x 2 x 2
```

This is, in effect, 2^n.

To multiply by 2^{n+1}, examples being 3, 5, 9, 17 etc., use:

```
ADD R0, R0, R0, LSL #n
```

Again where n is the value. Conversely to multiply by 2^{n-1}, examples being 3, 7, 15 etc., use:

```
RSB R0, R0, R0, LSL #n
```

Where n is the value.

To multiply a number by 6 first multiply by three and then by two:

```
ADD R0, R0, R0, LSL #1
MOV R0, R0, LSL #1
```

14: Register 15

Register 15 is the Program Counter, and it is important. If you don't treat it with respect your program can crash. If this happens your Raspberry Pi will most likely freeze and will not recognise anything you do until you turn the power switch off and re-boot. Time consuming, annoying and frustrating. It will happen occasionally, but it's good for the soul to keep those occasions limited!

R15 performs a simple function. It keeps track of where your program is in an executing machine code program. It holds the 32-bit addresses of a physical memory location. In fact, the Program Counter (PC) holds the address of the next instruction to be fetched. So, if you happen to load it with a number which relates to your calorie count for the day, you will understand why the program might crash.

The PC can be used within instructions in a variety of ways. R15 can be used in data processing instructions, which means it can be used as either Operand1 or Operand2.

Example:

```
ADD R0, R15, #8
```

This is an example of R15 acting as Operand1. This line would add 8 to the value (address) in R15 and save the result in R0.

```
SUB R0, R9, R15
```

Here, as Operand2, the value in R15 is subtracted from R9 and the result stored in R0.

R15 can also be used as the destination register in an instruction. In such instances, it should expect to be loaded with an appropriate value for the Program Counter as it will seek to fetch the next instruction from it.

```
MOV R15, R14
```

Places the value held in R14 into R15. As R14 is the Link Register, this is an effective way of returning from a previously called routine. In fact, it is the preferred way to hand control from machine code back to BBC BASIC, and has been used many times in sample programs already.

Pipelining

It is important to understand how the ARM goes about fetching, decoding and executing instructions. The instruction pipeline is a design feature of the ARM that is fundamental to its execution speed. This is because when it comes to executing machine code the ARM is doing three things almost simultaneously: fetching, decoding and executing. As these operations cannot be performed on the same instruction at the same time, the ARM has three instructions on the go at once. It is executing one, decoding a second and fetching a third. When an instruction is executed everything gets shuffled along one place as a new instruction is fetched. The instruction that was previously fetched is then being decoded, and the one that was being decoded is now being executed. There is a continuous stream running through the pipeline as illustrated in Figure 14a.

	Fetched	Decoded	Executed
Cycle 1	Op1	empty	empty
Cycle 2	Op2	Op1	empty
Cycle 3	Op3	Op2	Op1
Cycle 4	Op4	Op3	Op2

Figure 14a. The Fetch, Decode and Execute cycle of the ARM.

It takes three cycles for the ARM to fill the pipeline when it starts operating. Once an instruction has been executed it is discarded as the next instruction overwrites it. It is because of this multi-tasking process that the ARM can achieve great processing speeds. During the process of decoding, the ARM is identifying what registers are going to be used in the instruction, when it is executed.

In Figure 14a, on Cycle 4, the PC holds the address of Op4 — the next one to be fetched. Figure 14b shows where each cycle of the pipeline is relative to the PC.

This three-stage pipeline was the original design of the ARM chip. In fact today's ARM processors are even more sophisticated and the ARM chip in your Raspberry Pi has a pipeline that is no less than eight instructions long. But for the purpose of this book the original concept remains sound for evaluating the pipeline effect.

Contents	Action
PC	Next instruction to fetch
PC-4	Being decoded
PC-8	Currently executing
PC-12	Previously executed

Figure 14b. The PC relative to instruction processing.

Program 14a illustrates the effect of pipelining on the Program Counter.

Program 14a. The effect of pipelining on the program counter

```
 10 REM >Prog14a
 20 REM RPi ROAL
 30 REM Pipelining Demo
 40 :
 50 DIM code% 100
 60 P%=code%
 70 [
 80 .instruction
 90 MOV R0, R15 ; Move current PC into R0
100 MOV R15, R14
110 ]
120 PRINT
130 PRINT "Address of MOV R0,R15 instruction: &"; ~instruction
140 PRINT "Address of PC when instruction executed: &";
~USR(code%)
150 END
```

The program stores the contents of R15 in R0 for BBC BASIC to print out. This allows the address of the MOV instruction to be compared with the contents of the Program Counter when the instruction is executed. The value of R15 is eight bytes (two words) greater than the address of the MOV instruction.

The effect of pipelining must always be taken into account, otherwise in certain circumstances your program may not function as you might expect. Program 14b illustrates this. It might first look as though the MOV instruction in line 90 does nothing and all that the program does is print an asterisk onto the screen (line 100). It doesn't even do that. In the program, the instruction:

```
MOV R15,R15
```

causes the next instruction to be skipped. This is because the address accessed from the PC is two words (eight bytes) more than the address of the MOV instruction. When written back into the PC by the operation, execution resumes a couple of words (instructions) further on, thereby skipping the instruction in between.

Program 14b. Demonstrating the effect of pipelining.

```
 10 REM >Prog14b
 20 REM RPi ROAL
 30 REM Skipping Instructions
 40 :
 50 DIM code% 100
 60 P%=code%
 70 [
 80 .start
 90 MOV R15, R15              ; Move current PC into PC
100 SWI 256+ASC("*")
110 MOV R15, R14
120 ]
130 END
```

Remember that the address held in the PC is always eight bytes more than the address of the instruction being executed.

Calculating Branches

We looked at branches in Chapter 10. Let's examine how they are handled by the Program Counter.

A branch typically takes this format:

> **BAL start**

Here 'start' is taken to be a label or a marked position in the assembly language program. There is a physical limit to the distance a branch can occur. This is plus or minus 32 Mb as this is the largest address that can be represented in the space allocated for the label position. An absolute address is not stored — what is stored is the offset from the current position. When the ARM encounters the Branch instruction it treats the value following as a positive (forward) or negative (backward) adjustment to the PC from the current position.

Program 14c is a program that generates a forward branch.

Program 14c. Generating a forward branch.

```
 10 REM >Prog14c
 20 REM RPi ROAL
 30 REM Forward branches
 40 :
 50 DIM code% (100)
 60 FOR pass =0 TO 3 STEP 3
 70 P%=code%
 80 [
 90 OPT pass
100 .start
110 MOV R0, #255
120 BAL forward
130 MOV R0, #1
140 MOV R1, #2
150 MOV R2, #3
160 .forward
170 MOV R15, R14
180 ]
190 NEXT pass
200 END
```

The program does nothing more than execute the forward branch in line 120. However, we are not actually interested in CALLing this machine code. The key is to look at the assembled listing. If you RUN this, you will get something a little like the listing shown in Figure 14c. (over) As always, the memory address where it is assembled is irrelevant — we need to look at the machine code itself in the second column.

The machine code assembled for BAL forward is:

EA000002

The coding of instructions and conditional suffixes is not a topic for this book. For illustration at this stage we'll concentrate on the rightmost byte of the word, which provides the offset which here is 02. Being positive it indicates a forward direction. The label 'forward' actually means three words forward after three instructions. However, you will recall that the Program Counter does not contain the address of the next instruction to be executed but the next one to be fetched, so it is already one in front. When this is added to the PC, the branch is calculated correctly.

```
00009024                                OPT pass
00009024                    .start
00009024    E30000FF                    MOV R0, #255
00009028    EA000002                    BAL forward
0000902C    E3A00001                    MOV R0, #1
00009030    E3A01002                    MOV R1, #2
00009034    E3A02003                    MOV R2, #3
00009038                    .forward
00009038    E1A0F00E                    MOV R15, R14
```

Figure 14c. Assembly listing for a forward branch.

If you were to add in an additional line thus:

155 MOV R3, R3

and re-RUN the program, you will notice that the machine code assembled for BAL start is:

EA000003

This takes account of the one extra instruction to be negotiated.

Program 14d shows how a backwards branch is calculated. Several lines have changed from Program 14c, and this time the key is to see the assembler listing produced when it is run. This is shown in Figure 14d.

Program 14d. Generating a backward branch.

```
10 REM >Prog14d
20 REM RPi ROAL
30 REM Backward branches
40 :
50 DIM code% (100)
60 FOR pass =0 TO 3 STEP 3
70 P%=code%
80 [
90 OPT pass
100 .start
110 MOV R0, R0
120 MOV R1, R1
130 MOV R2, R2
140 BNE start
150 MOV R15, R14
160 ]
170 NEXT pass
```

The machine code assembled for BNE start is:

1AFFFFFB

The offset byte is now:

FB

This is a negative signed value, with a displacement of four words. Taking into account that the Program Counter will already have the fetched address of the instruction after the BNE one:

MOV R15,R14

this works out correctly.

0000900C			OPT	pass
0000900C		.start		
0000900C	EAA00000		MOV	R0, R0
00009010	E1A01001		MOV	R1, R1
00009014	E1A02002		MOV	R2, R2
00009018	1AFFFFFB		BNE	start
0000901C	E1A0F00E		MOV	R15,

Figure 14d. Assembly listing for a backward branch.

By using relative or offset values as branch destinations, it is possible to write machine code programs that are totally re-locatable. In other words, they can be loaded into and run in any part of memory. Only when you hard code the actual definitive address into place does it tie the machine code into one location.

The description of forward and backward branch calculations are correct in principle, although in these examples, I have limited the process to just the low byte in the word. The actual process, for those wishing to investigate further for branches of greater distance, proceed as follows: Take the difference between the branch instruction and the target address minus 8 (to allow for the pipeline). This gives a 26-bit offset which is right shifted by two bits. The bottom two bits are always zero as instructions are word aligned. The shift effectively saves the sign bit so it is accounted for when it is added to the Program Counter and thus generates forward or backwards branch.

15: Data Transfer

In most of the examples we have used so far, all data instructions used have come from either the contents of a register or an immediate constant — a specified value, like these examples:

```
ADD R0, R1, R2
SUB R0, R1, #7
```

There is only so much information that can be held in a set of registers, and registers have to be kept clear to perform operations on data. In general, data is created and then held at known memory locations. In such cases, we need to manage these memory blocks. To load and store data in memory we must know two things. First, the actual address of the data, and second, its ultimate destination – where it's coming from or going to. Registers are used in both circumstances, and the method of doing so depends on the addressing mode used. There are three addressing modes offered by the ARM:

- Indirect Addressing

- Pre-Indexed Addressing

- Post-Indexed Addressing

These methods load or store the contents of a specified register, but in each case the data source or destination is different.

ADR Directive

In Chapter 6 we examined the use of immediate constants and saw that although the MOV and MVN instructions can be used to load constants into a register, not all constant values are accessible in this way. The knock-on of this is that they cannot be used to generate every available memory address for the same reason. Therefore, the BBC BASIC Assembler provides a method that will load any 32-bit address. In its simplest form it looks like this:

```
ADR <Register>, <Label>
```

An example would be:

```
ADR R0, datastart
```

Despite its appearance, the ADR is a directive and not an ARM instruction. It is part of the assembler. What it does is take the hard work out of calculating the right number for you. When the assembler encounters this directive it does the following:

- Notes the address of where the instruction is being assembled.

- Notes the address of the specified label.

- Calculates the offset between the two memory positions.

It will then use this information as part of an appropriate instruction, normally ADD or SUB, to reconstruct the location of the address or label containing the information.

It's worth looking at what we write in an example program and what actually gets assembled to illustrate the point. Look at the listing given in Program 15a:

Program 15a. Use of the ADR directive.

```
 10 REM >Prog15a
 20 REM RPi ROAL
 30 REM USING ADR DIRECTIVE
 40:
 50 DIM code% (100)
 60 FOR pass=0 TO 3 STEP 3
 70 P%=code%
 80 [
 90 OPT pass
100 .start
110 ADR R0, data
120 MOV R1, #255
130 MOV R15,R14
140 .data
150 ]
160 NEXT pass
170 END
```

Program 15a does nothing really, other than point ADR at the data label and show R0 as the destination register. When this is assembled it will produce something similar to what is shown in Figure 15a.

```
00008FF8
00008FF8
00008FF8                                OPT pass
00008FF8                  .start
00008FF8    E28F0004                    ADR R0,PC, #8
00008FFC    E3A010FF                    MOV R1, #255
00009000    E1A0F00E                    MOV R15, R14
00009004                  .data
```

Figure 15a. Assembly listing of Program 15a.

The ADR directive has not assembled an address. It has assembled a relative address that will be used as an offset for the Program Counter,. Here the ADD instruction is used to add 8 to the PC, the address of value which comes right after the last instruction.

Indirect Addressing

The ARM is constructed with a 'load and store' architecture, but you cannot access memory locations directly. You can only access them indirectly via a register. The beauty of indirect addressing is that it enables the whole of the ARM's memory map to be reached through a single register.

There are two instructions that read and write memory data:

```
LDR        LoaD Register from memory
STR        STore Register to memory
```

Indirect addressing provides an easy method to read or write to a memory location. The address of the location is held in a register. So the address location is accessed indirectly. The advantage of this method is that you can change the source or destination location simply by changing the contents of the register. This makes it a handy way to dip into tables of data. Rather than writing a separate routine for each, a general purpose one can be developed, with the address operand being 'seeded' on each occasion that the routine is called.

In its simplest form indirect addressing takes the format:

LDR (<suffix>) <Operand1> [<Operand2>]

STR (<suffix>) <Operand1> [<Operand2>]

For example:

LDR R0,[R1]   ; Load R0 with contents at location in R1

STR R0,[R2]   ; Store R0 at memory location in R2

Executing the above two instructions would effectively transfer a word of data from one point in memory to another. Figure 15b illustrates this and is based on the instruction:

```
LDR R0, [R1]
```

At the onset R1 holds the memory address, here &9308, and that memory address contains the value &F80A. This value is loaded into R0. So on completion of the instruction R0 will contain &F80A. The value in R1 is unaltered.

All the addressing modes allow use of suffixes to effect conditional execution. So, for example:

```
LDREQ R0, [R1]
```

Here, the load operation into R0 from the address in R1 will only take place if the Zero flag is set.

```
          Register                              Register
  R0   | undefined |                    R0   |  &F80A  |
  R1   |   &9308   |                    R1   |  &9308  |

          Location       Contents
       |   &9300   |   |           |
       |   &9304   |   |           |
       |   &9308   |>> |   &F80A   | >>
       |   &930C   |   |           |
```

Figure 15b. Indirect addressing of memory using LDR R0, [R1].

Program 15b uses indirect addressing. Here the BBC BASIC program stores a simple character string into memory and uses the ADR directive to assemble a program to extract it and printed to the screen.

Program 15b. Using indirect addressing.

```
10 REM >Prog15b
20 REM RPi ROAL
30 REM SIMPLE INDIRECT ADDRESSING
40 :
50 DIM code% (100)
60 DIM string (20)
```

```
 70 $string="ABCD"
 80 FOR pass=0 TO 3 STEP 3
 90 P%=code%
100 [
110 OPT pass
120 .start
130 ADR R1, string
140 LDR R0, [R1]
150 SWI 0
160 MOV R15,R14
170 ]
180 NEXT pass
190 END
```

The space for the string has been reserved by the DIM instruction in line 60. The memory will be located above the BBC BASIC workspace and will be calculated and assembled through the ADR directive. The instruction in line 140 loads R0 with the contents of R1. R1 is the address of $string, so the hex value of the ASCII characters of the string are placed in R0, (&44434241). The SWI 0 instruction of line 150 prints out the ASCII character held in R0. If you RUN the program you will see that 'A' is printed. This is because the SWI 0 routine only looks at the least significant byte of the value in R0.

If you plan to run machine code program as a stand alone entity, you will need to make sure that when you save it, you also save all the data it may need if you are storing this in memory for it to use.

Immediate Constants

Although we have used ADR to provide the correct address, it is still possible to use immediate constants with the MOV and MVN commands. The only problem that will arise is when you encounter a constant that you can't load. In these instances you will need to work out ways to synthesise the address. This might be as the nearest immediate value to which you would then add or subtract an appropriate amount to arrive at the required address.

Listing 15c shows the use of MOV with an immediate constant address.

Program 15c. Using MOV with an immediate constant.

```
10 REM >Prog15c
20 REM RPi ROAL
```

```
 30 REM INDIRECT ADDRESS USING MOV
 40 :
 50 REM CHOOSE MEMORY LOCATION
 60 !&9300=65 ; !$9302=0
 70 DIM code% (100)
 80 FOR pass=0 TO 3 STEP 3
 90 P%=code%
100 [
110 OPT pass
120 .start
130 MOV R1, #&9300
140 .loop
150 LDR R0, [R1]
160 SWI 0
170 MOV R15,R14
180 ]
190 NEXT pass
```

This assembles and executes as expected. The "!" (Pling) operator in line 60 is used to write a value into memory.

All the addressing modes allow use of suffix's to effect conditional execution. So, for example:

```
LDREQ R0, [R1]
```

Here, the load operation into R0 from the address in R1 will only take place if the Zero flag is set.

Pre-Indexed Addressing

Pre-indexed addressing provides the ability to add an offset to the base address to give the final address. The offset can be an immediate constant or a value in a register, or indeed, the shifted contents of a register. The format of the instruction is:

```
LDR  (<suffix>) <destination>, [(<base>,(<offset>)]
STR  (<suffix>) <destination>, [(<base>,(<offset>)]
```

The modifying constant or register is simply placed as part of Operand2, separated by a comma, within the square brackets. For example:

```
LDR R0, [R1, #8]
```

Here, &08 is added to the address in R1 and the four-byte value at that address (R1+8) is placed in R0. Note that the value of R1 is not changed or adjusted by the constant. This is depicted in Figure 15c. R1 contains the memory address &9300. This is added to the specified constant value 8, to give a final source address of &9308. The contents of this location, &FBOA are loaded into R0.

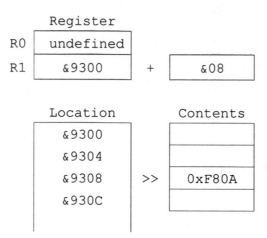

Figure 15c. Pre-Indexed Addressing.

You can use two registers inside the square brackets too:

```
STR R0, [R1, R2]
```

This instruction, when executed, would store the value in R0 at the address given by adding the contents of registers R1 and R2 together. R1 and R2 are not adjusted in any way.

You can also subtract the offset as well, simply by placing a minus sign in front of the offset:

```
LDR R0, [R1, #-8]
STR R0, [R1, -R2]
```

Finally, the offset operand may be rotated using one of the shift operations thus:

```
LDR R0, [R1, R2, LSR#4]
```

The value in R2 is shifted right by two bits and added to R1. This gives the address of the data to be loaded into R0. This final construction is useful when it comes to moving through data held in memory, given that it is located in four-byte blocks (ie, 32-bits and the size of a register) and that an LSL #2 operation (which is 2 x 2 = 4) moves you elegantly to the next word boundary.

The following segment replaces the third item in a four-byte wide list with the second item in the list, with the address of the start of the list held in R1, in this example held as &9300:

```
MOV R2, #4              ; four byte offset
LDR R4, [R1, R2]        ; load R4 from (&9300+4)
STR R4, [R1, R2, LSL #1] ; store R4 at(&9300+8)
```

Here, 4 is given as the offset as the first item is stored at offset #0 (ie, the base address). Then the LSL #1 shifts the bits along by four places. The #4 in R2 becomes #8 which is added to the address in R1. The value in R2 does not change itself. If you wanted to locate the next item in this list you would need to increment either R1 or R2 by four. But there is a far more elegant way as we shall see.

Accessing Memory Bytes

Program 15d illustrates the use of pre-indexed indirect addressing, using an offset to extract characters from a string located at a base address. It also uses the instruction, LDRB to load a register with a single byte.

Program 15d. Use of pre-indexed indirect addressing.

```
 10 REM >Prog15d
 20 REM RPi ROAL
 30 REM PRE INDEXED INDIRECT ADDRESS
 40 DIM string 32
 50 $string="ABCDEFGHIJKLMNOPQRSTUVWXYZ"
 60 DIM code% (100)
 70 FOR pass=0 TO 3 STEP 3
 80 P%=code%
 90 [
100 OPT pass
110 .start
120 ADR R1,string
130 MOV R2, #26
140 .loop
150 LDRB R0, [R1,R2]
160 SWI 0
170 SUBS R2, R2, #1
180 BPL loop
190 MOV R15,R14
200 ]
210 NEXT pass
```

ASCII characters are represented in single bytes, so the string defined in line 50 will occupy just 26 bytes of memory – as there are 26 characters in the alphabet held in the string. The LDRB will allow us to load single bytes of memory, rather than a word, at the location specified. To start with, R1 is loaded with the address of the string, and 26 as an offset into R2. So the first time:

```
LDRB R0, [R1,R2]
```

is executed, the value of R2 will be added to R1, and this will form the address of the byte, the contents of which are loaded into R0, which is then printed. Line 170 then subtracts one from the contents of R2, and if the value is still positive the BPL re-runs the loop. (If you used a BNE in place of the BPL the routine would not print out the letter 'A' from the string. Why?)

When you run this program you should get the string displayed on screen in reverse sequence. How would you make it print out in the correct sequence and maybe even convert the letters all to lower case at the same time?

The STRB instruction is complementary to LDRB in that it writes a single byte of information into memory. Program 15e uses both of these commands to overwrite one string with another:

Program 15e. Overwriting a string with Pre-Indexed Addressing

```
10 REM >Prog15e
20 REM RPi ROAL
30 REM PRE INDEXED INDIRECT ADDRESSING
40 DIM string 32
45 DIM numbers 32
50 $string="ABCDEFGHIJKLMNOPQRSTUVWXYZ"
55 $numbers="12345678901234567890123 4567890"
60 DIM code% (100)
70 FOR pass=0 TO 3 STEP 3
80 P%=code%
90 [
100 OPT pass
110 .start
120 ADR R1,string
130 ADR R3,numbers
140 MOV R2, #26
150 .loop
160 LDRB R0, [R1,R2] ; get byte at R1+R2
170 STRB R0, [R3,R2] ; write byte to R3+R2
180 SUBS R2, R2, #1
190 BPL  loop
```

```
200 MOV R15,R14
210 ]
220 NEXT pass
230 CALL start
240 PRINT "$string is: "; $string
250 PRINT "$numbers is: "; $numbers
```

RUN this program. The $numbers string does not contain numbers, it now has the alphabet stored in it.

The LDRB instruction loads the byte at R1+R2 into R0 and this is then stored at R3+R2. So first time around the last character in string: is stored over the last character in numbers: R2 is decremented by one and while the number is not zero or below the loop cycles again. When R2 reaches zero, the read/write is completed and the _write routine prints the new string out.

Although we haven't used immediate constants in these examples, they are certainly available to you and may also be specified as negative values. Here are a couple of examples:

```
STR R0, [R1, #&F0]
LDR R0, [R1,#-4]
```

In the latter example, R0 would be loaded with data taken from an address which is one word lower than the address contained in R1.

Address Write Back

In calculating the location in memory of the word or byte, the ARM adds the contents of the items held inside the square brackets, the first being a register with an address, and the second being a register or immediate constant. Once the result of the addition of these values has been used it is discarded.

It is sometimes useful to retain the calculated address, and this can be done in pre-indexed addressing, using a method called write back. This is done by including a '!' at the end of the instruction, after the closing square bracket:

```
LDR R0, [R1, R2]!
LDRB R0, [R2, #10]!
```

In the first example, if we refer to our earlier programs, let's assume that R1 holds the address &9300 and R2 contains the index initially set at 26. Now, on the first iteration R1 and R2 point to the address given by &9300+26 which is &931A. This address is used to source the information and then &931A is written back into R1.

To step through an array of data held in memory we might use the instruction:

```
LDR R0, [R1, #4]!
```

The value 4 will be added to R1 and thus create a single word step. The value in R1 is updated to reflect R1+4. By including this in a loop we can quickly step through memory with little hindrance.

Post-Indexed Addressing

Post-indexed addressing uses the write back feature by default. However, the offset field isn't optional and must be supplied. The offset is also handled differently. Post-indexed addressing takes this format:

```
LDR (<suffix>) <Destination>, [<Operand1>],<Operand2>
```

The first thing to note is that the compulsory Operand2 is based outside the square brackets to signify the difference in addressing mode. Here are a few examples of how the instruction is formatted:

```
LDR R0, [R1], R2
STR R3, [R4], #4
LDRB R6,[R1], R5, LSL#1
```

When post-indexed addressing is used, the contents of the base register alone are taken as the source or destination address (word or byte depending on the format of instruction). Only after the memory has been extracted or deposited are the contents of the offset field (Operand2) added to the base register and the value written there. Thus the offset is added post and not pre memory access. Figure 15d below illustrates this diagrammatically for the command:

```
LDR R0, [R1], #8
```

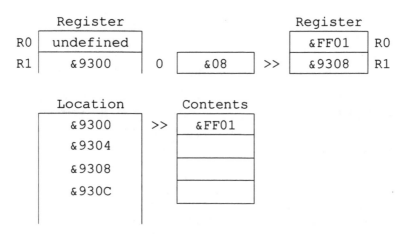

Figure15d. Post indexed addressing process.

The left hand side of the diagram shows the situation before the command executes. The contents of R0 are undefined at this stage. R1 contains the address &9300. The contents of &9300 contain &FF01, and this is taken and placed in R0. The intermediate value 8 is then added to the contents of R1 (&9300+08) and the result written back into R1, leaving R1 now containing &9308 as now reflected on the right hand side of the diagram.

Program 15f. Using post-indexed addressing.

```
 10 REM >Prog15f
 20 REM RPi ROAL
 30 REM POST INDEXED INDIRECT ADDRESSING
 40 REM STRING CONCATENATION EXAMPLE
 50 :
 60 DIM code% 256
 70 str1=0: str2=1 : char=3
 80 DIM string1 100
 90 DIM string2 100
100 FOR pass=0 TO 3 STEP 3
110 P%=code%
120 [
130 OPT pass
140 .start
150 LDRB char, [str1],#1
160 CMP char, #13
170 BNE start
180 SUB str1, str1, #1
190 ;
200 .copyloop
210 LDRB char, [str2], #1
220 STRB char, [str1], #1
230 CMP char, #13
240 BNE copyloop
250 MOV R15,R14
260 ]
270 NEXT pass
280 A%=string1
290 B%=string2
300 INPUT "First string: "; $string1
```

```
310 INPUT "Second string: "; $string2
320 CALL start
330 PRINT "Concatenated string is: "$string1
```

If the LDR line was executed again then the contents of &9308 would be extracted and deposited in R0, and after 8 is added to it R1 would contain &9310.

Program 15c will create a machine code routine that uses post-indexed addressing to join two strings to create one single string.

Byte Conditions

Conditional suffixes may be used with the load and store instructions in a similar fashion to others. However, when you are using the byte modifier with conditionals, you should express the conditional instruction first, thus:

```
LDREQB R0, [R1]
```

Note the condition test EQ comes before B, the byte modifier. If they are not in this order, an error message will result when you try to assemble the program.

PC Relative Addressing

Besides pre and post index addressing, the assembler implements an additional pseudo-addressing mode itself – PC relative addressing. We have already used this in previous examples, but it is worth highlighting its usefulness under a separate sub-heading here.

The general format of instructions that use PC relative addressing is as follows:

```
LDR <dest>, <address>
```

As before, the destination is always a register, into which — or from which — the data is transferred. The address is either an absolute number or an assembler label. In the latter case, the label marks the address from where the data will be placed or gathered. Let's look at a couple of examples:

```
LDR R0, &9300
STR R0, data
```

In the first case, the word located at &9300 would be loaded into R0. In the second, the location which the label 'data' was assembled at would be used as the destination of the word to be held in R0.

When the Assembler encounters an instruction in such a format it looks at the address or location of the address and calculates the distance from where it is to the specified location. This distance is called the offset, and when added to the program counter would provide the absolute address of the data location. Knowing this, the assembler can compile an instruction that uses pre-indexed addressing. The base register in this instruction will be the program counter, R15. If we ignore effects of pipelining, the PC will contain the instructions address when executed. The offset field contains the absolute offset number as previously calculated by the assembler, with a correction for pipelining.

It is important to remember that there is a set range restriction in the offset that can be used in pre-indexed addressing. This is -4096 to 4096, and the offset in PC relative addressing must be within this range.

16: Block Transfer

Efficiency is one of the key design concepts behind the ARM chip. With the large number of registers and the consistent need to manipulate and move data, it would be very inefficient to have to sequence a whole series of instructions to transfer the contents of a set of registers from one place to another. The LDM and STM instructions simplify multiple load and store between registers and memory.

The format of the instruction is:

```
LDM <Options>(<Suffix>) <Operand1>(!), {<Registers>}
STM <Options>(<Suffix>) <Operand1>(!), {<Registers>}
```

Registers is a list of the registers, inside curly brackets and separated by commas, to be included in the transfer. The registers can be listed in any order, and a range of registers can be specified with the use of a hyphen, ie, R5-R9.

Operand1 is a register which contains the address marking the start of memory to be used for the operation. This address is not changed unless the write back operator ! is used in the instruction.

Here's an example:

```
STM R0, {R1, R5-R8}
```

Here, the contents of the registers R1, R5, R6, R7 and R8 (five words or 20 bytes in total) are read and stored sequentially, starting at the address held in R0. If R0 held &9300 then R1 would be stored here; R5 at &9304, R6 and &9308 and so forth as illustrated in Figure 16a.

Reg	Contents		Memory	Contents
R0	&9300	>>	&9300	&FF00FF00
R1	&FF00FF00		&9304	&2A0D4AA
R2	&FF		&9308	&953A
R3	&A8FB		&930C	&F36BCA
R4	&AF2		&9310	&101
R5	&2A0D4AA			
R6	&953A			
R7	&F36BCA			
R8	&101			

Figure 16a. Storing register contents in memory.

Counting Options

The example in Figure 16a assumes that we want data to be stored in successively increasing memory address locations, but this need not be the case. The ARM provides options that allow memory to be accessed in an ascending or descending order, and also in which way the increment step is handled. In fact, there are four options as listed in Figure 16b.

Suffix	Meaning
IA	Increment After
IB	Increment Before
DA	Decrement After
DB	Decrement Before

Figure 16b. Suffixes for memory direction setting.

The I or D in the suffix defines whether the location point is being moved forwards (increasing) or backwards (decrementing) through memory. In other words, the base address is being increased four bytes at a time or decremented four bytes at a time.

After each instruction, the ARM will have performed one of the following:

Increment: Address = Address + 4 * n

Decrement: Address = Address - 4 * n

where 'n' is the number of registers in the register list.

The A or B options determine where the base address has the defined adjustment before or after the memory has been accessed. There is a subtle difference, and if you are not careful it can lead to your information being a word askew to what you might have expected. This is illustrated in Figure 16c and Figure 16d.

```
     STMIA Base,{R0-R6}          STMIB Base,{R0-R6}

                                  R6        Base+28

    R6        Base+24            R5        Base+24

    R5        Base+20            R4        Base+20

    R4        Base+16            R3        Base+16

    R3        Base+12            R2        Base+12

    R2        Base+8             R1        Base+8

    R1        Base+4             R0        Base+4

    R0        <<Base                       <<Base
```

Figure 16c. The effect of IA and IB suffixes on STM.

In Figure 16c the left hand model shows the storage pointer in Incrementing After mode. After the first register has been stored (R0), the storage pointer has four added to it and is incremented to Base+4 where the contents of R1 are placed. On the right hand side of the model Incrementing Before is in operation. When the command is executed 4 is added to Base and the contents of R0 is stored at that address.

In Figure 16d the actions are the same except that in each case 4 is subtracted from Base either After or Before as illustrated.

STMDA Base,{R0-R6}　　　　STMDB Base,{R0-R6}

			<<Base
R0	<<Base	R0	Base-4
R1	Base-4	R1	Base-8
R2	Base-8	R2	Base-12
R3	Base-12	R3	Base+16
R4	Base-16	R4	Base-20
R5	Base-20	R5	Base-24
R6	Base-24	R6	Base-28

Figure 16d. The effect of DA and DB suffixes on STM.

Write Back

Unless the instruction asks for write back to occur, then the address held in the specifying register remains unaltered. Its contents remain the same as they were when the command was first fetched. If we want write back to take place, the '!' operator must be included. For example:

```
LDMIA R0!,{R2-R4}
STMDA R0!,{R5-R8, R10}
```

The value written into the address register (R0) is the address calculated after the last register in the list has been processed.

The STM and LDM instructions have a variety of applications. One of the most obvious is that used in combination they can be used to preserve and restore the contents of all the registers. If R0 holds the address of a free memory block then save all the registers with:

```
STMIA R0, (R1-R14)
```

And restore them later with:

```
LDM R0, {R1-R14}
```

assuming that R0 again has the address of the memory block.

A word of caution about including R15 in a list like this. If you block restore with LDM and include R15 you will most likely set your program into a continuous loop. A real case of Ground Hog Day.

This write back feature in this block data transfer instruction is provided to simplify the creation of stacks, which is the subject of the next chapter.

Block Copy Routine

Program 16a shows just how simple it is to copy a block of data from one place in memory to another. In fact, just four lines of assembler is all it takes, and this routine is robust enough to copy a block of memory that can be any length provided it is divisible by 40 (10 words=40 bytes).

It uses registers R3 through R12 to first load and then store the data, so any information in them will be destroyed unless preserved first. R0, R1 and R2 hold addresses that point to the start and end of the data and the start address of its ultimate destination, respectively.

Program 16a. Moving blocks of memory.

```
 10 REM >Prog16a
 20 REM RPi ROAL
 30 REM Block Memory Transfer
 40 REM Block copy of memory
 50 :
 60 DIM code% 256
 70 DIM memory 256
 80 DIM dest 256
 90 FOR pass=0 TO 3 STEP 3
100 P%=code%
110 [
120 OPT pass
130 .start
140 ADR R0, memory          ; addr of source data
150 ADR R1, (memory+80)      ; addr of end of data
160 ADR R2, dest             ; addr of destination
170 .loop
180 LDMIA R0!, {R3-R12}
190 STMIA R2!, {R3-R12}
200 CMP R0, R1
210 BNE loop
220 MOV R15,R14
```

```
230 ]
240 NEXT pass
250 END
```

To check this works as expected you could use the DIM variables in lines 70 and 80 to store strings, and try printing $dest after the program has run.

Note that if your memory blocks are not correctly partitioned – in this case in blocks of 40 bytes as we are transferring registers – you may get a memory violation error of some sort when you CALL the machine code. Give it a go, change line 150 to:

```
150 ADR R1, (memory+96)
```

Run the program and it should generate an 'abort on data transfer' error.

17: Stacks

Stacks have been a fundamental feature of computer systems since just after the day dot. In many respects they are exactly what you might think them to be, stacks of data, but they are stacks of data that you as the programmer own and control. Their management is a fundamental component of designing programs. Do it well and the program flows well. Do it badly and you'll be reaching for the power switch.

The general analogy is a stack of plates. In theory, you can continue putting a plate on top of a plate. Unless you are attempting a trick, if you want to take a plate off the stack it will be the last one you placed on it. In this respect the last one on is the first one off. We refer to this as a LIFO structure, last in, first out. Try to take a plate out from the middle (or the bottom!) and, unless you do so very carefully, the lot comes crashing down. It's a good analogy.

Push and Pull

In the early days of home computers on systems such as the BBC Micro, stacks were built in a simple fashion. You pushed data onto the stack and pulled data off the stack. For the most part you didn't even know where the stack was — that was managed by the CPU. However, as a programmer you did need to keep track of what order things went on to the stack. Generally the concept is still true today in that a sequence of data pulled from the stack is always pulled from it in the reverse order it was pushed.

The instructions STM and LDM and their derivatives are what we use for pushing (STM) and pulling (LDM) data onto and off ARM stacks. These stacks are areas of memory that we as the programmer define. There is no limit to the number of stacks that can be used. The only restriction is the amount of memory available to implement them.

R13, also known as the Stack Pointer or SP, is designated to be used to hold an address relating to the location of the stack, but you can use any of the available registers for the purpose. If you are running several stacks you will need to allocate more registers or manage where you store the addresses in memory. Figure 17a illustrates a very simple stack.

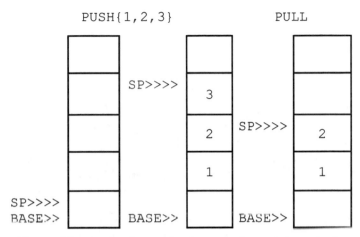

Figure 17a. A simple stack where each stack item is four bytes wide.

To implement a simple stack we can use the following instructions. The important thing to note is that the options for the STM instructions are always reversed for the LDM instruction.

```
STMIA SP!,{R0-R12, LR}  ; push registers onto stack
LDMDB SP!,{R0-R12, PC}  ; pull registers from stack
```

The IA and DB suffix options (introduced in the last chapter) are used in tandem to move up through memory to push them on, and then down through memory to pull them off. The LR and PC registers are used to save the Program Counter's address — therefore this two line combination is an effective way to save register contents before calling a subroutine and restoring everything on return.

The use of the write back function is absolutely vital. Without write back the Stack Pointer will not be updated, and the stack will effectively be corrupted as we will not know our relative positive within it.

You may implement a stack with two pointers. The first is the base point, and this locates to the memory location where the stack begins. The second is the stack pointer which is used to point to the top of the stack. The base pointer remains a static address; the stack pointer might be a moving address or an offset from the base pointer. Hopefully, you can now understand how different addressing modes could be used to organise different types of stacks. Whichever way you fall, you will always need to keep a record of where the stack starts and the point where it must end. Without defining these two end limits, you could get into all sorts of trouble. Also, does the Stack Pointer provide the address of the next free space in the stack or the last space used? To make this situation easier to manage and to manage the balancing of pushes and pulls more easily some additional options are provided.

Stack Growth

In ARM architecture stacks are grouped by the manner in which they grow through memory. Stacks can ascend through memory as items are pushed onto them, and they can descend through memory as data is pushed onto them. It's like being in space — there is no up and down, and the term is relative. Stand on the 10th floor of an empty 20 storey building. The 10th floor is the only entry and each floor, above and below, has four apartments. Eight families arrive; you can accommodate them on two floors up or two floors down. How do you want to do it?

In computer memory terms a stack that grows up — or ascends through memory — is one where the address grows larger. So as an item is pushed into it, the Stack Pointer increases its address by four bytes. A stack that grows in memory by going down the memory address decreases; this is called a descending stack.

In all, there are four types of stacks as listed in Figure 17b:

Postfix	Meaning
FA	Full Ascending stack
FD	Full Descending stack
EA	Empty Ascending stack
ED	Empty Descending stack

Figure 17b. The four types of ARM stack.

When the stack pointer points to the last occupied address on the stack it is known as a full stack. When the stack pointer indicates the next available free space on the stack, it is called an empty stack. Note that in this empty stack scenario the stack can have data on it; it is used to signify the condition of the next free word on the stack.

The option of full, empty, ascending or descending will often force itself on you and may just be decided by the way you are looping through your data. It may be easier to implement a descending stack as your code lends itself to a decrementing count and it's easier to test for the Zero flag.

There are instructions in the instruction set that cater for these types of stacks and these are shown in Figure 17c.

Instruction Pair	Stack Type
STMFD / LDMFD	Full Descending stack
STMFA / LDMFA	Full Ascending stack
STMED / LDMED	Empty Descending stack
STMEA / LDMEA	Empty Ascending stack

Figure 17c. Instruction set to access stacks.

Here are some examples:

STMED R13!, {R1-R5, R6}

LDMFD R13!, {R1-R4, R6}

There is nothing to stop you using different types of stacks within the same program. Just don't mix them up! Equally, you will understand now why write back is compulsory in the construction of these instructions.

Examples of these stacks are illustrated in Figure 17d and Figure 17e. By default, the ARM implements a full descending stack if a format is not specified.

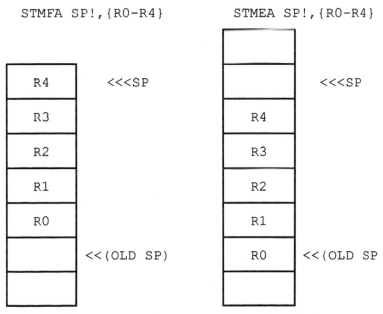

Figure 17d. Full and empty ascending stacks.

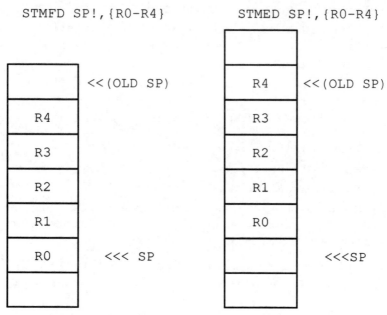

Figure 17e. Full and empty descending stacks.

The best way to understand stacks and their manipulation is to experiment with them. Try seeding an area of memory with known values, and then see if you can move this section of memory to another location via a stack, with the information and its order remaining intact.

Program 17a implements a full ascending stack. When the code is run it will read in characters typed in at the keyboard and push them onto a stack. It will do this until you hit the return key at which point the characters will be pulled from the stack and printed to the screen.

Program 17a. Implementing a full ascending stack.

```
10 REM >Prog17a
20 REM RPi ROAL
30 REM Full Ascending Stack
40 :
50 DIM code% 100
60 DIM stack 256
70 return=13
80 count=2
90 FOR pass=0 TO 3 STEP 3
100 P%=code%
```

```
110 [
120 OPT pass
130 .start
140 ADR R7,stack          ; get addr of stack base into R7
150 MOV count, #0         ; set counter in R2 to 0
160 .readkeyboard
170 SWI "OS_ReadC"        ; read keyboard
180 SWI 0                 ; echo character to screen
190 STMFA R7!, {R0}       ; push character onto stack
200 ADD count, count, #1  ; increment char count
210 CMP R0, #return       ; is it a Return?
220 BNE readkeyboard      ; continue loop if not
230 SWI "OS_NewLine"      ; Echo a return
240 ;
250 .pullstack
260 LDMFA R7!, {R0}       ;get char from stack
270 SWI 0
280 SUBS count, count, #1 ; decrement char count
290 BNE pullstack         ; loop if not zero
300 SWI "OS_NewLine"      ; Echo a return
310 ;
320 MOV PC, LR            ; BASIC
330 ]
340 NEXT pass
```

The program instigates two simple loops, one to push data onto the stack and the other to pull data from the stack. You can see just how simple this is to facilitate. The stack is defined by the DIM command in line 60. Note the push routine makes no check at to the limit of the stack. Because the 'DIM stack' command is after the 'DIM code%' command, the stack will be placed after the machine code. If the stack was defined before the space for the machine code, there is the potential that the stack could overflow into the machine code, thereby corrupting the code.

When you CALL the program it will wait for your response at the keyboard. Press "123456789" and hit RETURN. The response will then be that "987654321" is displayed, showing the information was pulled from the stack in the reverse order it had been pushed onto it.

Stack Application

Stacks have a multitude of applications, and we have already mentioned a few of them:

- Saving register contents

- Saving and processing data

A third use is to save link addresses when subroutines are called. By pushing the link addresses from the Link Register onto the stack, it is possible to create nested (one inside another) routines without fear of losing control in the program. As you link to a routine you push the link register onto the stack. You can then return from each subroutine by pulling the link addresses off the stack and popping them back into the Program Counter.

The stack also makes it relatively simple to swap register contents around without ever having to go through another register. You simply push the required registers in the stack and then pull them in the order you need them. Imagine this situation where register contents need to be swapped:

Source	Destination
R0	R3
R1	R4
R2	R6
R3	R5
R4	R0
R5	R1
R6	R2

At first sight, this looks complex. However, the following four lines will manage it:

```
STMFD  SP!, {R0-R6}
LDMFD  SP!, {R3, R4, R6}
LDMFD  SP!, {R5}
LDMFD  SP!, {R0, R1, R2}
```

The first line pushes R0 to R6 onto the stack. The top three items on the stack are (in descending order) R0, R1 and R2. From the chart above these have to go into R3, R4, and R6 respectively, and this is what line two does.

The Stack Pointer is now positioned at R3, which is transferred into R5. This leaves just R4, R5 and R6 on the stack which, in the final line, is pulled into R0, R1 and R2 respectively. What looks to be a complex task at the onset is in fact a simple one.

18: BASIC Assembler Revisited

The BBC BASIC Assembler provides many additional tools to help in the writing of machine code programs. This includes instructions that allow you to store data within your programs as well as the ability to pass information to them when they are called from the prompt. The Assembler also allows you to control exactly how and where your machine code is assembled.

OPT Settings

In Chapter 4, we looked at the structure of a BBC BASIC Assembler program so this should be familiar to you now. In that wrapper, the OPT function was introduced. Look at the segment of code below:

```
110   .start
120   MOV R0, R1
130   SUBS R3, R3, #1
140   BPL start
150   BNE skip
160   MOV R1, R3
170   BAL somewhere
180   .skip
190   SUB R2, R2, R3
```

The instructions in this are nonsense — what is important here are the labels. When the program is assembled it is done so sequentially, line by line. When the Assembler reaches line 150 it has not yet encountered the label 'skip'. It knows nothing about it so it cannot calculate the offset to 'skip'. As such it aborts the assembly with an error along the lines of 'Unknown or missing variable at line 150'. It will have assembled line 140 perfectly as it will have already encountered the label 'start' at line 110 and knows exactly where it is located.

One use of the OPT function is to allow forward references to be calculated. In the examples we have used so far, each program is assembled twice or in two passes. The first pass has all error reporting suppressed and allows all labels to be located and assigned addresses. The second pass has the error reporting switched back on, but as the locations of labels are now known, their offsets can be correctly calculated. Figure 16a details the full range of OPT settings.

OPT Value	Range Check	Offset Assembly	Error Reports	Listing
0	No	No	No	No
1	No	No	No	Yes
2	No	No	Yes	No
3	No	No	Yes	Yes
4	No	Yes	No	No
5	No	Yes	No	Yes
6	No	Yes	Yes	No
7	No	Yes	Yes	Yes
8	Yes	No	No	No
9	Yes	No	No	Yes
10	Yes	No	Yes	No
11	Yes	No	Yes	Yes
12	Yes	Yes	No	No
13	Yes	Yes	No	Yes
14	Yes	Yes	Yes	No
15	Yes	Yes	Yes	Yes

Figure 18a. The full range of OPT settings.

If you substitute No and Yes for 0 and 1 respectively in the table, you should see a direct correlation between the OPT number and a binary representation. OPT 15 relates to 1111 in the table. Effectively if the option is off then the bit is 0, and if it is on then the bit is 1. As you can see from the table, you can use OPT to decide if you actually even want an assembly listing produced. If no OPT directive is used, then the default value is OPT 0.

Offset Assembly

The BBC BASIC variable P% is used to control where in memory the machine code will be assembled. P% can be assigned to a label (as we have done in most of the examples in this book), or it can be assigned an absolute address memory. For example:

```
P%=&9300
```

The location of P% defines how the offset to labels are calculated, how absolute addresses are referenced and other how position-dependent factors are calculated. It determines to a large degree where your program will be loaded and run if you are making it a standalone executable file.

However, there might be occasions when you will want to assemble your code so that it will load and run in another area of memory which, at the time of writing it, you can't do. For instance, in the same space as your BBC BASIC program or if you were going to write your own machine code module or environment. This can be catered for with offset assembly. Here, P% is set to the address of where the machine code will be run, its final destination address, but O% is used to point the assembler to the area of memory where the code can be assembled. This can be DIMEnsioned space.

Offset assembly is controlled by the OPT settings defined by bit 2 (see Figure 18a). To implement the equivalent of OPT 0 TO 3 STEP 3 assembly with offset switched you would use OPT 4>7. Program 18a shows how it works in practice.

Program 18a. Using offset assembly to generate relocatable code.

```
 10 REM >Prog18a
 20 REM RPi ROAL
 30 REM Offset Assembly
 40 :
 50 DIM code% (100)
 60 FOR pass=4 TO 7 STEP 3
 70 P%=&8F00
 80 O%=code%
 90 [
100 OPT pass
110 .start
120 ADR R0,string
130 SWI "OS_Write0"
140 MOV R15,R14
150 .string
160 EQUS "Offset Assembly"
170 EQUB 0
180 ]
190 NEXT pass
```

Here, O% is where the code will be assembled, inside the space dimensioned in line 50. P% is set to the location where we actually want to use the code. Note that P% is inside the FOR…NEXT loop as it will need to be reset to its original value on the second pass through. In this example, P% is placed where BBC BASIC is being used (on my system anyway), so saving and then loading the machine code file in order to run might well corrupt what you are doing. So if you do want to try this, make sure you have saved everything first.

If you tried to run the machine code by typing:

```
CALL start
```

You will get an error as 'start' is pointing to &8F00, and nothing is there. Instead use:

```
CALL code%
```

This is where the machine code was actually assembled.

In reality offset assembly on the ARM should not be required. The instruction set is sophisticated enough to allow you to write your machine code as standalone modules which can be loaded and run just about anywhere there is free memory.

Range Check

Here, machine code is assembled into space allocated by a dimensioned label, eg:

```
150 DIM code% (100)
```

We have to be careful the code does not exceed the space allocated for it. If it did it could have repercussions if the memory contained important data, for example. The final control offered by OPT is a range check in which it will flag if the space is exceeded by aborting the listing and issuing a suitable error message like:

```
Assembler list aborted at line …
```

Bit 3 of the OPT control determines whether range checking is on or off (refer to Figure 16a), so OPT values of 8 and greater incorporate it. It is worth using for all but the smallest programs.

Data Storage Directives

As your programs become more sophisticated and have real application you will need to store information in them. This might be in the form of constants, addresses or messages to be printed. In the case of the latter, we have used the string operator for this purpose. The drawback of this is that the data is placed outside the bounds of the machine code in space dimensioned by BBC BASIC, and we must remember to save this as well if we are gathering everything. By placing the data within the body of the machine code, we can be safe in the knowledge that it is protected.

There are four directives to do this provided by the Assembler and these are listed in Figure 18b.

Directive	Function
EQUB	Reserve one byte
EQUW	Reserve one word - two bytes
EQUD	Reserve double word - four bytes
EQUS	Reserve string space (0-255 bytes)

Figure 18b. The four EQU directions.

A couple of things: First, these are not part of the ARM instruction set; they are pseudo-commands in the same way that ADR is used to assign addresses. Secondly, for the assembler purpose, a word is two bytes and not four and therefore to use an ARM word the double word directive EQUD must be used. This is to keep compatibility with those directives that were available on earlier Acorn-produced computers such as the BBC Micro.

ALIGNing Data

Except for the EQUD function, these directives can create word block alignment problems. For example, a string might end up being 15 characters long, so if the assembler is then looking to assemble instructions after the EQUS directive the program counter will not be on a word boundary and it will fail. To correct this, we can use the ALIGN directive. When the assembler encounters ALIGN it checks the value in P% and will add any necessary bytes to it to ensure that the next instruction is assembled on a word boundary. Program 18b illustrates these EQU directives in use.

Program 18b. Using EQU and Align directives.

```
10 REM >Prog18b
20 REM RPi ROAL
30 REM USE OF EQU & ALIGN
40 :
50 DIM code% (100)
60 FOR pass=0 TO 3 STEP 3
70 P%=code%
```

```
 80 [
 90 OPT pass
100 ;
110 .start
120 ADR R1,string1
130 MOV R2,#0
140 .printloop
150 LDRB R0, [R1, R2]
160 SWI 0
165 ADD R2, R2, #1
170 CMP R0, #13
180 BNE printloop
190 ;
200 MOV R15,R14
210 .string1
220 EQUS "ARM Assembly Language"
230 EQUB 13
240 EQUB 0
250 ALIGN
260 ;
270 .donothing
280 MOV R0, R0
290 ]
300 NEXT pass
```

The EQUB 0 operator is the standard way of marking the end of a string. The ALIGN directive is used to reset the word boundary to allow the rest of the program to assemble. The lines in 240 and 250 do nothing other than to illustrate the point. A good habit to get into is to use ALIGN at the end of any sections of data storage. It does not slow your program down in any way and is good housekeeping.

Call Parameters

To this point we have used the CALL command in its simplest form:

```
CALL start
```

This will execute a machine code program located at 'start'. On passing control from BBC BASIC to the machine code, the values in BBC BASIC's integer variables A% to H% are placed in registers R0 to R7 respectively. However, CALL can do much more. The format of the CALL command is:

```
CALL <Expression> (,Variable(s)...)
```

Here, 'Expression' is the address of the routine to be called. It can be a variable holding the address, it can be the address itself or it can be a calculated value giving the address. Beyond this, separated by commas can be multiple variables, or immediate values which will be passed into the program. The variables may be of any type, but they must exist when the CALL statement is executed. For example:

```
CALL start, B$, value%, count
```

On execution BBC BASIC confirms that all parameters exist and then seeds various registers with the details of a parameter block which BBC BASIC has constructed before entering the CALLed address. Figure 18c defines the format of this parameter block.

Register	Contains
R0	A%
R1	B%
R2	C%
R3	D%
R4	E%
R5	F%
R6	G%
R7	H%
R9	Address of parameter list
R10	Number of parameters
R14	Link back to BASIC

Figure 18c. Register designations when BASIC executes a CALL statement.

R9 contains the address of a memory block where BBC BASIC has created a parameter list. R10 holds the number of parameters that are passed with CALL.

The list pointed to in R9 is arranged in the reverse order that it was arranged in the CALL statement, so the last parameter is given first. Each variable is assigned two words (eight bytes) in this list. The first parameter is the address where the variable value is stored, and the second word contains the type of variable it is. The key ones to know are listed in Figure 18d.

Type	Address Gives
0	Single byte number
4	Four byte integer value
5	Real number in five bytes
128	String information block
129	Terminated character string

Figure 18d. Common parameter types.

For types 4, 5 and 129, the address points to the actual variable value. However, in the case of type 128, which are BBC BASIC string variables, the address in the parameter block points to a String Information Block, or SIB. This SIB address is word aligned, however, for the other variable types the values of variables are not guaranteed to be stored at word-aligned addresses.

The SIB is five bytes in length. Bytes 0-3 hold a pointer to the actual string, and byte 4 has the number of characters in the string.

Anatomy of a Parameter Block

Let's examine how the parameter block would be arranged in a hypothetical case. Using the CALL example above:

```
CALL start, B$, count, value%
```

We'll assume the following definitions:

```
B$="ARM Assembly Language"
value%=&F00F
count=10
```

On entry to 'start' R9 and R10 would contain:

```
R9          =              <address of parameter block>
R10         =              3
```

The address of the parameter block will vary but for this example let's say it is &9500. R10 holds the value '3' as three variables were passed with the CALL statement. The parameter block will be six words in length as each variable is assigned two words. Using our mythical address of &9500, Figure 18e shows how this block of memory would be arranged:

Knowing where the variable type is will allow you to identify what type it is. By comparing the type, you can then invoke a subroutine in your code to get and process the data you require. Here, Word 0 and Word 2 contain addresses to the actual value of the variables (10 for 'count' and &F00F for 'Value%').

Word Address	Contains	Description
&9500-&9503	<Addr>	Word 0: Pointer to value of 'count'
&9504-&9507	5	Word 1: 'count' is a variable of 'real' type
&9508-&950B	<Addr>	Word 2: Pointer to value of value%
&950C-&950F	4	Word 3: 'value%' is a variable of 'integer' type
&9510-&9513	<Addr>	Word 4: Pointer to String Information Block
&9314-&9417	127	Word 5: 'B$' is a variable of type 'string variable'

Figure 18e. The CALL parameter block.

The value in Word 5 identifies B$ as a string variable. The word before it (Word 4) contains the address of the string and the number of characters in the string. The high byte provides the number of characters in the string, and the other three bytes provide the address of the characters in the string itself.

Program 16d provides a routine that will print out the contents of a string variable whose name is passed to it through a CALL statement such as:

```
CALL start, test$
```

The program makes no check to see whether any other variables are passed in with CALL, if they are the routine may well fail. Its intention is to illustrate how the String Information Block works and can be used. The body of the routine could certainly be used to extract the information. Constructing similar routes to deal with other variables would form the basis of a good library, the relevant portions of which could be called once the variable type has been identified.

Program 18c. Printing a string via SIB from a CALL parameter.

```
10 REM >Prog18c
20 REM RPi ROAL
30 REM Access CALL String Information Block
50 :
60 DIM code% (100)
```

```
 70 FOR pass=0 TO 3 STEP 3
 80 P%=code%
 90 [
100 OPT pass
110 .start
120 LDR R0,[R9] ;R9 has addr of SIB
130 LDRB R2,[R0,#3]            ;high byte of addr
140 LDRB R1,[R0,#2]
150 ORR R2,R1,R2,LSL #8
160 LDRB R1,[R0,#1]            ;low byte of addr
170 ORR R2,R1,R2,LSL #8
180 LDRB R1,[R0,#0]
190 ORR R2,R1,R2,LSL #8
200 ;
210 LDRB R1,[R0,#4]            ;string len 4th byte
220 .getstring
230 LDRB R0,[R2],#1
240 SWI 0
250 SUBS R1,R1,#1
260 BNE getstring
270 ;
280 SWI "OS_NewLine"
290 MOV R15,R14
300 ]
310 NEXT pass
320 DIM test(50)
330 test$="This was printed via a CALL"
```

Assemble the machine code, and then type:

```
CALL start, test$
```

The program is a little more complicated than might have been first thought as we cannot simply load the address of the SIB in a single instruction — it may not be on a word boundary. Therefore it has to be fielded byte-by-byte and adjusted accordingly. The ORR instruction uses an LSL by eight places to shift the address across.

19: SWI Routines

We had a first look at the basic use of SWI routines in Chapter 8, and we have also used a few in the example programs so far. The most common of these are OS_WriteC to write a character to the screen, OS_Write0 to write an ASCII string to the screen and OS_ReadC to read a character from the keyboard. I will reiterate that SWI calls are particular to the operating system you are running on the Raspberry Pi. The ones we are discussing in this book relate to RISC OS. If you are using another operating system then they are most likely to use SWIs in a different format. In Raspbian for example, all SWI calls are performed by calling SWI 0 and the value placed in R7 determines the OS call to be called. Registers are used to pass over information.

Program 8a in Chapter 8 printed out a list of the first 256 SWI calls provided by RISC OS. You could try increasing the loop number and see how many calls actually exist and their range. The names returned in the list will give you a key to their use. The number and range of SWI calls provided by RISC OS is vast, and we can't cover them all here, so we'll look at ones relating to the input-output on the Raspberry Pi plus a few other useful ones.

Some of the most fundamental operations provided by the operating system are those which allow input and output. In particular, reading characters from the keyboard and writing characters to the screen. These functions are essential to allow the user to interact with the OS, and they are also a vital component of all applications software.

Characters In

In communicating with the outside world, and indeed with applications programs, we need to be able to deal with anything from a single key press to multiple lines of text. The fundamental aspect of both of these is the ASCII character — a unit which may be a letter of the alphabet, a number or punctuation mark. These single characters may be combined into streams of characters, so allowing us to get what are effectively strings of text from the user in one form or another.

OS_ReadC (SWI &04) Wait for an ASCII Character

No calling parameters are required. The SWI returns with R0 containing the ASCII code of the character pressed on the keyboard, and the Carry flag C clear if it is valid. If the <ESCAPE> key was pressed then the Carry flag is set and R0 will contain the ASCII ESCAPE code &1B. The segment below shows how you might branch to deal with an <ESCAPE> key press.

```
SWI "OS_ReadC"    ; Read keyboard
CMP R0, #&1B      ; Was ESCAPE pressed?
BEQ escape        ; Yes, so deal with abort
                  ; Otherwise continue with program
```

OS_Byte (129) Return ASCII Key with Time Limit

OS_Byte is a SWI call which provides access to a subset of routines. The routine we are interested in is number 129. This call waits for a key press for a specified time limit. On entry, R0 contains the routine number; R1 and R2 contain a time limit (in centiseconds) with the low byte in R1 and the high byte in R2. When the call returns, R1 contains the ASCII code of the key pressed, or &FF if no key was pressed within the specified time. Also, R2 will contain a flag indicating the result, which will be zero if a valid key was pressed, &1B if an ESCAPE condition occurred or &FF if a timeout occurred. Program 19a demonstrates how to implement this call.

Program 19a. Wait for a key press within specified time limit.

```
 10 REM >Prog19a
 20 REM RPi ROAL
 30 REM Wait for key in time limit
 40 :
 50 DIM code% 256
 60 FOR pass=0 TO 3 STEP 3
 70 P%=code%
 80 [
 90 OPT pass
100 .start
110 MOV R0, #129 ; It is OS_Byte code 129
120 MOV R1, #100 ; wait 1 second
130 MOV R2, #0
140 SWI "OS_Byte"
150 CMP R2, #0 ; valid character?
160 BNE escape
170 SWI "OS_WriteS"
180 EQUS "You pressed :"
```

```
190 EQUB 0
200 ALIGN
210 MOV R0, R1 ; Move ASCII char to R0
220 SWI 0
230 MOV R15, R14
240 :
250 .escape
260 SWI "OS_WriteS"
270 EQUS "Timeout or ESCAPE pressed"
280 EQUB 0
290 ALIGN
300 MOV R15, R14
310 ]
320 NEXT pass
```

This program waits for a key press — lines 120 and 130 define exactly how long. On return, the program checks whether R2 contains 0 which would indicate a valid response (line 150). If not then we assume that either a timeout occurred or the <ESCAPE> key was pressed. If this is the case the escape routine deals with this (lines 250-300). Otherwise, the ASCII code of the character is moved from R1 to R0 (line 210) and printed to the screen. You could expand this by checking specifically for a timeout or escape and printing a specific message to deal with these conditions.

OS_ReadLine (SWI &0E)

This routine will read a line from the keyboard into a predefined area of memory. Before calling, four registers must be set up with the following information:

```
Reg   Contents
R0    Pointer to address of buffer to hold string
R1    Max number of characters allowed for string
R2    Lowest permissible ASCII code acceptable
R3    Highest permissible ASCII code acceptable
```

On entry, the address of the start of the memory buffer to hold the ASCII string is placed into R0. Characters will be accepted and entered sequentially, starting at the address of the buffer and then ascending through memory. The maximum number of characters that can be entered into the buffer is defined by R1. If you try to exceed this limit a beep will be issued and the character will not be accepted. The ASCII codes for the lowest and highest values you will accept are placed in R2 and R3 respectively. This is useful if, for example, you want to limit the characters. Placing 48 in R2 and 57 in R3 would mean that only numbers would be accepted into the buffer (48 and 57 being ASCII codes for 0 and 9 respectively). Using 97 and 122 in R2 and R3 respectively would limit input to the lower case letters of the alphabet. The <DELETE> key can be used to erase the last character from the buffer in the normal fashion. String input is ended by pressing the <RETURN> key.

On return from the call, R1 will contain the length of the string entered, and the Carry flag will be clear. If the <ESCAPE> key was pressed the Carry flag would be set.

Program 19b provides a machine code equivalent of BBC BASICs INPUT command that uses OS_ReadLine.

Program 19b. Simulate the INPUT command.

```
 10 REM >Prog19b
 20 REM RPi ROAL
 30 REM Simulating INPUT using OS_ReadLine
 40 :
 50 DIM code% 256
 60 REM Define Register names
 70 pointer = 0 : REM Must use R0
 80 length=1      : REM Must use R1
 90 minASC=2      : REM must use R2
100 maxASC=3      : REM Must use R3
110 base=4
120 :
130 FOR pass=0 TO 3 STEP 3
140 P%=code%
150 [
160 OPT pass
170 .start
180 ADR pointer, buffer ; Get line buffer start addr
190 MOV minASC, #32     ; accept all alphanum chars
200 MOV maxASC, #128    ; but no ext ASCII set
210 MOV length, #30     ; maximum string length is 30
220:
230 SWI "OS_ReadLine"   ; Input text at buffer
240 ADR base, buffer
250 .printloop          ; print string out
260 LDRB R0, [base],#1  ; Get next
```

```
270 SWI "OS_WriteC"
280 CMP R0, #13
290 BNE printloop
300 SWI "OS_NewLine"
310 MOV R15, R14
320 :
330 .buffer
340 EQUS STRING$(32, CHR$(0))
350 ]
360 NEXT
```

Lines 180 to 210 set up the relevant registers to hold the required parameters before OS_ReadLine is called. The printloop segment from lines 250 to 290 simply reprint the string that was typed in. The printloop routine is the obvious way to do this, but a smarter way would be to use the fact that OS_ReadLine returns the length of the typed string in R1. This could be used to add a 0 byte at the end of the input string and then set R0 up so that the OS_Write0 SWI can be used to output the string. You might like trying to re-write the printloop segment to include some code to check for the <ESCAPE> key, as well as issue a message to that effect if it is detected.

Characters Out

There are a few SWI calls that can be used to write information to the screen, most of which we have used in demonstration programs to date.

OS_WriteC (SWI 0) Write Character

On entry, R0 contains the ASCII code of the character to be printed. As this will only occupy one byte of the full register word it is held in the low byte. No information is returned by the routine. Any character can be written in this way. It is possible to use the call to print out strings of text although OS_Write0 is better suited for this.

```
MOV R0, #ASC("*")      ; place asterisk in R0
SWI "OS_WriteC"        ; echo it to the screen
```

If a particular character is required to be printed to the screen, it is better to use the SWI 256+ call (see below) as this does not require the use of any registers and is therefore a quick and easy way of producing fixed characters from the ASCII set. This is described below.

OS_Write0 (SWI 2) Write Zero Terminated String

This SWI prints an ASCII string to the screen. The string can be of any length but must be terminated by a zero. On entry, R0 holds the address of the string to be printed. On exit from the routine, R0 will hold an address that points to the byte after the end of the string. The string may contain any combination of ASCII codes, but will terminate on the first '0' (zero) it encounters.

All you need to do is to put the address of the string in R0 and call the routine. Program 19c shows how this can be put into practice.

Program 19c. Use of OS_Write0.

```
 10 REM >Prog19c
 20 REM RPI ROAL
 30 REM Use of OS_Write0
 40 :
 50 DIM code% (100)
 60 FOR pass=0 TO 3 STEP 3
 70 P%=code%
 80 [
 90 OPT pass
100 ;
110 .start
120 ADR R0,string1
130 SWI "OS_Write0"
140 SWI "OS_NewLine"
150 ;
160 ADR R0,string2
170 SWI "OS_Write0"
180 SWI "OS_NewLine
190 ;
200 MOV R15,R14
210 .string1
220 EQUS "ARM Assembly Language"
230 EQUB 0
240 .string2
250 EQUS "On the Raspberry Pi"
260 EQUB 0
270 ALIGN
280 ]
290 NEXT pass
```

Here OS_NewLine is used to generate a return after a string is printed. There is nothing to stop you from using EQUB 13 to include the <RETURN> character in the string before the 0, as in the previous example.. However, this method gives you the flexibility with the program to decide if you want a <RETURN> or not.

OS_NewLine (SWI 3) Generate a New Line
As described above, this routine simply issues a RETURN to the output stream. There are no entry or exit parameters.

OS_WriteN (SWI &46) Write String of 'n' Length
This call is identical in action to OS_WriteC but allows for the printing of '0' to the screen. On entry R0 points to the address of the string to be printed, and R1 holds the number of bytes in the string. As the string length is pre-defined by R1, there is no need or requirement to ensure that the string itself is terminated by a zero If you were to run the segment below you would only see the first 10 characters of the string "Print this".

```
.printstring
MOV R0, stringaddress
MOV R1, #10
SWI "OS_WriteN"
MOV R15, R14
.stringaddress
EQUS "Print this string"
ALIGN
```

OS_WriteS (SWI 1) Write String that follows
This routine provides a quick and simple way to print a string of characters to the screen. The only requirement is that the string is terminated by a zero. This call is different from the others in that there are no entry or exit parameters to seed as the string is expected immediately following the SWI call. This sounds strange but in fact is a very common way of inserting fixed messages into machine code. Indeed most error messages are dealt with in this way. On exit from the routine, the Program Counter is updated to fit to the next instruction to be fetched, and this will be immediately after the string. The ALIGN directive should be used in all such instances to ensure that the next instruction is located on a word boundary.

```
.printstring
SWI "OS_WriteS"              ; Call SWI 1
EQUS "Error Message #123"    ; String follows
EQUB 0                       ; Terminating byte
```

```
ALIGN                          ; Re-point to word boundary
MOV R0, #0                     ; Continue with program
MOV R1, #1
MOV R15, R14
```

Another practical use of this routine is to pause your program for a key press:

```
SWI "OS_WriteS"
EQUS "Press any Y to continue"
EQUB 0
ALIGN
SWI "OS_ReadC"
CMP R0, #ASC("Y")
SWIEQ "OS_WriteS"
EQUB 0
ALIGN
```

However, although it looks perfectly acceptable this section of code is not. The OS_WriteS instruction will write "Option Selected" only when 'Y' has been entered at the keyboard. It is certainly true that if a 'Y' is not entered, the SWI instruction will not execute. However, in this case, the Program Counter will not have been manipulated by the SWI to recommence program execution after the string. Therefore, the Program Counter will try to continue execution immediately after the SWI "OS_WriteS" instruction itself. It will attempt to interpret the characters in the string as opcodes and execute them! Therefore in practice and in order to avoid a spectacular crash, a conditional execution suffix should never be added to the SWI "OS_WriteS" instruction. The cause of this type of logical bug or failure is often hard to track down.

OS_WriteI (SWIs 256-512) Write Specific ASCII Character

This routine is normally called SWI 256+. The suffix is the ASCII code of the fixed ASCII character to be printed. For example to print 'A' on the screen you would take the ASCII code for 'A', which is 65, and append it to 256 thus:

```
SWI 256+65
```

The following would also produce the same result:

```
SWI 321
```

321 being the sum of 256 and 65.

There are no entry or exit conditions, and the call does not alter the contents of any of the registers or flags. This makes it useful as a debugging tool (see Chapter 20).

Conversion Routines

Another common requirement in machine code is converting the numeric value of a register or location into the string of characters representing that value. For example, a register might hold the value 255, but how do we get machine code to print the string "255" onto the screen? In BBC BASIC, this is taken care of by BBC BASIC itself, but that option is not available in machine code. Equally, how can we read a string of numbers from the keyboard and convert them into the appropriate value for the machine code to use? RISC OS provides SWI calls to do these things and much more. A few examples are provided here that will be useful and fun to experiment with.

OS_ReadUnsigned (SWI &21): Unsigned String to Number

This routine takes a string stored in memory and converts it into a binary number for internal use. It assumes that the number is unsigned and therefore has a positive value. The string can be in any number base in the range 2 to 32. Base 2 would of course be binary and base 16 would be hexadecimal.

On entry, R1 points to the address of the string of digits to be converted while R0 has a value in the range 2-32 representing the base that the string should be converted to. On exit, R1 points to the end of the string (if it was valid) or is unaltered if the string was invalid. R2 contains the converted value or zero if an error arose. The Overflow flag 'V' will be set if the string was not in the specified format.

The string may also contain the base to be used for the conversion in the following format:

```
<base> <number>
```

For example, to convert the ASCII string "F0FF" into a hexadecimal value, you can use the following string:

&F0FF

To convert a binary string, 11110000 you would use:

2_11110000

If a base is not specified the default used is decimal. If a base is specified at the start of the string, this overrides any value that might be seeded into R0.

The string is analysed up to the first invalid character for the given base. So, for example, the string '92A' will return 92 if decimal was specified.

All numbers are taken as being unsigned, and no check is made otherwise. Program 17c shows how this routine can be used. The assembler also contains a routine that will check to see if you have entered a negative value as well — in other words if it is preceded by a '-'. For example:

```
-     &FFFF
```

When RUN, Program19d requests a string and calls the conversion routine which returns the value via the USR function.

Program 19d. Read signed ASCII string and convert to hex

```
 10 REM >Prog19d
 20 REM RPi ROAL
 30 REM OS_ReadUnsigned demo with signed numbers
 40 :
 50 DIM code% 256
 55 str=1 : result=2 : neg=3: char=4
 60 FOR pass=0 TO 3 STEP 3
 70 P%=code%
 80 [
 90 OPT pass
100 .start
110 MOV neg, #0 ; clear negative marker (R3)
120 :
130 .nospaces   ; move past leading spaces
140 LDRB char, [str], #1
150 CMP char, #32
160 BEQ nospaces
170 :
180 CMP char, #ASC("-")       ; Is it negative
190 MOVEQ neg,#1              ; Set negative marker
200 CMPNE char, #ASC("+")     ; Is it positive
210 SUBNE str, str, #1        ; If not "+" move back one
220 :
230 MOV R0, #10               ; Base is 10 - can be 2-32
240 SWI "OS_ReadUnsigned"
250 :
260 CMP neg, #1 ; Was neg marker set
270 RSBEQ result, result, #0 ; If so make negative
280 :
290 MOV R0, result           ; Return result in R0
300 MOV R15, R14
310 ]
320 NEXT pass
330 :
340 REM Pass string addr into R1 via B%
```

```
350 DIM string 100
360 B%=string
370 INPUT LINE "Enter number string: " $string
380 PRINT "String was: " USR(start)
```

The address of the string is passed into R1 via the variable B% (line 370) and the machine code starts by stripping out any leading spaces. This is good housekeeping, and you should always include a routine like this in similar situations where leading spaces might have an adverse effect on the functioning of the program. This is done between lines 130 and 160.

Lines 180 to 210 check to see if the first valid character is '-' (this is also a reason for stripping out leading spaces, so that we can check the first real character for a sign). R3 is used as a flag register. If the '-' is found then a 1 is placed in R3 to signify the fact. The use of a '+' sign at the start of a positive number is also checked for in line 200. Note the conditional execution. If '-' was found, we don't need to waste time looking for this. If no '+' was included then we need to move back one place so that the address in R1 is correctly positioned.

Line 230 moves the immediate value 10 into R0. This is to signify a decimal base by default. Remember, this is overridden by any base specified in the string when it is entered. The SWI routine is called in line 240. Line 260 checks to see if the negative register flag (R3) was set and if so uses the Reverse SuBtraction instruction to make the value negative. If you are wondering why 0 is used in this instance, check back to Chapter 7 for a reminder of the instructions operation. The result is moved across into R0 as this is the value returned through USR.

There are some interesting techniques illustrated in this short program, so it is worth studying. You should now be capable of re-working this program so that you use SWI calls to read in a string from the keyboard and pass it for processing. This way you will be able to remove the final lines of BBC BASIC from the program and make it a full machine code operation.

OS_BinaryToDecimal (SWI &28): Unsigned Value to Decimal String

This call performs the reverse function to the previous one, converting an unsigned 32-bit number into an ASCII string. On entry, R0 contains a pointer to the 32-bit number, R1 is the address of memory being used as the string buffer and R2 is a value defining how big the buffer is. On exit from the call, the buffer (pointed to by R1) contains the string of ASCII characters and R2 has been updated to provide the length of the string. The string is not terminated by a RETURN character or a 0 so your routines should do this using the value in R2.

A 'Buffer overflow' error is generated if the resultant string will not fit into the defined buffer.

The segment below shows how the call and addition of a RETURN might be performed:

```
; R0 has address of value to be converted
MOV R2, #100              ; max length of buffer
SWI "OS_BinaryToDecimal"
MOV R4, #13               ; get RETURN character
STRB R4, [R2, R1] ; Place RETURN at end of string
```

As an extension to Program 17b you could try adding this routine in order to convert your original number string back from binary to decimal to ensure that the routine works both ways.

Executing OS Commands

There is also a method of executing OS commands from within machine code with the use of an SWI call. An OS command is any that would normally be preceded by a '*', for example:

```
*CAT
```

SWI "OS_CLI" (SWI 5) is used for this function. On entry to the routine R0 points to the address of the command line string which is terminated by &0D, a RETURN. (The normal 0 will also work.) If the command requires parameters passed with it, these should be included in the string buffer, with any delimiting spaces or commands included as required. In fact, the string buffer should be a carbon copy of what you would enter at the BBC BASIC prompt, minus the '*' as this is implied by use of the command.

Program 19e shows how easy this is to do. When run and called the machine code performs a *CAT of your disk.

Program 19e. Perfoming a * command using SWI 5.

```
10 REM >Program19e
20 REM RPi ROAL
30 REM OS_CLI demo to do a *CAT
40 :
50 DIM code% 256
60 FOR pass=0 TO 3 STEP 3
70 P%=code%
```

```
 80 [
 90 OPT pass
100 .start
110 ADR R0, command
120 SWI "OS_CLI"
130 MOV R15, R14
140 :
150 .command
160 EQUS "CAT"
170 EQUB &0D
180 ALIGN
190 ]
200 NEXT pass
```

Line 160 contains the OS command to be executed. You can re-run and retry the program with the various OS commands simply by editing the string in line 160.

You could call other machine code routines in this way by using their filenames in place of the command string.

20: Debugging

RISC OS comes with a set of debugging commands which you will find very useful when the time comes to unravel your programs, and when you try to understand why something doesn't work the way you expected. If you are not using RISC OS then it is likely that your programming environment will supply like minded tools as well, so the reasons and ways to use them outlined here are still relevant.

One of two things generally happens when your machine code program doesn't work correctly. The first possibility is that the result returned is not the one expected. The second is that no result is returned, and the system freezes and requires a hard reset. Of course, both situations can occur together as well!

If a wrong result is given, the likelihood is that one or more constants or addresses are out-of-kilter. The positive side is that your routine seems to be functioning, and there are no logical or branch errors. Here, it is a matter of trying to track down where the error is occurring. The type of result being returned might give you a clue, and you will need to examine this and make some deductions of your own. For example, if you are getting a result that is one more than you were expecting (and 'one' in this case might not be a number) then perhaps a loop is being executed one more time than it should. The loop counter might need adjusting, or your conditional branch instruction might need changing. Being able to see what a loop counter value is at this point would be useful. It may also be that values in registers have been mixed or not referenced correctly in your assembler — for instance, you used R1 when you should have used R3.

Frozen Cases

When a machine hangs up or freezes, things can be a bit more involved. It might be that a routine is trapped in a continuous loop. In this case, the loop counter may not be decremented and will continue to process while power is applied. It might also be that you have mismanaged a stack or corrupted the Program Counter. We saw an example in Chapter 19 where the OS_WriteS routine could be mismanaged and cause a crash that would be hard to locate.

Trapping all these types of errors will become an everyday programming task for you. It is part and parcel of programming. That is why it is useful to develop your programs in small sections, each of which have a specific purpose and importantly each of which can be tested independently.

Use of SWI 256 Plus

If you find that a program crashes or hangs, one key issue is to locate the point at which this happens. The best way to do this is to get some visual feedback on how far the machine code gets before being upset. This allows you to at least narrow your search. For example, if you are getting screen output from your code then you will have some idea and most likely you can ignore everything that went before the last item displayed.

One way to produce screen output that has absolutely no effect on any of the ARM registers (and this is the key) is to use the SWI 256+ call. Chapter 20 details how this works. If you populate these calls throughout your code at appropriate points, you can see how far the program gets before hanging.

For example, let's say a machine code program has five main areas of operation. We could place an appropriate SWI 256+ call at the start of each one thus:

```
.area1
SWI 256+65 ; Print A

...

.area2
SWI 256+66 ; Print B

...

.area3
SWI 256+67 ; Print C

...

.area4
SWI 256+68 ; Print D

...

.area5
SWI 256+69 ; Print E

...
```

Now when the program is run, as each area is reached, a letter will be printed to the screen. Let's say we had the following result:

ABC

before the program froze. This would show that the program had frozen somewhere in area3, because 'D' was never printed.

Now you can concentrate your efforts in this area. You might add in additional SWI 256+ calls to print out more letters or numbers inside area3. This will then narrow your search and allow you to concentrate your debugging efforts in the right area.

This method works because SWI 256+ does not change any registers or Status Register flags and so conditions are always preserved within your code.

The Debugger

RISC OS supplies some useful tools that can be a big help in debugging machine code. One of these halts the code at pre-defined points and displays the values of the registers and memory. The commands are listed in Figure 20a.

Command	Function
*BREAKCLR	Clear all breakpoints
*BREAKLIST	List all set breakpoints
*BREAKSET	Set breakpoint
*CONTINUE	Resume execution of program from break point
*DEBUG	Enter debugging module
*SHOWREGS	Display registers from last breakpoint
*QUIT	Exit debugger

Figure 20a. The Debug commands provided by RISC OS.

The major debugging facility at your disposal is without a doubt the use of breakpoints.

Breakpoints

Breakpoints are temporary halt signs to a program. When the debugger encounters a breakpoint, it stops the code executing at that point, and in the case of machine code displays the values of all the register and Status Register flags. By inserting one or more breakpoints in a machine code program, we can stop and look at register and flag contents at the appropriate point. This should provide the information required to help decide what changes we need to make to the assembler source in order to correct any problem. Breakpoints are set using memory addresses, or more exactly the memory address that contains the address of the instruction immediately after the one we are keen to review. This means that the program must be assembled before we set the breakpoints so we need to know these addressees. Look at the example in Program 20a.

Program 20a. Demonstrating Breakpoints.

```
 10 REM >Prog20a
 20 REM RPi Assembly Language HOG
 30 REM Breakpoint Demo
 40 :
 50 DIM code% 100
 60 P%=code%
 70 [
 80 MOV R2, #255
 90 CMP R2, #255
100 MOV R15, R14
110 ]
```

When this is RUN the output will be something like that shown in Figure 20b.

```
00008F6C
00008F6C   E3A020FF                    MOV R2, #255
00008F70   E35200FF                    CMP R2, #255
00008F74   E1A0F00E                    MOV R15, R14
00009000   E1A0F00E                    MOV R15, R14
00009004                     .data
```

Figure 20b. The assembly listing produced by Program 20a.

As always, the memory addresses in the first column will most likely be different on your system. What we are interested in here is looking at the register dump after the first two instructions have executed. The two addresses that follow each of these that we need to note from Figure 20b are:

```
00008F70 - address after MOV R2, #255
00008F74 - address after CMP R2, #255
```

The format of the BREAKSET command is:

```
*BREAKSET <address>
```

So to insert the two breakpoints, type the following at the BBC BASIC prompt (alter the addresses to those relating to your assembly listing):

```
*BREAKSET 8F70
```

167

```
*BREAKSET 8F74
```

You can check that the breakpoints are set using:

```
*BREAKLIST
```

which will list all breakpoints.

Now, call the machine code:

```
CALL code%
```

After the first instruction has been executed the first breakpoint will cause an interrupt and will dump out the registers. You should see something similar to what is shown in Figure20c.

```
R0=00000000    R1=00000000    R2=000000FF    R3=00000000

R4=00000000    R5=00000000    R6=00000000    R7=00000000

R8=00008700    R9=00007FD8    R10=00000000   R11=00008100

R12=0008270    R13=00A7FC0    R14=0392637C   R15=20008F70

Mode USR flags set:
nzCvif
```

Figure 20c. Register dump after Breakpoint 1.

In Figure 20c, we can see that R2 is set to 255 which is &FF in hex. The other registers are undefined at present although R13, R14 and R15 are all functioning and contain addresses. R15 in fact has the address of this first breakpoint. The Status Register flags are also undefined at this point as we have not tried to affect any.

The prompt after the register due should show:

```
Debug*
```

To continue to the second breakpoint type at the '*' prompt:

```
CONTINUE
```

Now respond with Y to the prompt. Figure 20d shows the register dump.

```
R0=00000000    R1=00000000    R2=000000FF    R3=00000000

R4=00000000    R5=00000000    R6=00000000    R7=00000000

R8=00008700    R9=00007FD8    R10=00000000   R11=00008100

R12=0008270    R13=00A7FC0    R14=0392637C   R15=20008F74

Mode USR flags set: nZCvif
```

Figure 20d. Register dump after Breakpoint 2.

This is the result after the CMP operation. R2 still contains 255, but now the Zero flag is set because the CMP will have resulted in a zero.

At the Debug* prompt type:

```
CONTINUE
```

And

```
Y
```

again to complete executing the program. You will then be dropped back to the BBC BASIC prompt.

You can use:

```
*SHOWREGS
```

at any point to re-display the registers from the last breakpoint executed.

To clear all breakpoints use:

```
*BREAKCLR
```

It pays to try to narrow down where in your program the problem lies otherwise it can be a long winded task to trace the error, although a simple one.

One final point about the Debugger: always exit the program by continuing through all the breakpoints. If you try to quit from the Debug* prompt before doing this, you may corrupt and lose any program held in memory.

Memory Manipulation

If your program manipulates memory in any way then it can be good to set or clear sections of memory so that you can see the effect your program has on that area. If you know that you have cleared memory, or filled a section with zeroes before running your program, you can be sure that what is there after you have run your code will have been generated by it. Checking what is there — and indeed exactly where it is — can help the debugging process. RISC OS provides some memory commands to help with this.

The format of the memory commands is:

```
<Command> <Addr1> <Addr2>
```

Addr1: Is the start of the memory area.

Addr2: This is the end of memory or may also be the size of memory if prefixed with a '+'.

For example:

```
*MEMORY 9000 +1000
```

Would produce a hexadecimal memory dump on the screen that started at &9000 and went for &1000 bytes. The dump would be in word widths (four-byte words here; not the two-byte byte words that RISC OS normally deals with.)

A similar result can be produced but with information displayed in single-byte chunks by using the B suffix thus:

```
*MEMORY B 9000 +1000
```

Note that there needs to be a space between *MEMORY and B otherwise the command will not be recognised. In both cases the dump also includes a display of ASCII data.

Setting Memory

Memory can be set to specific values using the *MEMORYA command. It takes the format:

```
*MEMORYA (B) <address> <data>
```

If the B suffix is included then the command will operate at the byte level. If omitted it will work on a full word basis.

<address> is the location to be altered.

<data> is the data to be placed at the <address>.

For example:

```
*MEMORYA 9000 40
```

This would cause the word at location &9000 to be set to &40. All numbers are in hexadecimal.

If <data> is omitted an interactive mode is invoked that allows memory locations to be altered directly. For example:

```
*MEMORYA 9000
```

Would display the contents at &9000 and then request a new value. Typing:

```
FF
```

Would place &FF at &9000.

Once you are happy with the set byte if you press <RETURN>. the editor will step to the next location which you can then edit. You can also work backwards (descending) through memory by pressing '-' and pressing <RETURN>. The '+' key reverts to the ascending mode of operation.

The Disassembler

A disassembler is a program that takes an address specified and produces an assembly language listing of the machine code located there. If you like, by converting the codes into mnemonics it disassembles the machine code into something that can be read. This can be a very useful tool.

The command to do this is:

    *MEMORYI   <addr1> <addr2>

The two parameters are the start and end address of the block of memory that you wish to disassemble. <addr2> may also be specified in word lengths.

The best way to try this out is to assemble a program and then run the disassembler. A typical output from the command can be seen in Figure 20e.

```
00008F7C:  E3A010FF    MOV       R1, #&FF
00008F80:  E3A00021    MOV       R0, #&41
00008F84:  EF000000    SWI       OS_WriteC
00008F88:  E1A0F00E    MOV       PC, R14
00008F8C:  00000000    ANDEQ     R0,R0,R0
```

Figure 20e. A typical disassembly dump produced by *MEMORYI.

The disassembler will not recognise some of the assembler directives. For example, when EQUS is used to insert a string into memory, the disassembler will try to interpret the string as instructions which will be nonsense even if it produces some apparent instructions in the listing. However, the string will show up in the ASCII fields column. The ADR will disassemble correctly and the address specified will be displayed rather than a displacement. In Figure 20e, the SWI call has disassembled to its actual name. The final line is interpreted as an instruction. But if not, you will need to recognise when you get to the end of the actual machine code; otherwise you may end up on a wild goose chase.

21: Assembly Types

The integration of the ARM Assembler and BBC BASIC allows for great flexibility when you are developing programs. This chapter looks at some additional enhancements that can be applied to your structured programming techniques, and looks at how you can use BBC BASIC to generate information for use in look-up tables. They include:

- Conditional Assembly

- Macro Assembly

- Look-Up Tables

Conditional Assembly

Conditional assembly is a technique that allows for selected parts of a program to be assembled in response to certain conditions being met. Entire segments of assembly language can be assembled, or not, dependent on the condition of program variables or user inputs. This technique allows for machine code to be assembled for particular needs or user requirements and — just as importantly for speed and space — segments can be ignored if not required. The segment below shows how this is typically structured:

```
If screen=0 THEN
      [OPT pass
      SWI "OS_WriteS"
      EQUS "This is the Screen routine"
      EQUB 0
      ALIGN
      ]
ENDIF
```

Here, if the variable 'screen' is 0 then the code is assembled. If 'screen' is not 0 then the segment is ignored and therefore not coded. Note the inclusion of 'OPT pass' within the structure. This is important to ensure that if assembled the segment complies with the prevalent OPT conditions assigned to the whole program.

Taking this segment a step further, Program 21a uses a similar process to assemble some machine code based on your response.

Program 21a. Demonstrating conditional assembly.

```
 10 REM >Prog21a
 20 REM RPi ROAL
 30 REM Conditional Assembly
 40 :
 50 DIM code% 256
 60 PRINT "Please select Assembly value: "
 70 PRINT "String 1 - Enter 1"
 80 PRINT "String 2 - Enter 2"
 90 PRINT "String 1 & 2 - Enter 3" ;
100 A=GET
110 IF A=ASC ("1") THEN PROCone :[: MOV R15,R14:]
120 IF A=ASC ("2") THEN PROCtwo :[: MOV R15,R14:]
130 IF A=ASC ("3") THEN PROCthree :[: MOV R15,R14:]
140 END
150 :
160 DEF PROCone
170 P%=code%
180 [
190 SWI "OS_WriteS"
200 EQUS "This is the String 1"
210 EQUB 0
220 ALIGN
230 ]
240 ENDPROC
250 :
260 DEF PROCtwo
270 P%=code%
280 [
290 SWI "OS_WriteS"
300 EQUS "This is the String 2"
310 EQUB 0
320 ALIGN
330 ]
340 ENDPROC
350 :
360 DEF PROCthree
```

```
370 P%=code%
380 [
390 SWI "OS_WriteS"
400 EQUS "This is the String 1"
410 EQUB 0
420 ALIGN
430 SWI "OS_WriteS"
440 EQUS "This is the String 2"
450 EQUB 0
460 ALIGN
470 ]
480 ENDPROC
```

This program calls the relevant PROCEdure to assemble machine code dependent on whether 1, 2 or 3 is pressed. Again, the code assembled is simple but it is the principle that is being demonstrated here. After each PROC call there is a small segment of assembler that places a MOV R15, R14 at the end of the code.

More exciting options for this program would be to use conditional assembly to create a simple compiler. A sequence of commands could be read into a string buffer, or taken from a simple text file, and as each command is identified, the relevant machine code to execute it would be assembled. This is a technique I used many years ago in my book *Mastering Interpreters and Compilers* (see Appendix B). With this technique, a simple string conversion language could be built using the routines listed in Chapter 19.

For such projects, always start out by keeping them simple. Ensure that the outer structure works and then — and only then — you can add and expand the machine code to be assembled. The structure of Program 21a would work for this string conversion project at a basic level. Once you have worked out how to pass addresses and parameters, you can then start to expand how you feed the commands to the routines from the outside world. The point is that you will know your routines work, so any issues that occur as you expand the compiler will be in the processing of the commands.

Macros

A macro is a section of assembler code which is identified by a name and which can be assembled again and again as required. When the name is provided in the assembler program, BBC BASIC will locate the correspondingly named macro and assemble the instructions that it defines.

Macros are not subroutines but are processed at assembly time and normally in-line as part of a series of machine code instructions. This means that they are normally used to create code that is linear in nature. If they are used to create subroutines then you must manage the insertion of BL instructions carefully.

The BBC BASIC Assembler does not implement macros directly. However, these can be synthesised effectively using the BBC BASIC function operator FN. A function could be called like this:

```
MOV R0, #4
FNinput
MOV R1, R0
```

When this code is assembled the assembly language contained in 'FNinput' would be assembled between the two MOV instructions. Program 21b shows how a macro can be implemented in order to assemble code. It actually breaks down sections of Program 19d into functions that can be assembled when required. If you recall the pseudo-code program example given towards the end of Chapter 2, you can see that this function approach starts to come close to the modular concepts being outlined here.

Program 21b. Macro assembly demonstration.

```
 10 REM >Prog21b
 20 REM RPi ROAL
 30 REM Macro demo
 40 :
 50 DIM code% 256
 55 str=1 : result=2 : neg=3 : char=4
 60 FOR pass=0 TO 3 STEP 3
 70 P%=code%
 80 [
 90 OPT pass
100 .start
110 MOV neg, #0 ; Clear negative marker (R3)
120 FNremovespaces
130 FNisitnegative
140 FNreadunsigned
150 :
160 MOV R0, result          ; Return result in R0
170 MOV R15, R14
180 ]
190 NEXT pass
```

```
195 END : REM temp END to see macros
200 :
210 REM Pass string addr into R1 via B%
220 DIM string 100
230 B%=string
240 INPUT LINE "Enter number string: " $string
250 PRINT "String was: " USR(start)
260 END
270 :
280 REM DEFINE MACRO FNs
290 :
300 DEF FNremovespaces
310 [OPT pass
320 .nospaces    ; move past leading spaces
330 LDRB char, [str], #1
340 CMP char, #32
350 BEQ nospaces
360 ]
370 =0
380 :
400 DEF FNisitnegative
410 [OPT pass
420 CMP char, #ASC("-")       ; Is it negative
430 MOVEQ neg,#1              ; Set negative marker
440 CMPNE char, #ASC("+")    ; Is it positive
450 SUBNE str, str, #1 ; If not "+" move back a char
460 ]
470 =0
480 :
500 DEF FNreadunsigned
510 [OPT pass
520   MOV R0, #10               ; Base is 10 - can be 2-32
530   SWI "OS_ReadUnsigned" ; Convert
540   CMP neg, #1              ; Was neg marker set
550   RSBEQ result, result, #0 ; If so make neg result
560 ]
570 =0
```

Each of the main sections of assembler from Program 19d is now listed at the end of Program 21b, defined as a named function. Now the relevant functions are called from within the main body of the program (lines 120, 130 and 140). When the program is RUN it will assemble as one listing, but in reality the machine code generated should be identical to that generated to Program 17b. Line 195 has an additional END in it so it will stop after being assembled. If you delete this line and then re-RUN, the program should operate as it did in its previous incarnation.

Macros become particularly useful if you start to build up an assembly language library. By defining your segments as macros, you can assemble them within your programs by calling the appropriate (named) function. In effect macros can be the building blocks from which you assemble your programs.

Look-up Tables

By mixing BBC BASIC and assembler, it is possible to generate a variety of look-up tables, as well as the code to dip into them. In such circumstances we use BBC BASIC to generate the values required by the table and the assembler to create the machine code to extract them. Program 21c illustrates this perfectly, providing an application that will convert Centigrade to Fahrenheit. The routine only works in whole integers but nevertheless is a good demonstration. The BBC BASIC portion is used to create the data table first, populating the space at 'base%' with the Fahrenheit equivalents of 0 to 100. The value entered for conversion is passed into R2 via C% which is used as the offset, to reach into the table, and extract the correct value.

Program 21c. Using Look-up Tables for conversion processes.

```
 10 REM >Prog21c
 20 REM RPi ROAL
 30 REM Centigrade to Fahrenheit Table
 40 :
 50 DIM code% 256
 60 DIM base% 256
 70 DIM result% 10
 80 FOR N=0 TO 100
 90 base%?N=(1.8*N)+32
100 NEXT N
110 :
120 FOR pass=0 TO 3 STEP 3
130 P%=code%
140 [
150 OPT pass
```

```
160 .start
170 ADR R1, base%
180 ADR R7, result%
190 ; On Entry C% has C value passed to R2
200 LDRB R0, [R1,R2]
210 STRB R0, [R7]      ; store result
220 MOV R15, R14
230 ]
240 NEXT pass
250 INPUT "Centigrade value: " C%
260 CALL start
270 PRINT "In Fahrenheit that is : "; ?Result%
```

This routine would be a good opportunity to write some practical standalone machine code. Using the techniques previously described, you could use machine code to ask for the value to be converted. You should do some appropriate checks and then provide the result. You could then create the look-up table right at the top of your assembled code and *SAVE the lot. If you use a file name like:

    CTOF

You could run the application using:

    *CTOF

to provide the conversion. As another exercise, what about including the option to convert from Fahrenheit to Centigrade within the same code?

Greater Accuracy

By taking more time creating the table it is possible to generate greater accuracy. For example, it would also be possible to include results to two decimal places. There are many ways to do this. Each value could be represented by three bytes in the look-up table. The first byte would give the integer values while the second and third would give the decimal parts. The offset into the table could then be stepped in jumps of three.

The accuracy of the conversion is predefined by the detail placed into the look-up table. Another way of generating the data would be to use a spreadsheet and then hard code the values using EQUD definitions.

178

22: Floating Point

In our everyday use of computers we take the use of floating point numbers for granted. After all what use would a bank have of a computer that couldn't work out decimal points? When we use spreadsheets, calculators and even some word-processing packages, the ability to perform simple calculations down to several decimal points is accepted without a second thought. But what about in assembly language? All the number action we have looked at to date, and there's not been that much in reality, has been dealing with integer numbers, values without any fractional part.

The management and manipulation of floating point numbers takes a great deal of processing grunt and this is not provided in the first instance by the ARM chip — it is supplied by something called a co-processor. As we will see in Chapter 27, the ARM chip used in the Raspberry Pi is also known as a SOC or System On Chip. It is more than just the ARM chip itself, and one of these additional items is some additional hardware circuitry that handles floating point maths. This co-processor as it is known is the VFP or Vector Floating Point co-processor and this supplies additional architecture, including registers and instructions to allow floating point to be included in assembly language programs. Better still GCC and GDB support these too, and do so as the IEEE 754 definition they conform to standardises the format of floating point numbers to provide a common format across computer platforms.

In these next couple of chapters we'll look at how the floating point architecture is implemented and the instructions which we can use to include real numbers in our own programs. This should provide you with more than enough information to use them in a practical way, and display your results for the world to see.

VFP2 Architecture

VFP2 is implemented on the ARM chip fitted to your Raspberry Pi. As you might guess from the number this is the second release of VFP. There is also a VPF3 but that is only available in later releases of ARM. VFP2 provides support for single precision and double precision numbers. As the name implies the latter can represent numbers in more detail than the former. To this end a single precision number occupies a word of memory (32-bits or binary32), whilst a double occupies two-words of memory (64-bits or binary64). You will recall that the ARM can use 32-bit numbers for its standard values and this begs the question: are the single precision floating point numbers that are available as big as the integer ones? The answer is yes they are and they can be much bigger as it boils down to the way in which they are represented. The following are examples of floating point or real numbers:

```
0.2345
546.6735268
1.001011010
4E7
```

In the latter case the number is 4*10 to the power of 7 or 4×10^7. The 7 is the exponent and means 'raised to the power of'. In single and double precision numbers the values can be encoded into the bits so that they have a sign bit, an exponent portion and a fractional or mantissa portion. In this way very large or very small numbers can be depicted.

Figure 22a below shows how a single precision and double precision number are laid out. In the circumstance of double precision numbers the two words must occupy consecutive memory locations and be word-aligned.

Single Precision format

31 30	23 22	0
S	Exponent	Fraction

Double Precision format

63 62	52 51	32
S	Exponent	Fraction

31	0
Fraction	

Figure 22a. Construction of single and double precision numbers.

Sign (S):   This can be 0 or 1 to represent positive or negative values respectively. It is held in the most significant bit of the number.

Exponent: The exponent is the value we need to shift the mantissa along to the left to restore it to its original value. It is held between the sign bit and fraction.

Fractional: Also called the mantissa, this is the number following the point and it can obviously be a binary value to represent the real number. The mantissa will have been normalised, that is shifted along to the right until we are left with a single digit on the left of the dot. In double-precision numbers it occupies the whole of the least significant word and part of the most significant word.

In a single-precision floating point the mantissa is 23-bits (+1 for the integer one for normalised numbers) and the exponent is 8-bits, meaning the exponent can range from -126 to 127. In a double-precision the mantissa is 53-bits (+1 as for single) and the exponent is 11-bits, so the exponent ranges from -1022 to 1023).

For completeness there is also a third type of number representation. This is called NaN which stands for Not a Number! This is used in special circumstances where a value cannot be represented in single or double precision manner. It is a fascinating topic — not least as there are also two different types of NaN, and is worth investigating further if you are interested. We will not be using them here and I am glad to take the cop-out on this one!

The Register File

The load and store architecture of the ARM chip persists in VFP and to deal with floating point values it provides a set of registers specifically for the purpose. There are 32 in all with the prefix S and numbered S0-S31. These registers are used to hold single precision values as they are all one word wide. For the manipulation of double precision numbers these registers can be paired up to form up to 16 two-word width registers. The prefix D is used to denote this and they are numbered D0 to D15. Figure 22b illustrates this in principle.

You should be clear that these registers are one and the same and although the values in registers may be either single or double they can only contain one value at a time. Thus S0 and S1 can be used individually for two single precision values or combined as D0 for a double prevision value. If D0 is loaded with a value then the contents of S0 and S1 are wiped. It is perfectly possible to have single precision value in S0 and S1 and a double precision value in D1 as D1 is composed of S2 and S3.

Please note that there are no warning devices or alarm systems to tell you what is in what register. That is up to you to look after — this is machine code after all. You are the manager. These registers are grouped into Scalar (S0-S7/D0-D3) and Vectorial banks (S8-S31/D4-D15) for usage purposes — and the group determines how they are accessed, which we'll look at with some examples later on.

S0	S1	<< >>	D0
S2	S3		D1
S4	S5		D2
S6	S7		D3
S8	S9		D4
S10	S11		D5
S12	S13		D6
S14	S15		D7
S16	S17		D8
S18	S19		D9
S20	S21		D10
S22	S23		D11
S24	S25		D12
S26	S27		D13
S28	S29		D14
S30	S31		D15

Figure 22b. The VFP Register File. The Sx registers may be used individually or paired to create a double precision register, Dx.

As you might expect there are instructions to deal specifically with moving both single and double precision values to and from memory and registers and a variety of instructions for arithmetic functions.

Load, Store and Move

As with the standard ARM instruction set the VFP instruction set provides a versatile set of instructions to shift information around. VLDR and VSTR load and store single register quantities using indirect addressing. Here are a few examples:

```
VLDR S1, [R5]       ;Load S1 with F32 value at addr in R5
VLDR D2, [R5, #4]   ;Load S2 with F64 value addr+4 in R5
VSTR S3, [R6]       ;Store F32 value in S3 at addr in R6
```

Here, pre-indexed addressing is used in the second example to add 4 to the address held in R5 before the operation completes.

We can also use pre-indexed addressing with write back as well, to update the address in the indexing register. This is useful when dealing with operations working on sets of registers, as shown here:

```
VLDMIAS R5!,{S1-S4} ; Copy S1, S2, S3, S4 & update R5
```

In this example the values in the four registers S1, S2, S3 and S4 are copied sequentially to the word location starting at the address held in R5. When the operation is completed the length of space used for the storage is added to R5. This means that R5 will now point to the next address — the one after S4. If the instruction had read:

```
VLDMIAS R5!, {D1-S4} ; Copy D1, D2, D3, D4 & update R5
```

then the same operation would have taken place, but the instruction would have allowed two-words (8 bytes) per register and added 16 bytes to the value in R5. If you do not wish to update R5 then exclude the '!' from the instruction.

The addressing modes in operation here are similar in fashion to those described in Chapter 15, but notice how the registers and information are arranged differently. Note also that there is no post-indexed addressing operation.

VPUSH and VPOP can be used with curly brackets to transfer several items to and from the stack:

```
VPUSH {S1-S4} ; put S1, S2, S3, S4 onto stack
VPOP {S5-S8}  ; pull them into S5, S6, S7 and S8
```

The VMOV instruction allows values to be freely transferred between different register sets. When there is a transfer between a VFP register and an ARM register then the transfer is done bit-by-bit and no conversion takes place.

```
VMOV S1, S2              ; Copy S2 into S1
VMOV S1, S2, R3, R5      ; Copy R3 to S1 and R5 to S2
VMOV R2, R4, D1   ; Copy loD1 to R2 & hiD1 to R4
```

In the last example a double precision value (8 bytes) is being transferred into two registers. In such instances it is important to be aware of the order of the hi and lo bytes of the floating point value as failure to do so can radically alter the value saved. Once again no conversion is performed and it is a bit-for-bit transfer. The value is preserved if the transfer is reversed as nothing has changed.

You can use the VMOV instruction to copy information from ARM to VFP registers and thus you can use the command to allow you to store ARM register contents in the Register File if you are looking for extra space:

```
VMOV S1, R1              ; Store R1 in S1
```

Precision Conversion

Both programs at the start of this chapter included conversion from single to double precision values. This was done as the printf function directive %f requires a double precision value as its source to work correctly. The VFP architecture allows for conversion to work in several directions. It can also perform double-precision to single precision transformation, but it can also simplify signed and unsigned integer values conversions. You should bear in mind that conversion can lead to a loss of precision and some rounding of values, particularly where a floating point number is transformed into an integer.

There are four operators that can be used with VCVT to define the conversion source and targets, two of which must always be used, one as the source and one as the target. These are detailed in Figure 22c

Suffix	Meaning
.F32	Single Precision, 32-bit one word width values.
.F64	Double Precision, 64-bit two word width values
.S32	Signed integer, 32-bit one word values width values
.U32	Unsigned integer, 32-bit one word values width values

Figure 22c. Suffixes which can be used in number conversion.

The basic syntax of VFP instructions are thus:

VCVT <Target><Source> <Reg-Target>, <Reg-Source>

The suffixes .F32 and .F64 can be appended to arithmetic or conversion instructions to determine whether the quantities being manipulated are single or double precision. We have already seen an example of this in the conversion process in both programs above.

Here is an example:

VCVT.F64.F32 D5, S14

This takes the single precision (F32) value in S14 and converts it into a double-provision (F64) value to be stored in D5. A few more examples with short explanations are listed below:

```
VCVT.F32.F64 S10, D2      ; Convert double in D2 to single
                         ; in S10
VCVT.F32.U32 S10, R2     ; Convert Unsigned integer in R2
                         ; to single in S10
VCVT.S32.D64 R2, D4      ; Convert signed integer in R2
                         ; into double in D4
```

Vector Arithmetic

The VFP instruction set provides a comprehensive range of instructions to perform all the arithmetic operations you might expect. The format follows the standard form illustrated so far with F32 and F64 being used to specify single and double precision values. Operations are performed on one precision format value in each instruction line as single and double precision values cannot be missed. An example for each instruction available is given below, remembering that there are .F32 and .F64 flavours of each:

```
VADD.F32 S0, S1, S2      ; Addition S0=S1+S2
VSUB.F64 D0, D2, D4     ; Subtraction D0=D4-D2
VDIV.F64 D4, D5, D1     ; Divide D4=D5/D1
VMUL.F32 S2, S4, S1     ; Multiply S2=S4*D1
VNMUL.F64 D4, D3, D2    ; Multiply and negate
                        ; D4=-(D3*D2)
VMAL.F64 D4, D3, D2     ; Multiply and accumulate
                        ; D4=D4+(D3*D2)
VSUB.F64 D0, D1, D2     ; Multiply and Subtract
                        ; D0=D0-(D1xD2)
VABS.F32 S0, S1         ; Absolute S0=ABS(S1)
VNEG.F32 S2, S3         ; Negate S2=-S3
VSQRT.F64 D0,D1         ; Square Root D0=SQR(D1)
```

Staying Legal

Although the mnemonics may be different the basic concept of operation and use of addressing modes should be very familiar to you.. One thing that is very different though when calling a VFP program is that there is an overhead in additional housekeeping that needs to be done to remain compliant with various RISC OS protocols. This involves *context switching*.

23: Context Switching

A context switch is a procedure that a computer's processor follows to change from one task to another while ensuring that the tasks do not conflict and data is preserved. In this case the term 'context' refers to the data in the registers and program counter at a specific moment in time. At any one moment in time on the ARM that is a large amount of data. We often deal with this by pushing everything on the stack and then pulling it off before we return to the original task. In some cases we know and are aware (the PRMs tell us) that the data in some places is going to get trashed.

Now refer back to the VFP2 architecture and in particular the register file. That's an awful lot of information — add to this the three system registers and the amount of data we are looking at is growing. Being able to preserve this information as we switch from task to task becomes complex and poses the question: where should it be placed?

This is even more conflicting if, for example, you are trying to run two VFP processes on the Desktop and have the Wimp to deal with at the same time — lots of data and none of it dealt with automatically. There is the additional fact that the two VFP co-processors must be switched on for RISC OS to recognise and use them. This can become an involved process especially given the need to identify whether they are already in use, and are therefore switched on.

The issue is that multiple context switches may be required every second and this starts to impinge on memory and processing time. Things get slow and at the end of the day effective context switching is critical if the system is to provide a user-friendly multitasking interface.

VFP Support Module

The VFP Module supplies a number of SWI calls that will handle and deal with all these issues. Provided all users adhere to this official way of accessing the VFP instruction set then all housekeeping is taken care of for you as is the RISC OS way. It does this by providing a context environment for individual VFP operations to run in, each identified by its own context handle.

The SWI calls provided by the module allow:

- Contexts to be created

- Contexts to be destroyed (removed)

- Switching between existing contexts

- Context features and values to be interrogated

For each run situation you will need to create a context for your VFP program to operate in regardless if it is a standalone routine, an application or a module. Like so many things, it is relatively straightforward once you know how to do it. The various VFPSupport SWIs and functions which start at &58EC0. are summarised below:

VFPSupport_CheckContext
Checks whether it's possible to create a context with the indicated settings, and how much memory is required for the context save area if the application is to manage memory allocation itself.

VFPSupport_CreateContext
Creates and potentially activates a context as defined and set up by the above call.

VFPSupport_DestroyContext
Destroys a context, potentially activating the indicated context if the context being destroyed was the active one.

VFPSupport_ChangeContext
Activates the specified context.

VFPSupport_ExamineContext
Returns in a descriptor block a list of words describing the format of a VFP register dump.

VFPSupport_FastAPI
FastAPI can be used as a fast way of context switching from privileged modes.

VFPSupport_ActiveContext
Returns the currently active context pointer.

VFPSupport_Version
Returns the current module version number * 100. At time of writing the version was 0.02 which is not backwardly compatible with the original version 0.01.

VFPSupport_Features
Returns the values of the FPSID, MVFR0, & MVFR1 registers.

Creating A Context

Two calls are involved in creating a context. First we ensure that the context can be created with the required parameters and then, assuming there are no errors, we create the context. VFPSupport_CheckContext is called first and has the following entry and exit conditions with R0 acting as a flag register:

On Entry:
R0 Flags:
Bit 0:   = 0 User Mode access required.
          = 1 User Mode access not required
Bit 1:   = 0 Context not saved in Application space.
          =1 Context saved in application space
Bits2-29 = 0
Bits 30-31 = not used
R1 = Number of double-word registers required (1-16)

On Exit
R0 Number of bytes required to contain context.
All other registers preserved

The following segment of code would check to see if a context could be created that reserved the first two double-word registers for use and at the same time ensured that the VFP co-processors were available for use in User Mode, allowing us to create the context in our own memory space. Bit 0 of R0 allows the programmer to determine where VFP code is executed. By setting this bit you can ensure that VFP code can only be executed when the ARM is in a privileged mode (such as SVC) from the context being created. Bits 30-31 are not used. This is so that you can pre-seed information into these two bits that will be required when the context is created, as outlined shortly.

```
MOV R0, #2
MOV R1, #2
SWI "VFPSupport_CheckContext"
BVS context_error
```

When the call returns R0 will contain the amount of space required for managing the context. This can be saved and used to manually manage the space if required. If the context cannot be created an error is returned.

After checking that the context can be created VFPSupport_CreateContext can be called with the following conditions.

```
Entry:
R0 Flags:
Bit 0:     = 0 User Mode access required.
           = 1 User Mode access not required
Bit 1:     = 0 Context not saved in Application
space.
           = 1 Context saved in application space
Bit 30     = 0 Leave context inactive.
           = 1 Activate lazily
Bit 31     = 0 Leave context inactive.
           = 1 Activate now
R1 = Number of double-word registers required (1-16)
R2 = Pointer to buffer for use with context, or 0
R3 = Value with which to initialise FPSCR

Exit:
R0 = Context pointer
R1 = Previously active context - if R0 bit 30 or b31
was previously set on entry.
```

Bits 0 and 1 of R0 have the same function as they do in creating the context. Bits 30 and 31 of R0 are used to determine how the context is activated. If bit31 is set then the context will be activated immediately and the co-processors will be switched in if they are not already active. If bit 30 is set then the context will be activated when a VFP instruction is encountered. Using this so-called 'lazy activation' can provide improved performance in some situations by avoiding redundant save/restore operations, for instance where VFP code might only be executed in certain conditions. It would be a waste of processor time and memory space if those conditions were not met. The set condition of bit 30 supersedes the value of bit 31.

The value in R1 is the same as is passed in creating the context. R2 is a pointer to where the context data should be saved if bit 1 is set. If you are not providing your own memory space then bit 1 of R0 should be clear and R2 can contain 0. If you are creating your own memory buffer then the value returned in R0 by the create context call will need to have been saved. If you do not provide your own space management then the VFP Support module will manage the memory process for you.

The value passed in R3 will be copied to the FPSCR. This allows you to set up any flags and conditions that you might require prior to entering the VFP code. If you have no seeding requirements then this register can be cleared to zero. However there is a caveat here — the VFP support module is still in its infancy and does not provide full software support for all VFP instructions so this can cause it to crash. To ensure that this does not happen, bits 24 and 25 of the

FPSCR should be set to place the co-processors in RunFast Mode. Amongst other things, this forces the default result specified by the IEEE 754 standard for actions such as overflow, division by zero and invalid operations that would otherwise require software support to handle. So, in reality, for virtually all instances the results returned will remain accurate.

The segment below shows how a context can be created based on the previous information:

```
MOV R0, #1<<31      ; Activate context immediately flag
ORR R0, R0, #2      ; Allow in user mode & context space
MOV R1, #2          ; Allow D0, D1 and S0, S1, S2, S3
ADR R2, buffer%     ; load address of context buffer
MOV R3, #%11<<25    ; set RunFast Mode
SWI "VFPSupport_CreateContext"
ADR R4, context     ; Save context handle somewhere safe.
STR R0, [R4]        ; save context pointer
```

At this point the VFP instruction set is ready to be utilised. When you have completed your requirements you should remove the context by calling VFPSupport_DestroyContext and the context handle in R1 identifies the context to be removed:

```
LDR R0, [R4]
MOV R1, #0; Null context
SWI "VFPSupport_DestroyContext"
```

The entry and exit conditions are:

On Entry
R0 = Context to destroy
R1 = Context to activate in its place

On Exit
R0 = Context that's now active
All other registers preserved

If the context in R0 is currently active, then the context given in R1 will be activated in its place. Specify 0 to switch to the null context. If the context in R0 is not currently active then R1 is ignored and the active context will not be modified.

You are not required to call VFPSupport_DestroyContext in order to destroy the context if you are managing your own context space, but you should ensure that you have finished all your VFP activity before attempting to reuse any of the context memory, otherwise you will find your data corrupted which could lead to a crash. If the VFP Module is managing space for you then to free up module workspace it is best to destroy the context when you are finished with it.

Demonstration

Program 23a brings together the segments of code discussed above in order to create a program that demonstrates the use of creating and using a context. The lines 250-290 include a few VFP operations to prove that the process works, moving some floating point data around. Note the use of the DCFS directive in line 280 to store a real value in memory. Unfortunately at this stage RISC OS does not support any floating point SWI print equivalent so interrogating data is not as straightforward as it might be unless you include suitable conversion routines with the program for use. If you do want to have a look at the information returned take a note of the address where the .size label is assembled (line 360) and dump the 12 bytes of memory that are there thus:

```
*MEMORY xxxx +12
```

where 'xxxx' is the aforementioned address. Typical output might look like this:

```
00000028 00009400 48BFAE14 48BFAE14
```

Here &28 is the size of the context space required, &9400 is the address of the buffer% space (line 60) and &48BFAE14 is the single precision value 5.99 (line 380)

It is worth saving the program before you run it (if you have not downloaded from the website) as any errors may result in a freeze.

Program 23a. Demonstration of Context Switching.

```
 10 REM >Prog23a
 20 REM RPi ROAL
 30 REM VFP Context Switching
 40 :
 50 DIM code% 512
 60 DIM buffer% 256
 70 FOR pass=0 TO 3 STEP 3
 80 P%=code%
 90 [ OPT pass
100 .start
110 MOV R0, #2
120 MOV R1, #2
130 SWI "VFPSupport_CheckContext"
140 ADR R5, size
150 STR R0, [R5]
160 :
170 MOV R0, #1<<31
180 ORR R0, R0, #2
```

```
190 ADR R2, buffer%
200 MOV R3, #%11<<25
210 SWI "VFPSupport_CreateContext"
220 ADR R4, context
230 STR R0, [R4]; save context pointer
240 :
250 ADR R1, value1
260 VLDR S2, [R1]
270 VCVT.F64.F32 D0, S2
280 ADR R1, store
290 VSTR S2, [R1]
300 :
310 LDR R0, [R4]
320 MOV R1, #0; Null context
330 SWI "VFPSupport_DestroyContext"
340 MOV PC, LR
350 :
360 .size EQUD 0
370 .context EQUD 0
380 .value1 DCFS 5.99
390 .store EQUD 0
400 ]
410 NEXT pass
420 CALL start
```

Summing Up

This chapter is provided to introduce you to one of the most challenging areas of development in floating point use (and abuse) in RISC OS. If you wish to find out more then you should look at the RISC OS Open website and some of the discussions and documentation provided there. The book support pages on the website contain direct links which include a link to the VFP datasheet.

Now we know how to use VFP legally from RISC OS let's get back to programming the co-processor. with a real example.

24 : VFP Control Register

The VFP2 co-processor provides three system registers. The most important of these from our perspective is the Floating Point Status and Control Register or FPSCR. You can think of this as the CPSR for the normal ARM instruction set, in that it provides flag status information. Indeed the N, Z, C and V flags are all present and have the same application. Figure 24a shows how the register is set out for the programmer whilst Figure 24b details the function of the register bits that we'll be discussing here.

FPSCR Format	Rd			Vector			Exception		CEB	
31 28 24	23	22	21	20	1 8	1 7	1 6	12 7	4 0	
N Z C V			Rmode	Stride	Len					

Figure 24a. Floating Point Status and Control Register layout.

The operation and function of several of these flag sets will be covered in these pages. However, the operation of exceptions, although introduced in a forthcoming chapter for the ARM chip itself is not detailed to any degree.

Bit	Flag Set	Detail
31–28	Condition Flags	Negative, Zero, Carry, Overflow
23–22	Rounding Mode	Controls how values are rounded.
21–20	Stride	Controls the step size taken in vector banks
18–16	Len	Controls the Vector length
12–8	Exception Status	Enables trapping of exception types.
4–0	Cumulative Exception	Trap cumulative exceptions

Figure 24b. Register function summary.

Conditional Execution

We first looked at these condition codes in Chapter 10 The precise meanings of the condition code flags differ depending on whether the flags were set by a floating-point operation or by an ARM data processing instruction. This is because floating-point values are never unsigned, so the unsigned conditions have no meaning. (There is also another reason involving NaN values but as we have not delved into these in this overview they are not significant at this point.)

Without exception the only VFP instruction that can update the status flags is VCMP and this sets the relative bits in the FPSCR. However, condition flags and instructions are controlled by the APSR (Application Program Status Register — CPSR) and so the FPSCR flags have to be copied across into the APSR. There is a specific instruction to do this:

```
VMRS APSR_nzcv, FPSCR
```

The VCMP instruction comes in .F32 and .F64 flavours and can be used thus:

```
VCMP.F32 S0, S1          ; S0-S1 and set condition flags
VCMP.F64 D2, D3          ; D2-D3 and set condition flags
```

The entire contents of the FPSCR can also be transferred to an ARM register thus:

```
VMRS R4, FPSCR           ; Copy FSPCR into R4
```

And likewise the FPSCR can be loaded with the contents of an ARM register allowing the bits to be pre-determined and set:

```
VMSR FSPCR, R4           ; Copy R4 into FPSCR
```

Using the bitwise operators (AND, ORR, EOR) this instruction allows you to mask individual bits and also provides a mechanism to test specific condition flags with the FPSCR. This is used specifically in dealing with the bits associated with 'len' and 'stride' which we'll discuss shortly. Figure 24c overleaf details the meanings of the condition code mnemonics for both ARM and VFP side by side for comparison.

Remember that one of the huge befits of using conditional execution is to reduce the number of branch instructions required and thereby reduce the overall size of your code. Branch instructions also carry a bigger overhead in execution timings — typically three cycles to refill the processor pipeline. For example:

```
VADDEQ.F32 S0, S1, S2    ; Execute only if C=1
VSUBNE.F64 D0, D2, D4    ; Execute only if negative
```

Mnemo nic	Meaning after ARM instruction	Meaning after VFP VCMP instruction
EQ	Equal	Equal
NE	Not equal	No equal, or unordered
CS	Cary set	Greater than or equal, or unordered
HS	Unsigned higher or same	Greater than or equal, or unordered
CC	Carry Clear	Less than
LO	Unsigned lower	Less than
MI	Negative	Less than
PL	Positive or zero	Greater than or equal, or unordered
VS	Overflow	Unordered
VC	No Overflow	Not unordered
HI	Unsigned Higher	Greater than, or unordered
LS	Unsigned Lower or same	Less than or equal
GE	Signed Greater than or equal	Greater than or equal
LT	Signed Less Than	Less Than, or unordered
GT	Signed Greater Than	Greater Than
LE	Signed Less Than or equal	Less Than or equal, or unordered
AL	Always	Always

Figure 24c. Condition code comparison ARM v VFP

Program 24a shows how easy it is to use these commands. This simply loads values into S14 and S15 and then compares them using the VCMP instruction. This sets the flags in the FPSCR. The VMRS instruction is then used to copy the NZCV flags across into the ARM Status Register. Then depending on the status of the C register R0 is loaded with 0 or 255.

You can play with the values of the constants being loaded into the two single-precision registers and use GDB to check the register values to watch the process for yourself. You might like to try extending the program to create a loop that counts down in 0.1 increments, printing them on the screen as you do so and exiting when zero is reached.

Program 24a. Demonstrating conditional execution based on the outcome of a VFP operation.

```
 10 REM >Prog24a
 20 REM VFP Conditional Test
 30 REM RPi Assembly Language RISC OS
 40 :
 50 DIM code% 512
 60 DIM buffer% 256
 70 FOR pass=0 TO 3 STEP 3
 80 P%=code%
 90 [ OPT pass
100 .start
110 MOV R0, #2
120 MOV R1, #2
130 SWI "VFPSupport_CheckContext"
140 ADR R5, size
150 STR R0, [R5]
160:
170 MOV R0, #1<<31
180 ORR R0, R0, #2
190 ADR R2, buffer%
200 MOV R3, #%11<<25
210 SWI "VFPSupport_CreateContext"
220 ADR R4, context
230 STR R0, [R4]; save context pointer
240 :
250 ADR R1, value1
260 ADR R2, value2
270 VLDR S1, [R1]
280 VLDR S2, [R1]
290 VLDR S3, [R2]
300 VADD.F32 S0, S1, S2
310 VCMP.F32 S0, S3
320 VMRS APSR_nzcv, FPSCR
330 BNE over1
340 SWI "OS_WriteS"
350 EQUS "Value is 4.50!"
```

```
360 EQUB 0
370 ALIGN
380 B exit
390 .over1
400 SWI "OS_WriteS"
410 EQUS "Calculation Error!"
420 EQUB 0
430 ALIGN
440 .exit
450 LDR R0, [R4]
460 MOV R1, #0; Null context
470 SWI "VFPSupport_DestroyContext"
480 MOV PC, LR
490 :
500 .size EQUD 0
510 .context EQUD 0
520 .value1 DCFS 2.25
530 .value2 DCFS 4.50
540 .store EQUD 0
550 ]
560 NEXT pass
570 CALL start
```

Scalar and Vector Operations

In the previous chapter when looking at the Register file I mentioned that the registers can be divided into scalar and vectorial banks for access purposes. Figure 24d illustrates how this architecture is arranged.

In the earlier examples we have implied that all operations are working on individual registers. However, the VFP can group registers into vectors or groups of registers. For vector operations, the VFP register file can be viewed as a collection of smaller banks. Each of these smaller banks is treated either as a bank of eight single-precision registers or as a bank of four double-precision registers. The number of registers used by a vector is controlled by the LEN bits in the FPSCR. Practically the register banks can be configured as one of the following:

- Four banks of single-precision registers, S0 to S7, S8 to S15, S16 to S23, and S24 to S31

- Four banks of double-precision registers, D0 to D3, D4 to D7, D8 to D11, and D12 to D15

- Any combination of single-precision and double-precision banks.

Bank 0	Bank 1	Bank 2	Bank 3
S1 S7	S8 S15	S16 S23	S24 S31

D0 D1 D2 D3	D4 D5 D6 D7	D8 D11	D12 D15

Figure 24d. The four VFP2 banks and associated registers.

Normally the value of LEN is set to 1 so that an instruction will only operate on the registers defined in the instruction. However, by increasing the value of LEN we can make the instruction operate on the rest of the registers in the associated bank of registers. So, a vector can start from any register and wrap around to the beginning of the bank. In other words if a vector ends beyond the end of its bank, it wraps around to the start of the same bank. Figure 24e shows how this works in tabular form.

It is important to note that a vector cannot contain registers from more than one bank, so if the length wraps back to the start the operation stops at that point, once the bank is full.

Referring to Figure 24e, the first entry has a LEN of 2. This means that the number of registers to be operated on is two. The start register is D11. Looking at Figure 23d we can see that D11 is at the last register in Bank 2. Wrap around means that the next register in the bank is in fact D8 (D12 is in Bank 3).

The first register used by an operand vector is the register that is specified as the operand in the individual VFP instructions. The first register used by the destination vector is the register that is specified as the destination in the individual VFP instructions.

LEN	Start Register	Registers Used
2	D11	D11, D8
3	D7	D7, D4, D5
4	S5	S5, S6, S7, S0
5	S22	S22, S23, S16, S17, S18

Figure 24e. LEN and its effect on bank wrapping.

In the table above the registers accessed have been consecutive ones, in other words they followed the numeric order allowing for wrap around. However, they can also occupy alternative registers and this is defined by the setting of the STRIDE bits in the FPSCR. In the examples given in Figure 24e the STRIDE setting would have been 1 as the registers used are consecutive. But a STRIDE setting of 2 would have forced alternative registers to be used. Figure 24f illustrates this in tabular form also.

LEN	STRIDE	Start Reg	Registers Used
2	2	D1	D1, D3
3	2	S1	S1, S3, S5
4	2	S6	S6, S0, S2, S4
5	1	S22	S22, S16, S17, S18

Figure 24f. How LEN and STRIDE affects vector wrap-around.

As we have said, a vector cannot use the same register twice, so the combinations of LEN and STRIDE settings are limited.

Consider the following instruction:

```
VADD.F32 S8, S16, S24    ; S8=S16+S24
```

By default LEN=1 and STRIDE=1 and so the contents of S16 and S24 are added together with the result placed in S8. However, if we set LEN=2 and STRIDE=2 and execute the same instruction, it will be the same as executing the following two instructions with 1+1 settings:

```
VADD.F32 S8, S16, S24    ; S8=S16+S24
VADD.F32 S10, S18, S26   ; S10=S18+S26
```

In turn setting LEN=4 and STRIDE=2 and performing the same instruction would actually execute as though the following four instructions had taken place:

```
VADD.F32 S8, S16, S24    ; S8=S16+S24
VADD.F32 S10, S18, S26   ; S10=S18+S26
VADD.F32 S12, S20, S28   ; S12=S20+S28
VADD.F32 S14, S22, S30   ; S14=S22+S30
```

As you can see this is a potent programming method and is especially useful when it comes to matrix operations on blocks of numbers.

Which Type of Operator?

Essentially VFP arithmetic can be performed on scalars, vectors or both together. When LEN=1 (default) then all VFP operations are scalar in nature.

When LEN is set to anything else then they can be any scalar, vector or mixed. How this works is in your control only by your selection of the register banks used or source and destination registers.

STR	LEN	Instruction	Result
2	4	VADD.F64 D0,D1,D2	D0=D1+D2. Operation is scalar as destination (D0) is in Bank 0.
1	1	VADD.F32 S4,S8,S20	S4=S8+S20. Operation is scalar as destination (S4) is in Bank 0.
2	2	VADD.F32 S10,S16,S24	S10=S16+S24;S12=S18+S26;S14=S20+S28;S8=S22+S30. Vectorial and notice wrap around on the last iteration.
2	2	VADD.D64 D4, D8, D0	D4=D8+D2; D6+D10+D0. Mixed as the second source registers is in Bank 0.

Figure 24g. Examples of Scalar, Vector and Mixed operations.

For most purposes Bank 0 (S0-S7/D0-D3) is a scalar bank and the remaining three banks are vector banks. A mixed operation (scalar and vector) occurs when the destination register is in one of the vector banks. Figure 24g provides some examples followed by brief descriptions of the type of action being performed and what is actually to be performed. Although VADD is used through these examples, the action is applicable to all VFP arithmetic instructions.

Len and Stride

The bits associated with LEN and STRIDE in the FPSCR can be set up using VMRS and VMSR instructions to transfer the required bit pattern into the FPSCR. This has to be done through an ARM register and is a two-part process, as the FPSCR must be copied across first so that the flag settings may be maintained and a mask applied just to affect the settings of LEN and STRIDE. Any ARM register can be used and the two-way process would look like this:

```
VMRS R4, FPSCR          ; Copy FSPCR into R4
                        ; carry out bit setting here
VMSR FPSCR, R4          ; Copy R4 into FPSCR
```

The LEN field occupies three bits (b16-b18) whilst the STRIDE field occupies two bits (b20-b21). Figure 24h (over) shows the various bit combinations for LEN and STRIDE and the outcomes for each as well as their reliability with single and double-precision numbers.

Not all combinations return predictable results and should be avoided. Use the table to select what combination works for the type of values you are dealing with. You will see from this that STRIDE bits are only ever 00 or 11 to represent 1 and 2 and so are one more than the actual value stored. LEN operates the same so a value of 1 is represented by 000.

Program 23b demonstrates how vector addressing delivers the third option listed in Figure 23g. The bulk of the listing is actually given over to first seeding values and then printing them out using printf. The theory behind the latter should be familiar to you now, and as we will ultimately be printing four double-precision values, three of these have to be pushed onto the stack so the main: function begins by reserving 24-bytes for just this purpose (24-bytes being three words).

The actual instruction being actioned is:

```
VADD.F32 S10, S16, S24
```

This involves three vector banks in Bank 1, Bank 2 and Bank 3. As we will be using STRIDE=2, LEN=4 as our vector control settings, Bank 1 is used to hold results (S10, S12, S14, S8), Bank 2 will hold the first set of values (S16, S18, S20, S22) and Bank 3 the second set of values (S24, S26, S28, S30).

Five values have been defined for use. To make things easier to check, a single value is assigned into the Bank 2 registers and then four separate values assigned to each of the registers in Bank 2.

The lenstride: entry point marks where the FPSCR is seeded with the settings for STRIDE and LEN. We require settings of 2 and 4 respectively. Looking at Figure 23h we can see in line 8 the binary settings to achieve this for single-precision are 11 and 011 (a 'normal operation for single-precision).

As STRIDE and LEN are separated by a single bit the bit pattern we need to seed is 110011. This in turn needs to be shifted so the leftmost bit starts at b21 in the FPSCR so a LSL #16 achieves this.

	STR	Bits	LEN	Bits	Single (Sx)	Double (Dx)
1		b00	1	b000	All scalar	All Scalar
2		b11	1	b000	Normal	Normal
3	1	b00	2	b001	Normal	Normal
4	2	b11	2	b001	Normal	Normal
5	1	b00	3	B010	Normal	Unpredictable
6	2	b11	3	b010	Normal	Normal
7	1	b00	4	b011	Normal	Unpredictable
8	2	b11	4	b011	Normal	Unpredictable
9	1	b00	5	b100	Normal	Unpredictable
10	2	b11	5	b100	Unpredictable	Unpredictable
11	1	b00	6	b101	Normal	Unpredictable
12	2	b11	6	b101	Unpredictable	Unpredictable
13	1	b00	7	b110	Normal	Unpredictable
14	2	b11	7	b110	Unpredictable	Unpredictable
15	1	b00	8	b111	Normal	Unpredictable
16	2	b11	8	b111	Unpredictable	Unpredictable

Figure 24h. STRIDE and Vector LEN combinations and their effect on single and double-precision numbers.

Looking at the program listing, the 'convert:' routine transforms the Sx registers in Bank 1 into double-precision values in Bank 0. In this program Bank 0 is not touched so these registers are free, but beware, you must ensure that you have at least one double-precision register that you can use if you plan to utilise printf, otherwise you will be doing a lot of register moving and restoring.

Program 24b is shown below. All source files are available on the companion website at www.brucesmith.info.

Program 24b Using LEN and STRIDE to sum vectors.

```
10 REM >Prog24b
20 REM Using LEN & STRIFD to sum vectors
30 REM RPi ROAL
40 :
50 DIM code% 512
60 DIM buffer% 1024
70 FOR pass=0 TO 3 STEP 3
80 P%=code%
90 [ OPT pass
```

```
100 .start
110 MOV R0, #2
120 MOV R1, #16
130 SWI "VFPSupport_CheckContext"
140 ADR R5, size
150 STR R0, [R5]
160:
170 MOV R0, #1<<31
180 ORR R0, R0, #2
190 ADR R2, buffer%
200 MOV R3, #%11<<25
210 SWI "VFPSupport_CreateContext"
220 ADR R4, context
230 STR R0, [R4]; save context pointer
240 :
250 ADR R1, value1
260 ADR R2, value2
270 ADR R3, value3
280 ADR R4, value4
290 ADR R5, value5
300 ;
310 VLDR S16, [R1]; load values into
320 VLDR S18, [R1]; registers
330 VLDR S20, [R1]
340 VLDR S22, [R1]
350 VLDR S24, [R2]
360 VLDR S26, [R3]
370 VLDR S28, [R4]
380 VLDR S30, [R5]
390 ;
400 .lenstride
410 ; Set LEN=4 %101 and STRIDE=2 %11 */
420 VMRS R3, FPSCR; get current FPSCR
430 MOV R4, #%11011; bit pattern
440 MOV R4, R4, LSL #16; move across to b21
450 ORR R3, R3, R4; keep all 1's
460 VMSR FPSCR, R3; transfer to FPSCR
470 VADD.F32 S10, S16, S24;Vector addition
480 :
490 ADR R4, context
500 LDR R0, [R4]
```

```
510 MOV R1, #0; Null context
520 SWI "VFPSupport_DestroyContext"
530 MOV PC, LR
540 :
550 .size EQUD 0
560 .context EQUD 0
570 .store EQUD 0
580 .value1 DCFS 1.0
590 .value2 DCFS 1.25
600 .value3 DCFS 1.50
610 .value4 DCFS 1.75
620 .value5 DCFS 2.00
630 ]
640 NEXT pass
```

I make no apologies for the simplicity of this program, but it does provide a good way to get to grips with using the FPSCR and the STRIDE and LEN bits. It is worth spending some time making copies of the source and editing the file to look at other combinations. Perhaps try to test the rest of the examples given in Figure 24g.

25: Modes Of Operation

This chapter provides an overview of the various modes of ARM operation, exception handling, and vectors and interrupts. This is a fundamental design aspect of the ARM chip and provides a clever and versatile way to customise the manner in which your chosen operating system works. It should be considered an advanced topic and as such its detail is beyond the scope of this book. However, it is fascinating as is the whole concept of interrupts which are fundamental to everyday Raspberry Pi operation. As such an overview here is provided which will certainly help you should you delve into areas such as bare metal programming, or look at writing your own OS to run on your Raspberry Pi. And these are all tasks you should consider as a next step in the learning curve.

As an operating system RISC OS is defensive in the way it is configured, and its core, the kernel, prevents you from accessing something that is not mapped into the process memory map. In other words, it will not let you just read and write to arbitrary memory locations. It is for this reason that the GPIO pins and other hardware components of the Raspberry Pi cannot be accessed from a standard machine code program running under RISC OS .

CPSR Mode Bits

In Chapter 5, we examined the Current Program Status Register and saw how the individual bits within it were used as flags to denote certain conditions. The figure presented then is shown again as Figure 25a.

31	30	29	28	27...8	7	6	5	4	3	2	1	0
N	Z	C	V		I	F	T	MODE				

Figure 25a. The Status Register configuration.

The N, Z, C and V flags should be very familiar by now. The ones we are concerned with now are held in the low byte of the register in bits 0 to 7.

The Mode bits are located from 0 to 4 (five in total), and their setting determines which of the six operating modes the ARM operates in. Figure 25b summarises these modes. Any of them can be entered by changing the CPSR. Except for

User Mode and Supervisor Mode all modes can be entered when an exception occurs.

Mode	Description
FIQ	Entered when a high priority (fast) interrupt is raised
IRQ	Entered when a low priority (normal) interrupt is raised
Supervisor and Reset	Entered on reset and when a Software Interrupt instruction is executed
Abort	Used to handle memory access violations
Undef	Used to handle undefined instructions
User	Unprivileged mode under which most tasks run

Figure 25b. The ARM's six modes of operation.

User Mode is the one used by default by programs and applications. This is the environment we work in, and in truth, we as programmers never have to leave it, unless we are looking to be more adventurous and take over total control of the ARM chip itself. This is not for the novice and care needs to be taken when that line is stepped over.

Referring back again to Figure 25a, bits 7 and 6 are used for enabling and disabling IRQ and FIQ interrupts respectively. If a bit is set the associated interrupt is disabled. If the bit is clear then the interrupt is enabled. Bit 5 is the Thumb mode bit and is discussed in Chapter 24. For all interrupts this bit is clear and the processor is operating in ARM State.

Vectors

Vectors play an important role in the operation of the ARM chip. A vector is a known location in memory that is exactly one word, or 32-bits wide. (Not to be confused with vectors in VFP , which we examined in previous chapters,

There are two types of vectors: hardware vectors and software vectors. Hardware vectors are hardwired to the ARM chip itself and they never change, and as Figure 25c shows, they are located at the very beginning of the memory map.

Hardware vectors control the ultimate flow of information and are a set of memory addresses that are 'known' to the ARM chip. The term 'known' here means that they are physically 'hard-wired' and are thus termed hardware vectors. Hardware vectors typically control the flow of abnormal events which the chip itself cannot deal with. They are often referred to as exception vectors and they reside smack bang at the start of the memory map from &00000000 to &0000001C. Figure 25c lists the hardware vectors.

Address	Vector
0x00000000	ARM reset
0x00000004	Undefined Instruction
0x00000008	Software Interrupt (SWI)
0x0000000C	Abort (pre-fetch)
0x00000010	Abort (data)
0x00000014	Address exception
0x00000018	IRQ
0x0000001C	FIRQ (or FIQ)

Figure 25c. The ARM Hardware vectors.

One common reason for manipulating the hardware vectors is to change the machine's response to memory access faults. If some non-existent memory is accessed then one of the memory fault vectors, &0000000C to &00000014, is called. The normal effect of this is for the Operating System to report a fatal error and stop executing the current task. Sometimes, for example when writing a memory editor, this is not a very desirable thing to happen. It would be better simply to warn the user that a particular location is invalid and allow editing to continue for the rest of memory.

Vectors are useful to the programmer as they allow programs to access standard routines without directly calling the physical address where the machine code for the routine is stored.

In the early days of computers operating systems were small and everything was 'hard-coded', meaning address where used in absolute terms. The problem with using absolute addresses and by this I mean a real physical address rather than a branch offset for example, is that you are always tied to that address. If the OS is updated then, a pound to a pinch of salt, that address will change. Now any external or third-party code that uses that absolute address might be snookered. If the code is updated and its execution point is changed, all that needs to happen is for the address in the vector to be changed.

The second advantage to using vectors is that we, as the programmer, can also change the address in the vector — we can intercept it. By intercepting vectors we can modify and even change the way the Raspberry Pi operates. This is not easy under RISC OS but if you plan to write bare metal code then you will be required to take control of the vector table yourself and manage its requirements.

When an exception interrupt occurs the processor stops what it is doing and jumps to the appropriate location in the vector table. Each location contains a branch instruction pointing to the start of a specific handling routine. These instructions normally take one of three forms as shown in Figure 25d.

Instruction	Description
B <address>	Jump to an address give as a relative offset to the PC.
LDR PC, {PC, #offset]	Load address from memory to the PC. This address si a 32-bt value stored close to the vector table. This is slightly slower than the previous method due to extra memory access. The bonus is that you can branch to any address in the memory map.
LDR PC, [PC, #-0xFF0]	Load address of a specific interrupt service routine from 0xFFFFF030 tp the PC.
MOV PC, #value	Copies an immediate value into the PC. This will normally be an single byte value that is rotated right by an even number of bits. Thus provides access to the full memory map but with gaps.

Figure 25d. Instructions that may be used in a vector.

For example, when an IRQ interrupt occurs it ultimately goes via the IRQ vector. This location is 32-bits wide (a word), and is just big enough to contain an instruction that facilitates an instruction to branch to another memory location.

Register Arrangements

Each of the modes has an associated set of registers available to it. The registers available to the programmer vary according to the current CPU operating mode.

When executing in User Mode the full set of registers, R0 to R15, are available for use. However, when the CPU switches into another operation mode, this all changes. Figure 25e shows the register arrangement depending on the mode of operation. All modes have dedicated stack pointers and link registers associated with them. Whilst all modes except for User Mode have a new register, the Saved Program Status Register, available to them, only FIQ mode has several dedicated registers from R8-R12. Otherwise registers remain unchanged.

User	FIQ	IRQ	SVC	UND	ABT
R0					
R1					
R2					
R3					
R4					
R5					
R6					
R7					
R8	R8_fiq				
R9	R9_fiq				
R10	R10_fiq				
R11	R11_fiq				
R12	R12_fiq				
R13 SP	R13_fiq	R13_irq	R13_svc	R13_und	R13_abt
R14 LR	R14_fiq	R14_irq	R14_svc	R14_und	R14_abt
R15 PC					

CPSR					
	SPSR_fiq	SPSR_irq	SPSR_svc	SPSR_und	SPSR-abt

Figure 25e. The ARM programmer's model.

The SPSR is used to hold a copy of the User Mode Status Register when one of the other modes is entered. The User Mode does not have and it does not need an SPSR. An important point to note here is that the CPSR is only copied into the SPSR when an exception or interrupt is raised; it is not changed if you physically write to the CPSR to change mode.

The idea behind this banked register system is that each processor mode has some private registers which it can make use of without affecting the values of the normal registers, thus ensuring that the programmer does not have to worry about saving the contents of their own User Mode registers when an alternative mode is entered.

Figure 25f shows how the low byte of the CSPR looks when one of the modes is invoked. With the exception of User Mode, all modes are privileged. When power is first applied to the ARM chip it starts off in Supervisor Mode.

	I	F	T		MODE			
	7	6	5	4	3	2	1	0
Abort	1	1	0	1	0	1	1	1
FIQ	1	1	0	1	0	0	0	1
IRQ	1	uc	0	1	0	0	1	0
Supervisor	1	uc	0	1	0	0	1	1
System	1	1	0	1	1	1	1	1
Undefined	1	uc	0	1	1	0	1	1
User	0	0	0	1	0	0	0	0

Figure 25f. Bit settings for Mode changes in CPSR.

Interrupts can be enabled and disabled very easily in ARM — using masking. Bits 7 and 6 enable or disable IRQ and FIQ interrupts respectively. If either bit is set then the associated interrupt is disabled and will not be processed. When an exception or interrupt occurs, the interrupt mask bit will normally be set by the chip. For a number of modes the FIQ bit remains unchanged (uc).

Exception Handling

An exception is a condition that requires the halting, temporary or otherwise, of whatever code is executing. A segment of code called an exception handler is called at this point. It identifies the condition and passes control to the appropriate route to handle the exception. When an exception causes a mode change the following sequence of events needs to happen:

- The address of next instruction is copied into the appropriate LR

- The CPSR is copied into the SPSR of the new mode

- The appropriate mode is set by modifying bits in the CPSR

- The next instruction is fetched from the vector table.

- When the exception has been dealt with, control can be returned to the code that was executing when the exception occurred. This is done as follows:

    The LR (minus an offset) is moved into the PC

The SPSR is copied back into CPSR and by default this automatically changes the mode back to the previous one

If set, the interrupt disable flags are cleared clear the interrupt disable flags to re-enable interrupts.

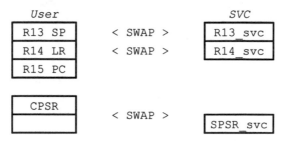

Figure 25g. Swapping registers on at a privileged exception.

The illustration above in Figure 25g illustrates what happens at a register level when a SWI call is made. The concept is the same for any of the privileged mode exceptions. The SP and LR of the accessing Mode are switched in over the User Mode ones to allow the exception to be serviced, whilst preserving the status of the interrupted program. The return address is copied from the User Mode PC and stored in the LR of the privileged mode being invoked. R14_svc in the example above.

By preserving the status of the three User Mode registers shown, the status quo of program execution can be maintained when the SVC Mode call has been serviced simply by swapping them back. As stated earlier the CPSR is only saved into the requesting mode's SPSR when an exception occurs. It does not happen when the mode is changed by flipping the Mode bits.

MRS and MSR

There are two instructions which can be used directly to control the contents of the CPSR and SPSR and they can be used on the whole contents or at bit level.

The MRS instruction transfers the contents of either the CPSR or SPSR into a register. The MSR instruction works the opposite way and transfer the contents of a register into either the CSPR or SPSR. The instruction syntax is as follows:

```
MRS (<suffix>) <Operand1>, <CSPR|SPSR>
MSR (<suffix>) <CSPR|SPSR|Flags>, <Operand1>
MSR (<suffix>) <CSPR|SPSR|Flags>, #immediate
```

Some examples will make their operation clearer. The following three lines of code could be used to enable IRQ Mode:

```
MRS R1, CPSR
BIC R1, R1, #&80
MSR CPSR_C, R1
```

First the CPSR is copied into R1 where it is then masked with 10000000 to set the bit at b7 — the position of the I flag. (see Figure 26a). R1 is then written back to CPSR. Note the use of the _C as an addition to the CPSR operand. For the purpose of programming, the CPSR and SPSR are divided into four different sectors. These are illustrated below in Figure 25h.

Flags (F) [24:31]								Status (S) [16:25]										Extension (X) [8:15]								Control (C) [0:7]				
N	Z	C	V																					I	F	T		Mode			

Figure 25h. The CPSR/SPSR segments to control updating.

By using the correct adjunct(s) on the appropriate instruction we can ensure that only the correct bits of the associated register are updated. The F, S, X and C suffixes may be used in like fashion.

To disable the IRQ, the following segment of code would suffice:

```
MRS R1, CPSR
ORR R1, R1, #&80
MSR CPSR_C, R1
```

The same commands can be used to effect a mode change thus:

```
MRS R0,CPSR        ;    copy the CPSR
BIC R0,R0,#&1F     ;    clear mode bits
ORR R0,R0,#new_mode ;   select new mode
MSR CPSR,R0        ;    write CPSR back
```

In User Mode you can read all the bits of the CPSR but you can only update the condition of the field flag, ie, CPSR_F.

Interrupts When?

Interrupt Request Mode (IRQ) and Fast Interrupt Mode (FIQ) are called when an external device pages the ARM chip and demands its attention. For example, the keyboard generates an interrupt whenever a key is pressed. This is a signal to the CPU that the keyboard matrix should be scanned, and the ASCII value of the key entered into the keyboard buffer. If the ASCII value is &0D (RETURN), the keyboard buffer must be interpreted.

The analogy here can be you, sitting at your own keyboard learning Raspberry Pi Assembly Language RISC OS. At some point your phone starts to ring. You have been interrupted. So, you stop what you are doing (you may make a quick note to remind you or you may save your work) and answer the phone (you deal with or process the interruption). When you have completed the phone call, you hang up and return to what you were doing before the interruption.

The process with the ARM chip is much the same. It receives an interrupt signal at which point it saves what it is doing in line with what we have already discussed and then hands control to the calling interrupt routine by invoking the appropriate mode of operation. When the interrupt has finished its work (in the keyboard example this would be reading the key press and placing the ASCII code in the keyboard buffer) it hands control back to the ARM which restores all its previously saved information and returns to User Mode, picking up where it left off.

So here the interrupt is a function of the ARM chip itself, but how it is dealt with and what happens thereafter is a feature of the software handling it — Raspbian in this case.

Without an effective interrupt system, the Raspberry Pi at software level would have to spend a lot of its time checking all attached components just to see if anything has happened, taking up time and resources. Think of all the connections to your Raspberry Pi — keyboard, mouse, USB ports, disk drives... They all require servicing, and often.

Fast Interrupts (FIQs) are deemed to be ones that have the highest priority and are the ones that must be serviced first. For example, any disk drive connected, otherwise data might be lost. The only time a FIQ is not serviced first is when another FIQ is in the process of being serviced. The Interrupt Request (IRQ) line is deemed to be of lower priority where a slight delay will not create any problems.

The need for speed in processing an FIQ interrupt is signified by its position in the hardware vector table. It is the last in the list. This is because it actually begins executing right at that point — the other vectors all perform other branch instructions further into the system software. The FIQ code resides in the space after the vector at &1C. It is then the job of the appropriate interrupt coding to identify which device caused the interrupt and process it accordingly and as quickly as possible.

Your Interrupt Decisions

When dealing with interrupts you need to make the decision about other interrupts. For example what happens if a new interrupt occurs whilst you are handling an existing interrupt? The easiest method is to invoke what is called a non-nested interrupt handling scheme. In this all interrupts are disabled until control is handled back to the interrupted task, The downside of this is that only one interrupt can be serviced at a time, and if a succession of interrupts are occurring you may lose some of the requests. This could have consequences.

A nested interrupt scheme allows more than one interrupt to be handled at a time and in this case you would look to re-enable interrupts before fully servicing the current interrupt. This is more complex but it solves the problems that can occur with interrupt latency, which is the interval of time from an external interrupt signal being raised to the first fetch of an instruction of the raised interrupt signal.

For an FIQ, the IRQs are disabled as the FIQ is deemed critical in relation.

In all cases the implementation of a stack for interrupt handling (interrupt stack) should be considered essential for context switching between the modes and preserving information. If several interrupts occur at the same time the details need to be stored somewhere for processing as the sequence is dealt with.

Returning From Interrupts

When the interrupt service routine has been performed, the operating system must return to the original program which was interrupted by the FIQ or IRQ. This is done by using the following instruction:

```
SUBS R15, R14, #4
```

This restores the program counter so that the interrupted program can be resumed from exactly the point at which it was suspended. The 'subtract 4' calculation is required to correct for the effects of pipelining. Providing that the interrupt handling routine has not corrupted any shared registers or workspace, the program will continue executing as if the interrupt had never happened. On the Raspberry Pi, interrupts are occurring and being serviced all the time without the user even realising it.

Writing Interrupt Routines

Usually, you will not need to create interrupt service routines of your own because the OS provides a well-defined system for doing so.

If you intend to write direct interrupt handling routines, you should observe the following rule to avoid potential disasters:

- Do not re-enable interrupts in the handling routine. If this is done, a second IRQ/FIQ could interrupt the processor before it has finished handling the first. Sometimes this may be permissible, but you could be walking on thin ice if you do it. Be very aware!

- The interrupt routine must be written as economically as possible. Processing the interrupt at maximum speed should be a major goal. If it keeps interrupts disabled for too long, then the normal Raspberry Pi background activities will grind to a halt. The keyboard will lock, various software clocks will lose time, and the mouse pointer will freeze.

- All shared processor registers should be preserved. They should contain the same values on exit from the interrupt routine as they did on entry to the interrupt. This is absolutely vital if the interrupted task is to be resumed correctly.

- The interrupt handling routine should avoid calling OS routines. It is possible that one of these routines would be only half executed when it is interrupted by IRQ/FIQ. If re-entered in the interrupt routine, workspace could be disturbed, causing the routine to corrupt when resumed.

26: GPIO Functions

One of the things making the Raspberry Pi so popular is the ability to connect external electronics to it and control them — everything from lights through to complete home automation systems. The sky really is the limit. So it makes sense to examine how we can control those attachments using from RISC OS.

In this chapter we'll look at how the GPIO interface is connected to the Raspberry Pi and how you can use machine code to access that connection, thereby enabling you to read and write to individual GPIO pins. We'll also look at one of the GPIO modules freely available to you if you want to experiment a bit with a proven interface.

While this isn't a primer on the GPIO interface, understanding how it sits with the Raspberry Pi is fundamental to understanding how to program it. Neither am I going to show you how to physically connect devices to your GPIO port.

Figure 26a. The Gertboard in its 'leds' configuration. Jumpers set to output.

There are plenty of other books and articles explaining how to do that and indeed there are dedicated expansion boards that provide a whole range of functionality simply by plugging them onto the GPIO connector. Just for the record, in testing these examples I have used a *Gertboard* which has been configured as described in its manual to run its own 'leds' test file. The photograph in Figure 26a illustrates this configuration. The same result should be achievable with one of the other expansion boards available or even through your own breadboard constructions. .

A far as the GPIO interface goes I would recommend that you download the BCM2835 datasheet, which contains just about everything you would want to know about — not just the GPIO interface but also all the other hardware-orientated aspects of the ARM chip fitted to your Raspberry Pi. The datasheet can be a little daunting if you have not looked at one before, but if you look at it in conjunction with the examples worked below, you will be able to follow it clearly enough, and that will enable you to investigate the numerous other GPIO functions for yourself. You can access a link to this via the Raspberry Pi website or through this book support website.

The GPIO Controller

The GPIO has its own controller and this contains no less than 41 registers. The first five of these registers deal with reading and writing to the 54 GPIO pins. These pins are numbered GPIO 0 through to GPIO 53 although only a handful or so of these are available to us to connect to on the GPIO expansion port itself (this is what the Gertboard and other similar boards connect to). The first five of these registers, their names and the pins they are associated with are listed in Figure 26b.

No	Name	Off	Pins
0	GPIO Function Select 0 (GPSEL0)	#0	0-9
1	GPIO Function Select 1 (GPSEL1)	#4	10-19
2	GPIO Function Select 2 (GPSEL2)	#8	20-29
3	GPIO Function Select 3 (GPSEL3)	#12	30-39
4	GPIO Function Select 4 (GPSEL4)	#16	30-49
5	GPIO Function Select 5 (GPSEL5)	#20	50-53

Figure 26b. GPIO registers and pin control.

It should be noted also that the GPIO Controller pin numbers do not run concurrently on the GPIO main GPIO header connector and may differ again on any expansion board you have attached. Please ensure you familiarise

217

yourself with the system you are using as the pin numbers here relate specifically to the numbers assigned by BCM.

Each of these registers is 32-bits wide and each pin has three bits assigned to it within each register. In GPSEL0 GPIO Pin 0 has bits 0, 1 and 2 assigned to it. GPIO 1 has bits 3, 4 and 5 and so on. In GPSEL1, then the first three bits (0, 1 and 2) are assigned to GPIO 10. In GPSEL2, then the first three bits (0, 1 and 2) are assigned to GPIO 20. Figure 25c illustrates the arrangement for GPSEL2.

(You may have noticed above that not all the bits in Register 5 are used. This is correct. Only the first 12 bits are used and the others are classed as 'reserved'. Likewise bits 30 and 31 in each of the other registers are unused)

Pin 29			Pin 28			Pin 27			Pin 26			Pin 25			Pin 24			Pin 23			Pin 22			Pin 21			Pin 20		
31	30	29	28	27	26	25	24	23	22	21	20	19	18	17	16	15	14	13	12	11	10	9	8	7	6	5	4	3	2	1	0

Figure 26c. Bit association with GPSEL2.

It is important to understand how these bits are assigned as we will need to address them individually at various times to make things happen in their associated registers.

To assign a pin as an input we must store a 0 in the three associated bits (000). To make the same pin an output we must write a 1 in those same three bits (001). For example, to make GPIO 21 an output we must place 001 in bits 3, 4 and 5 (see Figure 26c above). To achieve this we could write the binary value:

```
001000
```

(decimal 8) to GPFEL2. Of course we must preserve and not overwrite any other bits that may be set or clear so we would do this using a bitwise operator as we shall see in due course. (Other bit combinations assign other functions to the pins, so it is important to get this right. The Broadcom datasheet explains these other functions).

The base address for the GPIO controller in RISC OS is &20200000 and this address is where the first register is located — GPSEL0. If we want to get to the second register, GPFEL1, then we need to add four to the controller's base address. Figure 26a also contains a column called 'offset'. This is the number of bytes offset from the GPIO Controller start address where that particular register starts. GPSEL2 has an offset of 8, so its RICS OS address would be &20200000+8.

So far we have looked at configuring a pin as an input or an output. To turn the pin on (set) or off (clear) we have to write some values into another register. (In this case I am talking about turning a LED on or turning an LED off.)

There are four registers associated with setting and clearing pins and these are detailed in Figure 26d.

No	Name	Off	Pins
7	GPIO Pin Set 0(GPSET0)	#28	0-31
8	GPIO Pin Set 1(GPSET1)	#32	32-53
10	GPIO Output Clear 0(GPCLR0)	#40	0-31
11	GPIO Ouput Clear 1(GPCLR1)	#44	32-53

Figure 26d. GPIO registers for setting and clearing.

There is a single bit associated with each pin for the purpose of setting and clearing. For example, to set GPIO 21 we would write a '1' into bit 21 of GPSET0. To clear the same bit we would need to write a '1' into bit 21 of GPCLR0.

If you were to write a 1 to bit21 in GPSET0 but GPIO 21 was defined as an input nothing would happen. If you then set GPIO 21 to an output, an attached LED would light. The last value written to either GPSET0 or GPCLR0 in this case is remembered and actioned when the status of the pin is changed.

As we can see from Figure 26d the offset for GPSET0 is 28 and for GPCLR0 is 40 and this value added to the base address to the GPIO controller is where we need to write to.

Building the Code

That's quite a lot to take in, so let's work through an example. Here we'll assume that we are dealing with GPIO 21. We have an LED attached to it which we want to turn on. Before we can do that we have to initialise the pin by first setting it as an input, then as an output. Finally we can turn the LED on by setting the bit associated with the pin. The toggling of the input/output status of the pin enables it to record what the last action was (by order) when we set or clear its status.

The code segment that follows is pseudo-code just for illustrative purposes — if you try and use it 'as is' it will not work, for reasons which I'll explain shortly!

```
.input
LDR R3, #&2020000          \ get GPIO Base addr
MOV R5, R3                 \ save copy for later use
ADD R3, R3, #8             \ pin 21 in register 2 so add 8 offset
MOV R2, R3                 \ move address into R2
LDR R2, [R2, #0]           \ get value in Register 2
BIC R2, R2, #0b111<,3      \ clear 3 bits associated with pin 21
STR R2, [R3, #0]           \ and write value back to GPIO Base

.output
MOV R2, R3                 \ write GPIO addr to R2
LDR R2, [R2, #0]           \ get value at R2
ORR R2, R2, #1<<3          \ set lsb as output for pin 21
STR R2, [R3, #0]           \ and write to Register 2

.set
MOV R3, R5                 \ get base addr
ADD R3, R3, #28            \ set GPSET0 address for set
MOV R4, #1                 \ set bit
MOV  R2, R4, LSL #21       \ rotate to pin 21 and place in R2
STR R2, [R3, #0]           \ write to memory to set
```

The comments should help you follow this through. The key thing to remember here is that, for GPIO 21, we are dealing with Register 2 which has an offset of 8. This means that 8 must be added to the GPIO base address at &20200000. In Register 2 bits 3, 4 and 5 are associated with pin 21. Thus we must shift left any value we want to write into those bits by three places. Take a look at the BIC instruction below which is taken from the input part of the segment:

```
BIC R2, R2, #%111<<3
```

R2 contains the address of Register 2. If we shift the binary value 111 left by three places we get 111000. The result is that these three bits are cleared when we store this value back in the register. Remember BIC performs a logical bit clear or AND NOT on the value in R2. By effectively placing 000 in the three bits we have assigned the pin as an input. (We have used a slightly different way to perform the LSL here using '<<' which is one of many shortcuts that the BBC BASIC Assembler provides.)

The '.output' routine now programs the same pin as an output by writing a 1 into bits 3, 4 and 5 of Register 2. It does this with:

```
ORR R2, R2, #1<<3
```

We have now initialised the pin by getting it ready to act as an output.

Now we just have to place a 1 in the bit associated with the pin in the GPSET0 register. GPIO 21 is pin 21 so we have to place a 1 in bit 21 of GPSET0. GPSET0 is offset 28 bytes from the start of the GPIO Controller, so the 28 is added to the base controller address and then the left shifted bit stored there.

As I said, this program won't work, but assuming the LED attached was now illuminated, to turn it off we would use:

```
MOV R3, R5              \ get base addr
ADD R3, R3, #40         \ get GPCLR0 address for set
MOV R4, #1              \ set bit
MOV  R2, R4, LSL #21    \ rotate to pin 21 and place in R2
STR R2, [R3, #0]        \ write to memory to set
```

So why won't the program work? Because RISC OS will not allow us to write directly to the GPIO Controller (or other I/O space for that matter)! It is a self-protect mechanism that is built into it to try and ensure we don't corrupt anything that might otherwise cause it to crash. So we have to get around that.

Virtual Memory

If you look at the BDM datasheet (page 5) the diagram depicts that the I/O block at bus address &7Exxxxxx is mapped to ARM physical address &20xxxxxx. The Raspberry Pi actually has three address spaces – the ARM logical address, the ARM physical address, and the bus physical address. This is because all memory and I/O accesses go through both the ARM's MMU and the VideoCore's MMU before it actually hits the target device.

The way we get around this problem is to use a technique that allows us to create an area of memory that mirrors the protected space we want to access - *virtual memory*. Once we have ascertained what the virtual address is for the GPIO Controller we can read and write to it using a system call. The three calls we use are OS_Memory, OS_EnterOS and OS_LeaveOS.

OS_Memory

This call performs a variety of operations the exact nature of which is defined by a reason code passed in R0. For our purpose we are interested in reason code 13 (&0D) which I used to 'Map in IO permanent'. The entry and exit conditions are:

```
On entry:
R0=13
```

```
R1=physical address to map in
R2=size to map in

On exit:
R0-R2 preserved
R3=logical address assigned to R1.
```

So, R1 will contain &20200000 and R2 we can put &100 as this will more than cover the mapping the registers we need. On exit the address that we can use to access the GPIO Controller will be held in R3. This call can be performed from BASIC using:

```
SYS "OS_Memory",13,&20200000,&100 TO ,,, logical%
```

The variable 'logical%' will hold the logical address for the start of the GPIO Controller. It is this address we must utilise as the GPIO base address.

OS_EnterOS and OS_LeaveOS

The purpose of these calls is to allow the user to enter and leave Supervisor Mode cleanly. There are no register entry and exit conditions, in fact all registers are preserved. Interrupt and Fast Interrupt status is unaltered. Note that SWI calls while in SVC mode will alter R14, and will use R13 as stack.

Pin 21

Program 26a shows how this all comes together for the example we have worked above — GPIO 21. You can run and assembler this one ! Of course it is assumed that you have a Gertboard attached or have made the required changes to select the pins your require (more on this shortly).

Program 26a. Setting GPIO 21 to turn on an attached LED.

```
 10 REM Prog26a
 20 REM GPIO Pin 21 toggle on Gertboard
 30 REM RPi ROAL
 40 :
 50 DIM code% 256
 60 :
 70 FOR pass=0 TO 3 STEP 3
 80 P%=code%
 90 [
100 OPT pass
110 .start
120 \ First need to get logical address
130 MOV R0, #13
```

```
140 LDR R1, gpiobase
150 MOV R2, #&100
160 SWI "OS_Memory"
170 MOV R0, R3
180 \
190 SWI "OS_EnterOS"
200 MOV R5, R3
210 ADD R3, R3, #8
220 MOV R2, R3
230 LDR R2, [R2, #0]
240 BIC R2, R2, #%111<<3
250 STR R2, [R3, #0]
260 :
270 .output
280 MOV R2, R3
290 LDR R2, [R2, #0]
300 ORR R2, R2, #%1<<3
310 STR R2, [R3, #0]
320 :
330 .set
340 MOV R3, R5
350 ADD R3, R3, #28        \ #40 to run off
360 MOV R4, #1
370 MOV R2, R4, LSL #21
380 STR R2, [R3, #0]
390 :
400 SWI "OS_LeaveOS"
410 MOV PC, R14
420 :
430 .gpiobase
440 EQUD &20200000
450]
460 NEXT pass
470 CALL start
```

Lines 130-160 perform the OS_Memory call and on return the logical address held in R3 is moved into R0 so that the pin action can take place as previously described. As call 13 here performs a permanent map the virtual memory area remains in play until it is 'released' or there is a rebook. Thus we only need to make the call once.

To edit the program so that it turns pin 21 off all you need to do is to edit one line of code as follows:

```
350 ADD R3, R3, #40
```

And assemble again - that simple!

Using and Adapting

I tend to assembler these files into machine code and save them using a name indicative of the pin. For example, for Program 26a I would compile and save the executable using the name, 'on21'. I would also create a complementary file to clear the pin using the filename 'off21'. Creating a pair for each file gives you the immediate ability to set and clear individual pins as you wish:

```
*on21
*off21
```

You only require minimal changes to adapt the program to work on other pins, and you should have more than enough information to do this. If you make the changes listed below to Program 25a then you can have access to GPIO 17. Referring back to Figure 25a we can see that GPIO 17 is in GPIO Function Select 1 (GPSEL1) and the offset here is 4. This is the first change we must make.

Bits 21, 22 and 23 within GPSEL1 are linked to GPIO 17 so the logical shift left value associated with writing %111 and %001 is 21. Finally GPIO 17 is associated with bit 17 in GPSET0 so this is the final shift value we need to change in the assembler.

Program 26b. Changes: adapting for GPIO 17.

```
210 ADD R3, R3, #4        \ 8 is now 4
240 BIC R2, R2, #%111<<21 \ 3 is now 21
300 ORR R2, R2, #%1<<21   \ 3 is now 21
370 MOV R2, R4, LSL #17   \ 21 is now 17
```

Other GPIO Functions

There are a number of other registers that form part of the GPIO Controller that can be used and programmed using these methods. As already mentioned you will need to get a copy of the BCM2835 ARM peripherals datasheet to get the specific detail that you need relating to the other registers, their functions and what you need to do to use them. It is all there.

One final thing in relation to the datasheet: If you look at the memory maps at the start of the document you will see that the ARM peripherals are mapped as starting at &7E000000, whereas in RISC OS they start at &20000000. All operating systems implement their own memory addressing systems which overlay the ones provided by default by the CPU. This allows the OS in question to implement virtual memory mapping — a technique that allows program and applications to use more memory than is actually available to them by swapping data in and out of memory from the SD Card in use or the hard drive attached. From a practical point of view, when you access the Broadcom datasheet you should remember that all the peripheral addresses specified in the text are bus addresses and must be translated into physical addresses. Thus the GPIO Controller start address is given as &7E200000 but we implement as &20200000 in our programs — change the first two numbers from 7E to 20 if you like!

Finally a word of warning. The GPIO pins control a whole host of functions on your Raspberry Pi and if you are not careful you can crash RISC OS causing everything to freeze and necessitating a hard reset. Always save your work before you try to execute any machine code file for the first time.

27: GCC – An Introduction

The BBC BASIC Assembler is the ideal environment in which to learn ARM assembly language. I am probably in the minority but think BBC BASIC is a perfectly acceptable medium not just to learn programming, but to create sophisticated and complex applications. Indeed you might be surprised to learn that certain aspects of RISC OS are written in BBC BASIC.

That said, as you move towards more advanced usage of the ARM processor on your Raspberry Pi, you will find that programs are increasingly written in C and often contain a mixture of assembler and C. This fact will bear fruit if you start investigating the source code to Modules, for example. You will find that the source code for many 'free' applications is provided as standard. In the next chapters we'll look at this aspect of programming and illustrate how to use a C compiler in its various modes of operation, including as an assembler and a compiler to generate machine code.

This is not a book about learning to program in C, but the fact is as you delve deeper into ARM assembler on your Raspberry Pi you will probably be drawn towards it. At the very least you will probably want to learn more about the functions and routines that C can provide in libraries such as libc so that you can take advantage of them in your own programs. You might want to look at the machine code that constitutes the libc functions to see how they work, and learn from them. This is called reverse engineering and it plays a major part in all software development, as programmers look at how other programmers have achieved certain results and seek to improve on those themselves.

C Compilers and GCC

There are several C compilers available for RISC OS, some of which are available free of charge. The Desktop Development Environment (DDE) toolset for RISC OS dates back to when Acorn developed RISC OS and contains an excellent C compiler, assembler and associated tools. Though not free they are available at very low cost from RISC OS Open Ltd as part of the NutPI package. However, a free one is available as part of RISC OS and is perhaps perhaps the most widely used and supported of the free variety across all operating systems and computer platforms—GCC.

The original author of the GNU C Compiler (GCC) was Richard Stallman, the founder of the GNU Project. The GNU project was started in 1984 to create a complete operating system as free software, to promote freedom and cooperation among computer users and programmers. Every operating system needs a C compiler, and as there were no free compilers in existence at that time, the GNU Project had to develop one from scratch.

The first release of GCC came in 1987. Since that time GCC has become one of the most important tools in the development of free software and is available on almost every operating system platform in existence.

GCC is free software, distributed under the GNU General Public License (GNU GPL). This means that you have the freedom to use and to modify GCC, as with all GNU software. If you need support for a new type of CPU, a new language, or a new feature you can add it yourself, or get someone to do it for you.

GCC is still a work-in-progress on RISC OS but its popularity and availability will ensure that it will become one of the best supported. Many of the programs I had previously developed on GCC under Raspbian on the Raspberry Pi all transferred and ran first time out without any changes needed. This portability — across not just operating systems but also computer platforms — is one of the reasons why it will become a major player in the compiler market.

Downloading and Installing GCC

GCC can be loaded and installed using PackMan. The icon for PackMan is located on your desktop. Click on the PackMan icon to install it on the icon bar. The source for GCC will need to be added to your RISC OS installation. The steps to complete this, if necessary, are outlined below.

Menu click the PackMan icon located on the icon bar. Select 'advanced' and 'sources' to bring up a list of installed sources. Click add and enter the URL:

```
http://www.riscos.info/packages/pkg/autobuilt
```

Click OK then click Save. This will update the lists of all sources. When complete click on 'Close' thereby completing the addition of the new package source to PackMan.

Now proceed to install GCC and related tools. Click on the PackMan icon to open the PackMan window. Scroll down until you locate GCC4 and select this as shown in Figure 27a.

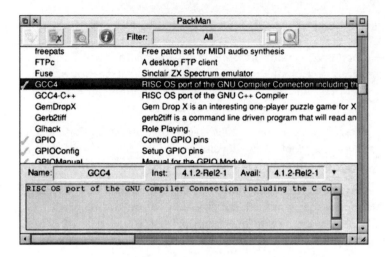

Figure 27a. Select GCC from the PackMan files list.

Next press the Menu button and select the 'Update Lists' option—Figure 27b. This will run through and ensure that you have the latest information about the GCC files (you will need to have an internet connection for this).

Figure 27b. Select 'Update Lists' to ensure that you have the latest file information.

Once this has completed select to install GGC4 by selecting 'Package GCC4>Install' from the menu button. Once downloaded and installed you will find the !GGC folder in the $.Apps.Development directory of the SD Card.

Figure 27c. GCC is saved to the $.Apps.Development directory of the SD Card.

Before you close PackMan you will need to do the same process with SharedLibs, SharedLibs-C and SharedUnixLibrary. The libraries may have been installed as dependencies of GCC. Scroll down to confirm the libraries have been installed, indicated by the presence of a tick illustrated in Figure 27d. If they are not installed repeat the installation process for each library.

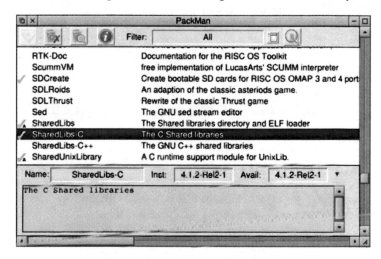

Figure 27d. Download and install the Shared Libraries.

Running and Testing GCC

GCC is memory thirsty and needs at least 6000k to run. Each time before you run it you will need to open Task Manager and drag the 'Next' slot up to at least 6Mb.

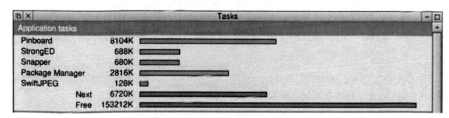

Figure 27e. Ensure that there is at least 6Mb set on the 'Next' slider before launching GCC.

Double click on the !GCC application icon and then open a new Task Window by pressing <CTRL>-F12. At the *prompt type:

```
gcc - v
```

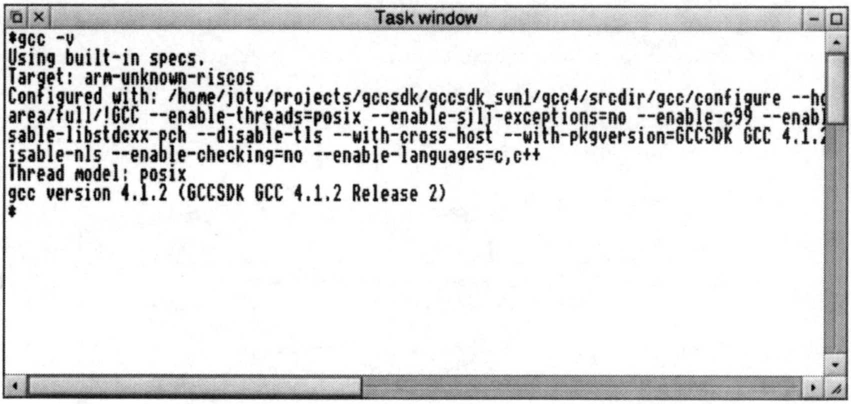

Figure 27f. GCC responding to the gcc -v command.

If you do not get any response then close the Task Window and repeat the steps again, from the Task Manager prompt. If GCC responds with a report then you are ready to continue. Leave this Task Window open as we'll be coming back to this shortly to compile and link our files.

This startup process is required only once and not each time a GCC tool is used. It must be repeated if the RISC OS machine is restarted.

Configuring the GCC Environment

To create programs with GCC we need to go through a write-compile-link process to generate a machine code file that can be executed. The first step is to write a source file in either c or assembler.

GCC comes from a Unix environment where files will use extensions such as .c for c source files. RISC OS extensions do not operate in this way and instead .c represents the c subfolder of the current directory. It is important to establish this folder structure prior to using GCC.

The following sub-folders should always exist in the current working directory used for program development:

c   This will contain C source files eg, file.c

s   Contains assembler input and output files e.g. file.s

h   Include files referenced by the program typically:"include.h"

An additional 'o' folder will contain object files and will be created automatically when any of the GCC tools generate an object file.

If you open the !GCC directory (<SHIFT>-click) and then open the examples and c directories the folder should look similar to that shown in Figure 27g below. As noted above the o and s directories may not exist if GCC has not yet generated any source or object files.

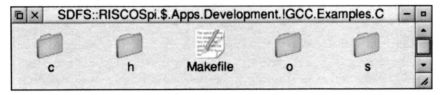

Figure 27g. Opening the Examples.C directory for locating files.

It is very easy to construct the directory structure to initially use GCC. The following set of commands issued from a Task Window will setup the required structure under the current working directory.

```
*cdir c
*cdir h
*cdir s
```

Ensure you select the correct current working directory in advance either by using 'Set Directory' from a filer window or issuing a relevant *dir from the Task Window. The directories can also be created from a filer window using the create directory menu option as shown in Figure 27h.

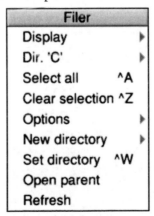

Figure 27h . Select the 'Set directory' option from the Filer menu.

For now you may wish to use the Examples.c and Examples.Asm folders within GCC until you are comfortable with the environment.

GCC - The Swiss Army Knife

GCC is a bit like a Swiss Army Knife, it has to be able to deal with all situations and it goes about it in a methodical manner. GCC isn't a single beast; it is more a controller for several GNU programs, running them one-by-one in order to produce a result. But the good thing is that we can stop the process at any point in that chain and this is to our benefit.

GCC can compile a C program to an executable file with just a single command line thus:

```
*gcc -o tornado   tornado.c
```

This will take a C program called 'tornado' located in the c sub-folder and convert it to an executable file called 'tornado' in the current working directory. It does this using a number of separate steps:

CPP   The C Pre-processor takes the C source and gathers information about the #defines and #includes so that it has a list of all the variables and additional bits of information and files it will need.

GCC   Creates the assembly language source listing. It does this by using some basic rules and building the sections of code needed as a series of building blocks which calls functions in any required libraries. It then assembles the code before starting the process again. Once this is complete the source file, in the '.s' folder, is complete.

AS   The assembler takes a source file and converts it into an object file (.o) in much the same way as the BBC BASIC assembler.

LD   The linker takes the object code file and adds to it all the additional files and libraries required.

What GCC does not give you is compact, refined machine code. If space and speed are critical to your code then you need to originate it directly yourself. Much of the core of RISC OS is written in assembly language resulting in the size and speed benefits RISC OS enjoys. Compiled code can be optimised at the source stage and GCC provides some automated options for doing this. However, this is outside the scope of this book. But in a way, when looking at the assembler source file created to execute a particular function, what we will be doing is to optimise the source, cutting away everything that is not needed, until we have the bare bones assembler to do what we need.

Assembly Language with GCC

As we are creating a machine code file we need to first create a source file that contains the assembly language that we wish to compile. For the most part the file contains the same mnemonics that we've been using, but there are a couple of additional requirements.

The source files can be created in any suitable text editor. !Edit and StrongEd are both suitable and when you create them, they must be saved in the 's' directory as shown in Figure 27g above.

Program 27a. A simple source file.

```
        .global   _start
_start:
        MOV R0, #65
        SWI 0x00              @ OS_WriteC
        MOV R8, #0
        SWI 0x11              @ OS_Exit R8=0 => No Error Block
```

The file name for this program, here prog27a, is not particularly special, and just follows the format used in this book. You should be comfortable with the mnemonics here. The program will print an 'A' on the screen. Shortly, we'll look at the two lines at the start. The last two lines demonstrate the preferred method of returning to RISC OS on completion and is discussed later in the chapter. One other thing you may have noticed is that '0x' is used to signify a hex number. The convention in BBC BASIC is to use an ampersand (&), however the standard in other assemblers and compilers such as GCC is to use 0x, known as the *hex introducer*, as the prefix.

Note the formatting with the indents. This is standard and a good habit to get into to aid readability.

Come to the Execution

The next step is to convert the source file into an executable file of machine code. We do this with two commands entered at the command line in the Task Window. Enter the following two lines, one after the other, at the * prompt:

```
*as -o prog27a.o prog27a.s
*ld -o prog27a prog27a.o
```

These two lines first assemble and then link the assembly language program. On completion the machine code can be executed, and the syntax for this is:

```
*prog27a
```

When the prompt reappears, the machine code program has completed and you should see an 'A' before the '*' prompt. It's as easy as that!

So we have just written, compiled and executed a machine code program in GCC—all the basic steps needed were involved in the process above. Of course, as the programs get more complex and we seek to make more use of the tools available in GCC then the process will itself become more involved, as we shall see.

Assembler Errors

If at any time during the above process you receive an error message — or any message at all — look carefully at what you have typed. First look carefully at the assembly language program and then the individual lines of code to assembly, link and finally run the program. If there was an error and you found it, congratulations! You have just debugged your first GCC assembly language program.

If you get an error message from the assembler (this will be after you have pressed <RETURN> at the end of the first line) it will normally provide you with a line number as a guide. Even if you do not know what the message means note the line number and then reload the source file back into your preferred editor such as !StrongEd. For example:

```
prog27a.s:5: Error bad expression
```

This would indicate there is an error in line 5 of the source file.

Source Components

Let's now look at the above process and understand a bit more the anatomy of the source file and what we did to make it all come together. Look at prog27a.s again. It consists of just six lines.

Each assembler source file must have a starting point, and by default in the GCC assembler this is the label:

```
_start:
```

So the first line of this program defines '_start' as a global name and available to the whole program. We'll see later why making it a global name is important. The second line defines where '_start:' is in the program. Note the use of the ':' at the end to define it as a label (which is different to what we do in the BBC BASIC Assembler). We've defined _start as global and now marked where _start is.

If you look at prog27a.s again you can see that it consists of two clear sections. (Notice the format for the filename I am now using which indicates its directory location as well as the type of file it is — 's' for source.) At the top (start), are some definitions, and in the lower half are the actual assembly language instructions. Assembly language source files always consist of a sequence of statements, one per line. Each statement has the following format, each part of which is optional:

```
<label:>   <instruction>      /* comment */
```

All three of these components can be entered on the same line, or they can be split across lines. It's up to you. However, they must be in the order shown. For example an instruction cannot come before a label.

The 'comment' component is new. When the assembler encounters the '/*' it ignores everything after it until a '*/'. This means you can use it to annotate your program and if you use StrongEd as your editor it will highlight these comment blocks for you. You can also use the '@' character to denote that a comment follows; in such cases everything from the '@' up to the end of that line is treated as a comment, as illustrated on the SWI lines.

To convert the source file into an executable file we needed two steps. The first was:

```
*as -o prog27a.o prog27a.s
```

The 'as' at the start invokes the assembler program itself, which expects several arguments after the command to define the files it will be working with and what it will be doing with them. The first of these is 'o' and this tells the assembler that we want to produce an object file, here called 'prog27a.o' from the source file 'prog27a.s' You can choose another name if you wish; the body of the name does not have to be the same, although making it the same makes it easier to keep track of your files. Of course, the directory is not the same! Here the '.o' and the '.s' are identifying the directory where the file will be saved or found.

The second and final step is to link the file object file and convert it into an executable file using the 'ld' command as follows:

```
*ld -o prog27a prog27a.o
```

You can think of linking as the final part of binding that makes the machine code work. What it produces is an executable file (called an ELF file and is described in a few pages) from the .o (object) file created in the assembly process. It is this ld command that uses the _start: label to define where the program is to be run from. (This may sound crazy, but sometimes the start point of a file may not be at the very front of it, as we shall see!)

Exiting to RISC OS

Until now all programs we have developed have been assembled and executed from the BASIC environment. BASIC has been the active application and our programs have returned to BASIC using the "simple return method" of MOV PC, LR. Programs assembled by the GCC tools are executed from the Task Window which is an interface to the operating system.

Programs executed from the Task Window become the active application and will return to the operating system rather than an existing active application. A correct exit is required to ensure control passes back to a well-defined place, which defaults to the Task Window * prompt but could be a location within the previous application. The simple "return from subroutine" method will not suffice and could result in execution errors at program termination.

The correct method of returning to the operating system is via the OS_Exit SWI Call (SWI 0x11). In this instance R8 is generally loaded with 0 to indicate no error prior to the call. The two instructions illustrated in Figure 27i achieve this will be used throughout our examples intended for GCC.

```
_exit:
      MOV R8,#0
      SWI 0x11   @ OS_Exit R8=0 => No Error Block
```

Figure 27i. RISC OS exit method

It is good practice to precede the exit section with an _exit label as shown. There may be a requirement to use the error block to report an error condition to RISC OS. Further information on this and other usage situations can be obtained from the RISC OS PRM or other references.

This exit method is only used at the program exit point. All other subroutines used internally within a program should continue to use the "simple subroutine return" method we have been using to date.

Lack of _start

You can learn a lot about the workings of the GCC assembler and linker simply by experimenting. What do you think would happen if we omitted the _start: label from the source file?

Open the prog27a.s file in your text editor and delete the line '_start:', thereby erasing the label. Save it and return to the Task Window to assemble the program:

```
*as -o prog27a.o prog27a.s
```

Now link the program:

```
*ld -o prog27a prog27a.o
```

The following error message (or similar) will be produced:

```
ld: warning: cannot find entry symbol _start; defaulting to
00008068
```

The error message is clear enough. Because it can't find a pointer to where the program starts, the linker is assuming that the program start point is right at the beginning, and the location of this in memory is at the address 00008068. This is a safety net, but not a fail-safe. Always use the _start: in your files to define the start of execution. This program will run perfectly well — others might not and probably won't!

Linking Files

The letters ld stand for link dynamic and the linking command is capable of linking or daisy-chaining several files together into one long executable program. In such cases only one '_start:' label should be defined across all these files, as there should be only the one start point, and this defines it. This is easy to demonstrate using our sample program.

Create a new text file and call it part1 and save it within the s folder. In this file enter the listing shown below as Program 27b.

Program 27b. Part 1 of the source file.

```
/* part1.s file              */
     .global _start
_start:
     MOV R0, #65
     BAL _part2
```

Save the file. Now create a new file, call it part2 and save it within the s folder. This should contain the lines in the listing below as Program 27c:

Program 27c. Part 2 of the source file.

```
/* part2.s file              */
     .global _part2
_part2:
     SWI 0              @ OS_Write C
     MOV R8,#0
     SWI 0x11          @ OS_Exit R8=0 => No Error Block
```

Save and exit this. We have written two source files that we will now compile and link to create a single file. At the end of the part1.s we added:

```
BAL _part2
```

In the second file we have defined a global variable called part2 and also marked the point where part2 begins. Because we have used the global definition, the location of the address made known by the global definition will be available to all the program parts.

The next step is to compile both new source files:

```
*as -o part1.o part1.s
*as -o part2.o part2.s
```

Now the labels must be identified and linked using the linker thus:

```
*ld -o allparts part1.o part2.o
```

Here the linker will create an executable file called 'allparts' from the files part1.o and part2.o. You can try running the file with:

```
*allparts
```

The order of part1.o and part2.o could have been swapped — it would not have mattered as the linker resolves such issues. The key here is that each source file is independently written, created but then joined together (we might say tethered) by linking. If you tried to link just one file on its own you would get an error message because when linking, each part references the other. So in this case the linker is also a safety check.

What this small demonstration shows is that if you start to think carefully about your source files, you can start to develop a library of files that you can dip into each time you need a particular function. Each source file does not need to be assembled/compiled each time the program is linked. A source file only requires assembly if it has been changed speeding modular development.

GCC provides an excellent tool called make for managing programs consisting of multiple source files. This is beyond the scope of this introduction to GCC and the reader is directed towards the excellent make documentation and the companion website for any additional information that may become available.

Tidying Up

If you look in the Examples.Asm directory (or any other folder you have configured as described) you will see the executable files sitting there. If you look in the o directory you will see the object files, and the s directory contains your source files. The object files are intermediary files and you can delete these. As with standard BBC BASIC Assembler files you can maintain your source program and machine code files as you wish.

Unlike the BBC BASIC Assembler there is no need to *SAVE the machine code as they are already generated to a file by GCC. Examination of this file will show it is an ELF file type. This refers to the Executable and Linkable File format, a widely used binary file format.

A Simple C Framework

As I mentioned this is not a book about programming in C. However a basic understanding and use of C can be very helpful in reverse engineering how library functions work, function calling methods and even how C creates assembly from higher level language constructs.

The framework for a C program is simple enough. Program 27d illustrates the use of the C function putchar to print a single ASCII character to the screen. It has seven lines.

Program 27d. A simple C program to print an asterisk.

```
/* prog27d.c */
#include <stdio.h>
int main()
{
        putchar('*');
        return 0;
}
```

The first line tells the compiler that the file stdio.h should be included in the compilation. Stdio.h references parts of the libc standard library that includes the standard input-output interfaces and includes functions such as printf and the one we are interested in now — putchar. This is the part of the file that would be handled by the pre-processor described earlier, and this is the case for any line that begins with a hash.

The actual program starts with the function named main(). All functions begin with an opening brace ({) and end with a closing brace (}). Everything between the opening and closing braces is considered a part of the function. main(), like all C functions, must state what kind of value it returns. The return value type for main() is int, which means that this function returns an integer to the operating system when it completes. Here, it returns the integer value 0. A value may be returned to the operating system to indicate success or failure, or using a failure code to describe the cause of failure.

Hopefully you will have already cottoned on to how the main() in the C program above ties in with the main function in our assembler source files to date (and to a lesser extent the start function in the assembler listings that we looked at earlier in this chapter).

In amongst all this we have the crux of the program — putchar — being instructed to print an asterisk to the screen.

Program 27d can be entered with an editor such as !StrongEd and the file should be placed in the c folder in the Examples folder or any other folder you have configured with the environment outlined at the start of this chapter.

To compile this C program into an executable and run it we use the Task Window and enter the following:

```
*gcc -o prog27d prog27d.c
*prog27d
```

You will see an asterisk printed on the screen before the prompt.

Note that in this case there is no need to invoke the linker as we have done when using the assembler. This is convenient for the single file, simple programs we will be using specifically to reverse engineer how C works. The normal linker tools will work with C and even allow C and assembly to be mixed. The reader is directed to some of the excellent books on C to expand their knowledge and use of C.

28: C Library and Directives

The assembler and linker we have been using to write and create machine code programs so far are just a small part of the GCC package. As I said at the onset the GNU GCC compiler is a C Compiler. It will take programs written in C and convert them into machine code. Broadly speaking, it takes the C source file and translates it into an assembly language source file, which in turn gets translated into an executable machine code program which is linked together with other files and libraries to generate an executable file. As you can see we have been dealing with the last couple of processes here. But that is only just the tip of the iceberg.

This is not a book about C programming, but that is not to say we cannot use many of the features that C and the GCC Compiler provides. This includes libc, which is the standard function library of C. As we saw in an earlier chapter we can use the RISC OS system to perform common operations such as input/output, memory management, string manipulation, and so forth; libc gives us a standard and mostly cross-platform compatible convenient C library method of accessing similar functions.

While the libc functions are well documented from a C programmer's perspective, there is not a lot of detail about using them at the lower machine code level. I guess this is understandable. But given that C is relatively straightforward and there are literally thousands of program examples available to you (in manuals, on-line and in forums) it is very easy to write a very small C program containing a particular function that you can compile into an assembly language source file and then examine it, investigate it and refine it for your own purposes.

Directives

The GCC Assembler provides many additional tools to help in the writing of machine code programs. This includes instructions that allow you to store data within your programs and the ability to pass information to them when they are called from the prompt. All assembler directives begin with a period or full-stop and there are a lot of them with GCC. We have already seen several of these in action in earlier programs. A key here as you may have already identified for yourself is that when switching between GCC and the BBC BASIC

Assembler you need to take care not to mix the delimiters for labels and directives otherwise you will get errors or incorrect code at the very least.

Data Storage Directives

To store character string information within our programs, there are two options:

```
.ascii "This is the string to print."
.asciz "This string has a zero added to the end"
```

A string is written between double-quotes. The 'z' in the second option stands for zero and a zero byte (0x00) is appended at the end of the string; this is known as a null-terminated string and is the C standard for strings This is a useful way to end mark a string in memory allowing a simple Zero flag test when you are looking for the end of it. Both directives allow for control or escape code characters to be embedded within them by use of a backslash character, '\'. Figure 28a gives some of the more popular and useful ones:

Option	Effect
\b	backspace
\f	formfeed
\n	newline
\r	return
\t	tab
\\	allows printing of '\' in the string
\"	allows " to be printed in the string

Figure 28a. Popular backslash controls for use in strings.

The following:

```
.ascii "1\t2\t3\r\n4\t5\t6\r\n7\t8\t9\r\n"
```

would print out a simple but neatly formatted table using any of the write routines shown in this book. (Remember to change the string length count accordingly.)

As your programs become more sophisticated and have real application you will need to store information in them. This might be in the form of constants, addresses or messages to be printed. By placing the data within the body of the machine code, we can be safe in the knowledge that it is 'protected'. There are numerous directives that can create space for data.

Program 28a shows two of these, .byte and .equ.

Program 28a. Using directives to create a set of numbers.

```
/* prog28a.s */
/* Use of byte and equ to sum a set of numbers */
      .global _start
_start:
      LDR R1, =values
      LDR R2, =endvalues
      MOV R0, #0
_loop:
      LDRB R3, [R1], #increment
      ADD R0, R0, R3
      CMP R1, R2
      BNE _loop
_exit:
     LDR R1, =buffer
     MOV R2,#6
     SWI 0x06                     @ OS_ConvertCardinal2
     SWI 0x02                     @ OS_Write0
     SWI 0x03                     @ OS_NewLine
     MOV R8,#0
     SWI 0x11                     @ OS_Exit R8=0 => No Error Block

.data
.equ increment, 1
values:
      .byte 1,2,3,4,5,6,7,8,9
endvalues:
```

The .byte directive allows for a sequence of values separated by commas to be stored sequentially in memory. As the directive suggests these values must be in the range 0-255.

The .equ directive allows an immediate value to be assigned to a name. The name can then be used in your source files. This is handy in that if you need to change the value at any point you just have to change the .equ definition and not any and every reference to it in the source.

If you look at the .data section of Program 28a you can see that the constant 'increment' has been assigned the value 1. You can see how this is used as the post-indexing counter at the start of the _loop routine.

The label values: is used to mark the start of the .byte definition. A second label called endvalues: is used to mark the end of the .byte sequence. This is a handy technique to use when dealing with tables or arrays of data as a simple CMP test sees if the end of the sequence has been reached. The program illustrates this.

Within the _exit section several RISC OS Calls are used to convert the integer to a string, display the string and a newline. Further information on these can be obtained from the usual reference sources or the book *RISC OS System Programming Revealed.*

If you assemble, link and run Program 28a you will get the value 45 displayed, which is the sum of the bytes. Figure 28b below summarises a few important data directives.

Directive	Function
.equ	Assign immediate value to named label. Example: .equ one, 1
.byte	Store byte sized values, separated by commas into memory. Example: .byte 1,2,3,55,255
.word	Store four-byte values, separated by commas into memory. Example: .word 0xFFFFFFFF, 0xFF
.ascii	Store an ascii string. Example: .ascii "String"
.asciz	Store a null-terminated ascii string. Example: .asciz "String"

Figure 28b. The common data storage directives.

ALIGNing Data

GCC provides the equivalent of the ALIGN directive in BBC BASIC to ensure you keep your assembling code on word boundaries in places where you might store text strings and data. If you see the error:

Unaligned opcodes detected in executable segment error.

Then this is almost certainly the cause. In GCC use the directive:

`.align 2`

This pads out the space with 0s to the next word boundary. Note that there is generally no reason to use the .align directive outside of the executable sections of your code. Any definitions made in data sections are normally stored at the end of the file by the assembler to avoid such problems.

Using C Functions in Assembler

The C language has no built-in facilities for performing these functions but provides the interface to allow access to them, without necessarily needing to know a lot about the underlying systems calls. In addition, many of the things you may be looking to program for yourself may already be found in libc or available in other C libraries, and they can be included and linked into your own assembly source. There are many libraries to be found that are pre-packed and ready to be included by the compile process.

The main reason for using the system calls directly and not using libc would be one of space and speed. Some might also consider it a purer method of programming and not the rather disjointed code that integrating libc creates. The libc library is of a certain size and much of its basic configuration might be redundant. This is not normally an issue, but for a tight, small routine where speed and memory overhead might be critical then it may be a critical consideration. Technically your own program becomes a procedure which uses the resource libc provides.

From a user point of view a copy of 'The GNU C Library Reference Manual' is essential. Not to learn C (but that is not a bad thing to do — you will become increasingly aware of how fundamental it is to system and application programming) but for the detail of the various functions you can access. This contains information required and returned. In this chapter we'll be looking at some worked examples on these and using the above document as our source. The GNU C Library Reference Manual can be found on the GNU website for download or a link to it is available on the book support website via www.brucesmith.info.

Source File Structure

The format of the source file used with the full GCC compiler is a little different from what we have been using to date. It is no more difficult to create and is in fact a lot simpler to compile as we do not need to do the assembly and link stages separately — they can be done with a single command. Have a look at Program 28b.

Program 28b. GCC source file structure.

```
/* prog28b.s */
/**    Printing a string using libc    **/
/**    entry requirements change       **/
/**    and string must end with 0      **/
/**    when using printf function       **/
       .global main
       .func main
main:
       LDR R0, =string          @ R0 points to string
       BL printf                @ Call libc
_exit:
       MOV R8,#0
       SWI 0x11                 @ OS_Exit R8=0 >= No Error Block
.data
string:
       .asciz "Hello World String\n"
values:
       .byte 1,2,3,4,5,6,7,8,9
endvalues:
```

The first thing to notice is that the global _start definition has been replaced with global main thus:

```
       .global main
       .func main
       main:
```

The structure used is important as this is used by the compiler to tell libc where the main program is located. Because all C and libc routines are written as named functions then we have to declare this main part of our code as a function and then use a label to part exactly where the function starts. These three lines do that. (As you can see they effectively undertake the same task that _start does when using the assembler-linker only, notwithstanding the addition of the function definition.)

The libc function printf is used to print the asciz string defined at the end of the listing. printf is not a C command but is a function defined in the library that we can use. It is a very versatile function and all that is required before we call it is for R0 to be given the address of the string. In all cases printf requires that the string be terminated with a zero and this is why the asciz directive is — and should always — be used.

The exit function uses the preferred SWI OS_Exit method limiting this to the main function as it will return to the operating system.

If you have tried to assemble and link this command in the way we have described so far it will have failed because there is no _start entry point. Assembling with GCC can be done in a single step thus:

> ***gcc <options> <destination_name> <input_name.s>**

So for Program 28b you might use:

> ***gcc −o prog28b prog28b.s**

and run the program with:

> ***prog28b**

There is no requirement to invoke the linker separately when assembling simpler programs with gcc in this way.

Using printf

The printf function is amazingly versatile and I could fill a book with examples. Program 28c shows how values can be passed into printf and used in printing results.

Program 28c. Passing parameters to printf.

```
/* prog28c.s */
/****   Printing a string using libc and ****/
/****   passing parameters to function   ****/
/****   for use in printf                 ****/
        .global main
        .func main
main:
        LDR R0, =string      @ R0 points to string
        MOV R1, #10          @ first value in R1
        MOV R2, #15          @ second value in R2
        MOV R3, #25          @ result in R3
        BL printf            @ Call libc
_exit:
        MOV R8,#0
        SWI 0x11             @ OS_Exit, R8=0=> No Error Block
.data
string:
        .asciz "If you add %d and %d you get %d.\n"
```

The string definition here includes three parameters within it. These are signified by the preceding '%'. If you compile and run this program you will see that its output is:

If you add 10 and 15 you get 25.

Looking at the listing for Program 28b we can see that these three values were passed in R1, R2 and R3. When using libc functions such as printf there is a standard way to pass and return information into them and we'll look at this in a following section which deals with functions. For now note that the register passing method as illustrated will work only for functions with a maximum of four parameters.

The table in Figure 28c below lists some of the output options available to use within printf. This list is by no means extensive but it does provide some options for you to experiment with, by editing the above program.

Directive	Function
%d	Print an integer as a signed decimal number.
%o	Print an integer as an unsigned octal number.
%u	Print an integer as an unsigned decimal number.
%x	Print an integer as an unsigned hexadecimal numbers using lower-case letters
%X	Print an integer as an unsigned hexadecimal number using upper-case letters.
%c	Print a single character.
%s	Prints a string
%%	Print a literal '%' character.

Figure 28c. Output parameters recognised by printf.

Number Input with Scanf

You could be forgiven for thinking that scanf performs the reverse task of printf, but it does not. scanf takes a string of characters entered at the keyboard and converts it into its numerical value and stores it in memory. For example, if when using scanf you typed:

255

when requested scanf would store the binary equivalent in memory. In hex this would be:

```
0xFF
```

The reason for discussing this routine at this point, rather than the string-input routine equivalent of printf is that it illustrates another way a libc function expects and uses data. Not all functions expect data in the same way. This is a concept that you will need to bear in mind as you come to learn how to access libc functions and write your own.

However, as with printf, scanf recognises many, many different formats and you could spend a great deal of time learning and experimenting with them both. For this example we'll stick with the use of integer values. This is the %d format introduced in the previous program example.

The format for use of scanf is as follows (this is stylised — it is not how it would be coded in C):

```
scanf <input_format>, <variable>
```

or:

```
scanf "%d", &integernumber
```

The steps for using scanf are these:

- Declare a memory variable holding the address of the formatting string. This will be a string "%d" for this example.

- Declare a memory variable holding the address of where the value is to be placed.

- Make space on the stack for the converted ASCII string to be stored.

Notice how in this case we are pointing to the information indirectly; we are passing the addresses of the relevant information - a technique commonly referred to as passing-by-reference as opposed to passing-by-value referring to passing information directly. This is important to know because it means that to use the indirect addresses we have to declare the variables, and here we are talking about the .word directive, within the text area, in other words within the executable code area. The string definitions themselves should remain outside the text section and be defined in the data segment of the code. The other thing you need to know is that scanf stores its result on the stack, so to prevent it being corrupted we need to adjust the stack point by a word to make a safe place for it. Program 28d should help disperse the mist.

The line numbers are there to help in the description of the program and should be omitted when you are entering the listing.

Program 28d. Reading and converting a number with scanf.

```
1        /* prog28d.s */
2        /******  Reading a number using scanf    *****/
3        /******  via registers and the stack     *****/
4              .global main
5              .func main
6        main:
7              SUB SP, SP, #4    @ Make room on stack
8              LDR R0, addr_format @ get addr of format
9              MOV R1, SP             @ place SP in R1 and
10             BL scanf              @ store entry on stack
11             LDR R2, [SP]
12             LDR R3, addr_number
13             STR R2, [R3]
14             ADD SP, SP, #4
15       _exit:
16             MOV R8,#0
17             SWI 0x11             @ OS_Exit R8=0 => No Error Block
18
19       /* as scanf needs addresses of strings we */
20       /* assemble them in the text area         */
21
22       addr_format:          .word scanformat
23       addr_number:          .word number
24
25       .data
26       number:               .word 0
27       scanformat:           .asciz "%d"
```

Let's look at the listing. *The line numbers should not be entered and are only there to make the description easier to follow.* Lines 6 and 15 should be familiar and should be considered part of standard procedure. Line 7 is where we adjust the stack pointer by four bytes to make some space for scanf. Before we call scanf we need to place the address of the location to store the result into R1, in this case SP+0 hence loading SP into R1 (line 10) and the address of the format string in R0 (line 8). The format string should indicate the details of the value that will be entered at the keyboard and read by scanf. This ensures that the value is converted correctly.

After calling scanf (line 10) the converted binary value is now held on the stack, so this is retrieved (line 11) and the address of where it is to be saved is placed in line 12. Then using indirect addressing the value is stored (line 13). To tidy up, we should reset the stack point by adding the 4 additional bytes we originally stole from it (line 14).

Lines 22 to 27 show how we create addresses to point to the actual data to be utilised. The actual data is in the .data subsection (lines 25-27) and the addresses of these two places are held in word length addresses within the text area defined by lines 22 and 23. Thus on assembly the four-bytes of space created by line 23 will hold the address of the string "%d". This is the format string we encountered earlier. Line 26 creates a place for the address of where the result returned by scanf will be placed.

When you run this program there will be no prompt. Just enter a number such as 255 and press the return key. The prompt will be returned.

Program 28e extends the above routine to provide some interaction using printf to request the value and then print the result.

Program 28e Reading a number using scanf.

```
/* prog28e s */
/****** Reading a number using scanf    *****/
/****** and printing it with prinf      *****/
          .global main
          .func main
main:
      SUB SP, SP, #4          @ make a word on stack

      LDR R0, addr_messin     @ get addr of messagein
      BL printf               @ and print it

      LDR R0, addr_format     @ get addr of format
      MOV R1, SP              @ place SP in R1
      BL scanf                @ and store entry on stack

      LDR R1, [SP]            @ get addr of scanf input
      LDR R0, addr_messout    @ get addr of messageout
      BL printf               @ print it all

      ADD SP, SP, #4          @ adjust stack
_exit:
```

```
        MOV R8,#0
        SWI 0x11                    @ OS_Exit R8=0 => No Error Block

addr_messin:    .word messagein
addr_format:    .word scanformat
addr_messout:   .word messageout

.data
messagein:      .asciz "Enter your number: "
scanformat:     .asciz "%d"
messageout:     .asciz "Your number was 0x%X\n"
```

Note that in this program the information is expected to be entered in decimal format, but the result is actually displayed in hex — see the very last line of the program.

Getting This Information

If you have no experience with C then you may be wondering how best to get all this information and then understand how to use it. Good question. The simple answer is that there is no central resource and that it comes down to investigation and interrogation. Websites and user forums are a good source of detail for one. The other way is to create the desired function call in C then compiler to assembly using gcc -S and inspecting how the compiler generates the function call. As your knowledge of ARM machine code increases then this will become a more common option and we'll have a look at just how to go about it in a later chapter.

Function Standards

The libc functions we looked at, print and scanf, both expected to receive and return information. We also saw that we can pass information into these functions using the registers R0, R1, R2, and R3. This is determined by a standard called the Application Binary Interface (ABI) which was carefully devised and defines how functions should run. The point being that if everyone follows the standard and writes their functions in the same way, then everyone will be able to use each other's functions. (C compilers use the ARM Procedure Call Standard (APCS) which goes into things in a little more detail). As far as we are concerned they achieve the same result at code level but it is worth getting online and investigating both in a little more detail at some point.

Reg	Alias	Role	Preserved
R0	A1	Argument 1, integer result and scratch register	No
R1	A2	Argument 2, scratch register	No
R2	A3	Argument 3, scratch register	No
R3	A4	Argument 4, scratch register	No
R4	V1	General register variable	Yes
R5	V2	General register variable	Yes
R6	V3	General register variable	Yes
R7	V4	General register variable	Yes
R8	V5	General register variable	Yes
R9	V6 or SB	General register variable or stack base	Yes
R10	V7 or SL	General register variable or stack limit	Yes
R11	FP	Frame pointer. Can be setup to point to bottom of stack frame - usually SP-4 on call to allow for argument storage on stack (GCC typically does this)	Yes
R12	IP	Intra procedure call or scratch register. Can be setup to SP on call before creating stack frame (GCC typically does this)	Yes
R13	SP	Stack pointer. Where local data is - lower end of stack frame	No
R14	LR	Link Register - return address to caller, scratch register	Yes
R15	PC	Program Counter	No

Figure 28d. Register designations in a function call—ARM Procedure Call Standard

Figure 28d details the purpose of each register when a function complying with the APCS is called. In summary a function should adhere to the following:

- It may freely modify registers R0, R1, R2 and R3 and expect to find the information in them that it requires to carry out its task.

- It can modify registers R4-12, providing it restores their values before returning to the calling routine.

- It can modify the Stack Pointer providing it restores the value held on entry.

- It must preserve the address in the Link Register so that it may return correctly to the calling program.

- It should make no assumption as to the contents of the CSPR. As far as the function is concerned the status of the N, Z, C and V flags are unknown.

The use of IP and FP are optional and not required as all local variables can be referenced from SP using pre-indexed addressing. Setting up IP and FP is typical of GCC generated code and should be expected when reviewing code assembled by GCC from C source.

The Link register does not need to be preserved if the function is the main function and the preferred exit method, namely OS_Exit, is used. Let's break this down in a bit more detail.

Register Use

It is this standard that says R0, R1, R2 and R3 (in that order) will be used as inputs to a function. But this is only if the function requires four inputs. If it only needs one then this goes in the first register — R0, if it needs a second that must be placed in R1 and similarly for R2 and R3. If it only needs one input then it does not matter what is in the other registers as they will not be used. If the function returns a value it will always go in R0.

The second point made is that the other registers R4-R12 inclusive must be preserved so that when the calling program gets control back from the function the contents of R4 through to R12 inclusive must be the same as when the function was called. Now that is not to say we can't use them. If your function needs them, then one of the first things it should do (but not necessarily the very first as we shall see) is to push their contents onto the stack and then restore them from the stack before finishing. These two complementary instructions would do the job:

```
STMFD SP!, {R4-R12} @ save registers R4 thro R12
LDMFD SP!, {R4-R12} @ restore R4 through R12
```

More Than Three

You may be asking at this point what happens if we need to pass more than four items to the function we are calling. The answer lies in the next 'rule' in that we can modify the Stack Pointer (SP) again provided we ensure that it is set correctly on completion of the routine. However, this is not always strictly true, because if we need to pass more information into the function the control of the SP has to be managed by the calling routine, especially if the amount of data is unknown. If a function must have an additional four items of data each and every time, then the function can manage the SP, but you need to be wary of this.

You will recall in Program 28b we called printf to display three items of information by passing the data through R1-R3. Program 28f extends this to pass six values to the calling routine. The listing has lines numbered for ease of discussion—these should not be entered.

Program 28f. Using the stack to pass parameters.

```
1        /* prog28f.s */
2        /** Printing a string using printf **/
3        /** and passing parameters to it   **/
4        /** via registers and the stack    **/
5             .global main
6             .func main
7     main:
8             LDR R0, =string  @ R0 points to string
9             MOV R1, #1       @ first value in R1
10            MOV R2, #2       @ second value in R2
11            MOV R3, #3       @ result in R3
12            LDR R7,=value1   @ get address of param
13            LDR R8, [R7]     @ load value1 into R8
14            PUSH {R8}        @ put on stack
15            LDR R7,=value2   @ repeat for value2
16            LDR R8, [R7]
17            PUSH {R8}
18            LDR R7,=value3   @ repeat for value3
19            LDR R8, [R7]
20            PUSH {R8}
21            BL printf        @ Call libc
22            ADD SP, SP, #12  @ balance stack
23     _exit:
24            MOV R8,#0
25            SWI 0x11         @ OS_Exit R8=0 => No Error Block
26
27            .data
28     string:  .asciz "Values are: %d, %d, %d and %d\n"
29     value1:  .word 4
```

```
30      value2:    .word 5
31      value3:    .word 6
```

The program is pretty much identical until we get to line 12 where we start taking the word values stored in lines 28-31 inclusive and pushing them onto the stack.

This introduces PUSH which is actually compiler directives and not ARM instructions. This has the same effect as the ARM instruction STMFD but is a lot easier to use as you don't have to think too much about what type of stack you are going to use and what order the stack adjusters are used in. (However, it is worth remembering that should you decide to use another assembler, directives may change and not be compatible with your existing code. That said, you will almost certainly have to make adjustments to your code format with a new assembly program.). The corresponding POP directive implements the reverse of PUSH.

By the time we reach line 21 we have the address of the string in R0 whilst R1, R2 and R3 hold the values 1, 2 and 3 respectively. Then the stack holds (at the top) 6, and below that 5 and below that 4. Despite being single digits these are all words with values and occupy four bytes each. If you run the program the result you will see on screen is:

Values are: 1, 2, 3 and 6

This is because we only instructed printf to print on an extra value, and it looked for it on top of the stack. Adding in a couple more %d into the printf string will provide the means to print the two additional values. You would also need to swap the push order onto the stack if you wanted to ensure that the numbers were displayed in the correct order.

Line 22 is interesting. We adjusted the SP by 12 bytes because of the three PUSH instructions. This line moves the SP back those 12 places and ensures that the system is hunky dory. This could have been achieved with three POP instructions equally as well; however, this is a neat way to restore the status quo if you are dumping a lot of data on the stack.

If this function had required the use of the other registers then we would have needed to save their contents as per the rule earlier. The simplest way to do this would have been to push the values straight onto the stack, but this would have forced the required data down the stack and out of sync with the function expectations. In situations such as these the best answer is to save them to an area of memory that you have set aside for workspace.

If you are writing a function that needs additional information passed to it on the stack and the registers saved, then you can use the stack for all of it as you are managing the stack. If your function expected three items on the stack and you needed to save R4 then you can access the stack directly at the three locations using a simple immediate offset, something like this:

```
LDR R4, SP+4 @ Get first data word on stack
```

The second item would be at SP+8 and the third at SP+12.

Remember that these instructions do not adjust the SP so you must reset it on completion as already described.

Preserving Links and Flags

One thing you must always remember when writing functions is that on completion the function is going to need to return program control back to whence it came. This means that it is imperative to preserve the integrity of the Link Register. If you intend to call another function or routine at some point then you may well use a BL or BLX instruction to do so. If you do this then the contents of the LR will be overwritten and lost. Therefore they must be stashed away safely in your memory workspace somewhere or pushed onto the stack for later restoration.

An exception to preserving LR is within the main program called from the operating system. There is no need to save and restore LR and the preferred exit method is outlined in the following section.

There is no requirement to preserve the Status Flags. As far as the function is concerned these are generally unknown. That said, your function may have a requirement for the flags as a signal back to the caller and this is a valid way to signal information, especially as R0 is the one standard way of returning a value. For example, the N flag might be set on return to signal that an error occurred.

29: C to Create Assembler

As we have seen, C can be a useful way to generate assembly language for the purpose reverse engineering the code. This can be useful when working out how to use library functions or looking at how higher level language structures are converted to assembly language. It can also be used to generate sections of code that may be difficult or time consuming to manually convert to assembly language, such as existing functions or code.

This is not a book on programming C and there are many excellent texts to assist the reader looking to gain familiarity with C. Our intended aim is to use GCC and the C compiler to learn more about assembly language and make use of the excellent C library functions.

This chapter will consider the use of C to create assembler that we can use, dissect and even interface to your assembly language programs.

Getting the Assembly Language

Given what we have learnt in the past few chapters you might be able to take a pretty good guess at what you would expect to see in the assembly language source code generated for the C program listed below as Program 29a.. The function prints a single character. We would expect therefore that, as specified by the AAPCS standard, the ASCII code for the character to be printed would be loaded into R0. No other information is passed. The routine will complete with a return value of 0, so we should also expect to find this passed back in R0 as per standard. Let's C!

Program 29a. C program to print a single asterisk using libc.

```
/* prog29a.c */
#include <stdio.h>
int main()
{
    putchar('*');
    return 0;
}
```

Prior to executing any GCC commands ensure the current working directory is set to the correct source directory using either filer or *dir from Task Window as outlined in Chapter 27. To create an assembler listing from a .c file we use the –S directive (note must be capital S), thus:

```
*gcc -S prog29a.c
```

GCC will create a file called prog29a located in the s folder in the current working directory. Open this in an editor such as StrongEd and you should see something very similar (it may not be identical) to what is shown in Figure 29a.

```
        .file"prog29a.c"
        .text
        .align    2
        .global   main
        .ascii    "main\000"
        .align    2
        .word-16777208
        .typemain, %function
main:
    @ args = 0, pretend = 0, frame = 0, outgoing = 0
    @ frame_needed = 1, uses_anonymous_args = 0
    mov   ip, sp
    stmfdsp!, {r9, fp, ip, lr, pc}
    sub   fp, ip, #4
    cmp   sp, sl
    bllt  __rt_stkovf_split_small
    mov   r0, #42
    bl    putchar
    mov   r3, #0
    mov   r0, r3
    ldmeafp, {r9, fp, sp, pc}
    .sizemain, .-main
```

Figure 29a. The assembler generated by GCC from the C program.

You should be able to identify quickly the body of the program in here. In fact of the 23 lines of assembler only a handful of them are of significance relative to what we are after. All the additional information can ultimately be discarded but was an important transformation step for GCC when it did the initial conversion. This conversion is very methodical and is a case of one size fits all using a brute force method of working. GCC has to create some workspace for each function it is dealing with in the conversion process, and has to protect this workspace for its needs. In broad terms it does this by partitioning an area on the stack for the function's use. This is called the stack frame and this has its own pseudo-register called the frame pointer, FP. This marks the start of the stack frame and each function creates its own stack frame to manage local variables. The stack frame is therefore an important aspect of a C program but they are less important in creating assembler. However, understanding what it does is important in allowing us to deconstruct C derived assembler.

Back to the listing above. It is good at this point to create a backup of this initial assembly file. You will want to start deleting lines and adjusting code to create a smaller compact source file that you can assemble and test. Thus either use Filer and copy the file or Task Window and execute

```
*copy s.prog29a s.prog29a-orig ~CF
```

would create a copy with the -orig indicating to you that it is source original.

Building Blocks

Our purpose here is to cut this source down so that we can assemble and link it directly and produce the same result as the original C program. GCC has constructed the assembler source using some basic building blocks. The first 15 lines provide various items of information. They are not important for our purposes and so can be deleted. There follows the file name and definition of the .text section. Again, for our small assembler construct these can both be deleted. The .size main directive is used by the linker to indicate the size of the function. Again, we do not need this and it can be discarded.

Having done all that we are left with the listing shown in Figure 29b, with line numbers for ease of reference. The first three lines define the main() function and we will need to edit these slightly for use in our assembly listing. This is followed by a couple of comments (lines 4 and 5) provided by the compiler in relation to management of the stack frame for this routine. Again, we will not need these and they can be deleted.

Lines 6-8 and 15 act in tandem to preserve the addresses held in registers including the frame pointer and link register. The FP is of no importance to us here but we do normally need to preserve the LR before calling the putchar routine so a suitable PUSH and POP instruction can be substituted here. Line 8 can also be removed as we do not need to process anything relating to the FP, but we can see from this instruction that the FP is being give the value of SP+4.

The exit method generated by the GCC compiler is not our preferred method. The linker will add code to call main and return to the operating system. As we are not using any other code to call our function we will replace the exit process on line 15 with our recommended RISC OS exit code.

As this is the main function there is no requirement to save and restore the Link Register. These have been left in the source to indicate they are normal function behaviour but commented to indicate the exception within the main function. These can be deleted if required.

```
        .global    main
        .type main, %function
main:
        @ args = 0, pretend = 0, frame = 0, outgoing = 0
        @ frame_needed = 1, uses_anonymous_args = 0
        mov  ip, sp
        stmfd sp!, {r9, fp, ip, lr, pc}
        sub  fp, ip, #4
        cmp  sp, sl
        bllt __rt_stkovf_split_small
        mov  r0, #42
        bl   putchar
        mov  r3, #0
        mov  r0, r3
        ldmea fp, {r9, fp, sp, pc}
```

Figure 29b. The C assembler source with directives removed.

Lines 9 and 10 check for stack overflow and link to a C library function if an overflow has occurred. As we are controlling the stack we will assume an overflow will not be permitted to occur and these lines can be deleted.

The crux of our code comes down to lines 11 and 12. The ASCII code for the asterisk (42) is moved into R0 and putchar is called. Lines 13 and 15 are then used to place a 0 in R0, You will recall that the original C function is to return 0. For our purposes, we do not strictly need these two lines and they can be removed. What we are left with is the listing presented as Program 29c.

Program 29c. The final putchar listing.

```
@ prog29c.s
        .global    main
        .type main, %function
main:
@       PUSH {LR}          @ Can be removed for main function
        sub  fp, ip, #4
```

```
        mov   r0, #42
        bl    putchar
@       POP {PC}        @ Can be removed for main function
        MOV R8,#0
        SWI 0x11        @ SWI OS_Exit, R8=0 => No Error Block
```

This listing will assemble and run correctly. Although the original C program was relatively trivial the methodology used to create and reduce the assembler source that it creates is sound and can be applied in virtually all cases.

A printf Example

We have already examined the use of printf in assembly language programs but we'll look at it again, this time from the C perspective as it provides a good insight into how C programs are constructed that will be useful when looking at the assembler. Program 29d is the C file for the famous "hello world" program. On the face of it, this is really not much different from our previous putchar example. But in fact it is.

Program 29d. C listing for the 'hello world' program.

```
/* prog29d.c */
#include <stdio.h>
int main()
{
    printf("hello world");
    return 0;
}
```

You can convert this to assembler using:

```
*gcc -S prog29d.c
```

Figure 29c lists the derived assembler minus the initial header and footer directives.

Given our knowledge of printf and applying what we learned above, the main: section of the program should be straightforward — nothing new to learn here. It is the other areas that are of interest —notably the areas marked by the labels LC0, L3 and L2. The L3 label is not required nor is the align 2 directive — the label will clearly be on a word boundary as it comes directly behind code. L2 marks a reserved word to hold the address of the 'hello world' text marked by

LC0. This was a technique that we used when playing with the scanf function in Program 28d but is different to the method we used in our original printf program, Program 28c. It is worth comparing the two side by side.

```
        .section    .rodata
        .align      2
.LC0:
        .ascii      "hello world\000"
        .text
        .align      2
        .global     main
        .ascii      "main\000"
        .align      2
        .word-16777208
        .typemain, %function
main:
        @ args = 0, pretend = 0, frame = 0, outgoing = 0
        @ frame_needed = 1, uses_anonymous_args = 0
        mov   ip, sp
        stmfdsp!, {r9, fp, ip, lr, pc}
        sub   fp, ip, #4
        cmp   sp, sl
        bllt  __rt_stkovf_split_small
        ldr   r0, .L3
        bl    printf
        mov   r3, #0
        mov   r0, r3
        ldmeafp, {r9, fp, sp, pc}
.L4:
        .align      2
.L3:
        .word.LC0
```

Figure 29c. The C assembler source with header and footer directives removed.

As a final exercise you might want to try compiling a scanf example, as this combines a few of these techniques and also accesses the stack for information. Program 29e is what you will need. If you compile and run this the keyboard will wait for you to enter a number. There will be no additional responses as it is the bare function we are concerned with.

Program 29e A C listing for using the scanf function.

```
/* prog29e.c */
#include <stdio.h>
int main()
{
    int myvariable;
    scanf("%d", &myvariable);
    return 0;
}
```

A reminder here that scanf uses the stack to store and pass its converted numeric value, so you will need to manage the stack pointer in the assembler.

Frame Pointer Variables

Just a word to the good about the frame pointer relative to dissecting your listings in this way. If the original C programs contains variables then the Frame Pointer will be used to point to these values, so it becomes important in your deconstruction. Consider these two lines of assembler:

```
LDR R2, {FP, #-8}
MOV R0, R2
```

The first line shows that a variable is located at the position given by FP-8 and this result is accessed and moved into R0. If the original C listing has several variables you will need to identify where each one is located on the stack, by seeking out similar code lines. Of course your assembler will not have a Frame Pointer, or it would be assigned a value it is often set equal to the SP by the code, so you will need to translate these into labelled locations.

In Summary

The examples above are ones we have encountered and already explained and this is done deliberately to make it easier to explain what GCC is doing in its compile process. You may not be forewarned with such knowledge when looking at new functions. But GCC goes about its business in a pre-defined way and the processes will not vary. Information is passed in registers and on the stack (and via the frame pointer) so it is often just a matter of identifying what is where and then working back from there.

30: Thumb Code

Thumb is the name given to a subset of the ARM instruction set. More significantly it is a 16-bit (two-byte) implementation, so instructions can in theory be coded in half the space of an equivalent ARM program but in reality achieving the same result in a third less space . This higher code density makes Thumb code popular where memory constraints are tight. You will probably not see a lot of Thumb programs around on the forums for RISC OS. It is commonly seen on GameBoy Advance development forums where the same GCC toolchain we have been using is widely used. Most Thumb code seems to be written and compiled from C though that isn't to say we can't hand assemble it.

In terms of hardware there is no real difference between the way in which ARM and Thumb instruction sets function — they are one and the same. Although Thumb is a 16-bit implementation register sizes do not change. R0 is still a word wide, as are the other registers. What is different is how they are fetched and interpreted before execution. Thumb instructions are expanded into their 32-bit equivalents internally by the hardware, so it doesn't slow down their execution in any way — ARM speed is maintained. This makes it perfectly acceptable to mix normal sections of ARM and Thumb code and jump from one to the other; in fact jumping from ARM to Thumb is the preferred way to enter Thumb code.

If you flick back to Chapter 6 and look at Figure 6c the diagram shows the Status Register configuration. Bit 5 is the 'T' bit and this is normally clear to indicated ARM State. When the T bit is set (T=1) then the chip is in Thumb State. We'll look how to move between states and write a simple program that can be the shell for any Thumb code you may wish to write. But first....

Differences

The Raspberry Pi allows the operation of Thumb 1 but not the newer Thumb 2 instruction set. For the most part the Thumb instruction set will be very familiar to you, but there are differences that need to be borne in mind. If you understand these you should have no difficulties implementing and writing a Thumb program from your existing ARM knowledge (which should be quite extensive at this point). The BBC BASIC assembler and the RISC OS Debugger do not support Thumb code. However GCC supports Thumb so the tools we have been using will allow us to investigate and use Thumb code. Programs using Thumb code will run normally within RISC OS.

The major architectural difference is that your code does not have direct access to all the ARM registers; only R0 to R7 inclusive are available. Registers R8 to R12 inclusive can only be used in conjunction with MOV, ADD, SUB and CMP. There is very limited access to R13 (SP), R14 (LR) and R15 (PC) and only indirect access to the CPSR. There is no access to SPSR and the VFP instructions cannot be accessed from Thumb State.

Thumb

R0
R1
R2
R3
R4
R5
R6
R7

Registers available to all Thumb instructions. Instructions assembled in two-bytes (16-bits)

R8
R9
R10
R11
R12

Registers only available to a few Thumb instructions. Namely MOV, ADD, SUB, CMP.

R13 SP
R14 LR
R15 PC

SP, LR, SP only have limited access and SP only accessible via PUSH and POP instructions.

CPSR
SPSR_xxx

Indirectly

None

Figure 30a. Thumb registers accessibility.

The registers and code that are not available can be accessed from the program, but only after ARM State is switched back in. In other words you have to first come out of Thumb State to execute what you want to do and then switch back into Thumb State to continue. Figure 30a summarises these register restrictions.

However, the advantage of all this is that when you move between ARM and Thumb State the contents of registers are preserved.

By definition, the other significant difference is that mnemonic representations of Thumb instructions are shorter, often with one less operand. Compare these ARM and Thumb versions of ADD:

```
ADDS R2, R2, #16    @ ARM State immediate addition
ADD R0, #3          @ Thumb equivalent, dest implied
```

The conditional code modifiers for instructions are not available, with only branch relative instructions conditionally executable. Therefore you cannot execute instructions like:

```
ADD CC R0, #3
```

in Thumb State.

The shift and rotate operators ASR, LSL, LSR and ROR are implemented as standalone instructions and are no longer available as a modifying operand. The following code segment illustrates the format for use:

```
LSL R2, R3    @ Shift R2 left number positions in R3
```

In the example above, if R2=4 and R3=1 then R2 would become 8.

Thumb includes just two branch instructions. Bxx and BX. The B variant (as used in Program 24a) is the only one that is conditional, but the range here is limited to a label that must be within a signed single byte value, effectively -128 to 127. A non-conditional branch instruction can be extended to a range within an 11-bit signed immediate value, -1024 to +1023 bytes.

The BL instruction is not conditional but because it can be used in an indirect manner the address range can be up to 4Mb centred on the branch instruction location. An example of this is provided at the end of the next section.

There are also significant changes to multiple load-store and stack access instructions and these are covered below separately.

Assembling Thumb

To switch between ARM and Thumb states, you should use the GCC directives:

```
.arm
```

or:

```
.thumb
```

These directives replace the oft seen older versions .code32 and .code16, which will work on the current version of GGC available on the Raspberry Pi, but these should be considered as old hat now. If necessary, these directives will also automatically insert up to three bytes of padding to align to the next word boundary for ARM, or up to one byte of padding to align to the next half-word boundary for Thumb. Thus use of .ALIGN is unnecessary.

Both .arm and .thumb must be used to direct the assembler what to compile. They do not assemble any instructions themselves; they just direct the assembler as to what follows. Rather than having to play with bit 5 directly in the CPSR the state change will be handled directly for you if you follow the correct protocol for doing so which involves using the BX instruction.

Program 30a. How to invoke Thumb State and run Thumb code.

```
@   Use of Thumb code in RISC OS on Raspberry Pi
@   This divide routine is R0/R1
@   with R2=MOD and R3=DIV
        .global main
        .func main
        .arm
main:
        MOV R0, #100           @ Seed R0 and R1 for demo purposes
        MOV R1, #5
        ADR R4, thumbcode+1
        MOV LR, PC
        BX R4

exit:
        MOV R8, #0
        SWI 0x11               @ OS_Exit, R8=0 => No Error Block

        @ All Thumb code to be placed here
        .thumb

thumbcode:
        MOV R3, #0
loop:
        ADD R3, #1
        SUB R0, R1
        BGE loop
        SUB R3, #1
        ADD R2, R0, R1
        BX LR                  @ Return to ARM
```

Essentially, if you load the link address of the start of the Thumb code into R4 and set the least significant bit of R4 (that is b0=1) then Thumb State will be invoked automatically when the Thumb code is branched to with BX. This implies that you must always start from ARM state, but that must be the case anyway as that is the state the chip fires up in. Program 30a above shows how this works in practice. (Note the use of '@' for comments. GCC Thumb code does not like the inclusion of '/* */' style comments and these can sometimes cause an error.).

The thumb instructions are located from the thumbcode: label. This address is loaded into R4 at the start of main: and 1 is added to the address to set the least significant bit of R4. The BX (Branch with eXchnage) is executed and the address in R4 is swapped into the PC. Because ARM and Thumb instructions are word or half-word-aligned respectively, bits 0 and 1 of the address are ignored because these bits refer to the half-word and byte part of the address.

The instructions at thumbcode perform a division routine (R0 and R1 are seeded with values for demonstration) before the BX LR returns code back to the calling ARM code. ARM state is switched back in due to the requirement to execute an ARM instruction. Note that you have to switch back to ARM State to execute an SWI call or a function such as printf.

You must use a BX LR instruction at the end of the ARM subroutine to return to the caller. You cannot use the MOV PC,LR instruction to return in this situation as it will not update the T bit for you thereby delivering the State change.

It would be helpful to disassemble the program to see how it conforms to the differences outlined earlier. However, as mentioned previously, the RISC OS debugger does not support Thumb code and will not disassemble the Thumb code section.

The process of mingling segments of ARM and Thumb code together is called *interworking* and you are free to write code that moves between the two instructions sets if you so desire. The same ADR-BX process can be used throughout. If for example an ARM routine was located at the label 'armroutine' then it could be called with:

```
ADR R0, armroutine
BX  R0                  @ Branch exchange to armroutine
```

Before making any calls that utilise the Link Register you should preserve its contents on the stack so that you can return to the original point of entry, and then recall the program originally entered at main, so that the program can complete its flow correctly.

Although BX is used in the examples above, the BLX instruction can also be used to jump into Thumb code. This instruction automatically saves the PC into the LR, so the MOV LR, PC instruction included in the listing is not needed. The +1 is still required for the entry address to switch State. The BX instruction should still be used to return from any called routine.

```
_start:
        ADR R4, thumbcode+1
        BLX R4
```

Program 30b shows how these come together in practice using the printf function to print the result of a division performed in an extended program. Note that the additional ARM code follows the Thumb code. This is necessary otherwise the compiler will create an error when trying to create the relative branch address to the ARM code. Note also that the .arm and .thumb directives should be before the label marking the section of appropriate code.

Program 30b. Using external functions by interworking code.

```
@ Interworking ARM and Thumb code to call printf
        .global main
        .func main
        .arm
main:
        ADR R5, thumbstart+1
        BX  R5


        .thumb
thumbstart:
        MOV R0, #9              @ Do 9/3
        MOV R1, #3
        MOV R3, #0
loop:
        ADD R3, #1
        SUB R0, R1
        BGE loop
        SUB R3, #1             @ R2=MOD
        ADD R2, R0, R1         @ R3=DIV
        ADR R5, divprint
        BX  R5


thumbreturn:
        @ Continue adding code as required
        @ Call ARM functions as and when needed
```

```
        ADR R5, exit
        BX R5                      @ Return to exit
        .arm
divprint:
        LDR R0, =string
        MOV R1, R3 @ DIV in R3
                                   @ MOD in R2 already
        BL printf
        ADR R5, thumbreturn+1
        BX R5

exit:
        MOV R7, #1
        SWI 0

.data
string:    .asciz "Result of 9/3 is: %d MOD %d\n"
```

Accessing High Registers

Only a handful of instructions can access the full set of ARM Registers. As already stated most Thumb instructions are limited to R0-R7 and automatically update the CPSR in doing so. Figure 30c lists the instructions and format use for accessing the higher registers R8-R14 and the PC. Apart from CMP these instructions do not update the CPSR.

MOV <Dest>, <Operand1>
ADD <Dest>, <Operand1>
CMP <Operand1>, <Operand2>
ADD <Dest>,   <Operand1>|<#Immediate>
ADD <Dest>, <Operand1>, <Operand2>|<#Immediate>
SUB <Dest>, <Operand1>|<#Immediate>
SUB <Dest>, <Operand1>, <Operand2>|<#Immediate>

Figure 30c. Thumb instructions that can access all ARM registers.

Stack Operators

The Thumb stack instructions are the most significant departure from the ARM instruction set, in fact opting to use the more traditional PUSH and POP mnemonics. We have seen these before as they are provided as pseudo-instructions by the GCC Compiler. In Thumb their action is similar so you should have little difficulties in getting to grips with them. However, there is a significant difference in that there is no stack pointer (SP) available to the instruction. This is because R13 is fixed as the Stack Pointer in Thumb operations and is automatically updated by the instructions. In other words, there is only one stack permissible in Thumb.

```
PUSH {R1-R4}          @ Push R1, R2, R3 & R4 onto stack
POP (R2-R3}           @ Pop top 2 items into R2 and R3
```

PUSH can include the LR in its list and POP can include the PC, otherwise registers are limited to R0-R7 inclusive. In the first instance the SP address is adjusted by four words; in the second by two words. In ARM terms PUSH performs:

```
STMDB SP!, <REGLIST>
```

and POP performs:

```
LDMIA SP!, <REGLIST>
```

Single and Multi-Register

The LDR and STR instructions are supported by Thumb but not all addressing modes are supported. In fact only three are available for use with these and other associated commands. Figure 30d lists these, which are based on the pre-indexed addressing concept, and supply offset by register or by an immediate operand.

Addressing Mode	Example
Load/Store Register	LDR R0, R1
Base + Offset	LDR R0, [R1, #5] LDR R0, [R1, R2]
Relative	LDR R0, [PC, #8]

Figure 30d Addressing mode samples in Thumb State.

Multi-register access is limited to the use of increment after addressing modes using LDMIA and STMIA instructions. Note also that the ! update operator is not an option as it is in ARM State - it is mandatory::

```
STMIA R1!, {R2, R3, R4}
```

Functions in Thumb

The example given in Program 30b illustrates how an ARM, or more exactly libc, function can be called from Thumb code. Effectively you have to go back to ARM State. There is nothing stopping you creating your own functions in Thumb code — in other words a function consisting entirely of Thumb code that runs exclusively in Thumb State. But when calling the function it must have the least significant bit of the pointer to it set. As the linker in the compiler cannot do this, you yourself must do it within your calling code, especially if you use an absolute address.

In other words when you call any standalone Thumb code from another section of Thumb code, the entry condition is exactly the same as if you were entering Thumb code from ARM State. You add one to the link address.

Interestingly, you can have two functions with the same name — one for ARM and one for Thumb. The linker allows this provided they operate within different instruction sets. However, this shouldn't be considered good practice and should generally be avoided.

31: System on a Chip

The square chip in the centre of the Raspberry Pi board is the one that this book has been all about. Everything we have been doing in the preceding pages has been taking place inside that square. Figure 31a below shows it in all its glory. In fact that bit of silicon is much more than just an ARM chip. It is actually a System On Chip device. Broadly speaking, a SoC is a microchip that has all the components required to drive a computer. In the case of the Raspberry Pi, the Broadcom BCM2835 chip contains a 700MHz ARM processor and a Videocore 4 Graphics Processing Unit.

Figure 31a. The Raspberry Pi with the SoC at its heart.

The technology is increasingly popular, and the packaging of numerous components onto a single integrated circuit (IC) means that the devices they are embedded into become ever smaller. If you have a close look at the Raspberry Pi board then you will see that much of the space is actually taken up by components that allow us to connect to it. The actual computer part probably occupies only about 10% of the printed circuit board!

Make no mistake, the SoC technology used on the Raspberry Pi is on the cutting edge, and you can expect to see it become prevalent in major advances in technology as the physical size of the SoC device continues to implode. Because of its great digital capabilities you might expect to see similar silicon devices restoring sight to the blind and providing sound for the deaf in the near future.

Another major advantage of the SoC design is the fact that it doesn't require a lot of power and it becomes very efficient because of the small distances that signals have to travel. Remember how much heat standard PCs throw out and where much of the space is given over to cooling?

There is a downside to SoC technology from the consumer point of view and a reason why those devices do not easily dominate the consumer and general market, and that is their lack of ability to be upgraded. Essentially you can't do this because everything is metaphorically glued into one place, so you can't readily add new memory or upgrade the core processor. When you are finished with the device, you effectively throw it away. So your Raspberry Pi will no doubt become out-dated but then you would have to simply replace it with the newer model. I am not sure if that makes the Raspberry Pi a disposable computer?

The ARM Chip & Instruction Sets

At the heart of the SoC on the Raspberry Pi is the ARM1176JZF-S core. SoCs are not limited to ARM chips but they are the processor of choice due to the use of RISC which offers power saving advantages. The ARM11 was launched in 2003 and is built around the ARMv6 architecture. The ARM chip itself has been around for over 30 years now and it has gone through continual development. The ARMv6 architecture in the Raspberry Pi isn't the latest release and neither will it be the last, but it does speak volumes for the design and original concept that today the ARM chip is at the centre of most things we use.

We have seen two of the instruction sets that ARMv6 provides on the Raspberry Pi, namely ARM and Thumb 1. There is actually a third instruction set called *Jazelle*. This is a combined hardware-software technology that provides a full-featured multi-tasking Java Virtual Machine (JVM) — Java being a sophisticated cross-platform application particularly useful for displaying graphics.

At the time of writing, Oracle (who produce Java) have released on their website a guide to getting started with Java SE Embedded on the Raspberry Pi which they say can be done in less than half an hour (although you will need access to a wired network and a host computer). A link to this site can be found on the book support website.

Incidentally, bit 24 of the CPSR is designated the J bit and when set places the chip into Jazelle State, allowing the running of A Java Virtual Machine through a combination of hardware and software technology. Java is an exciting development on the Raspberry Pi; this is an area that is sure to draw attention and one that could provide another unique platform for the credit card sized computer.

The ARM also includes a couple of other sub-instruction sets involved with media and digital signal processing and this is one of the reasons it is so popular in handheld devices.

Co-Processors

The ARM design allows for additional processing hardware to be connected to it. (Interestingly this was a unique design structure introduced by Acorn as early as 1983 with the launch of its Second Processor Tube interface which allowed additional CPUs to be literally bolted onto the side of the BBC Micro, and which would allow other processor dependent operating systems such as CP/M to be run. An ARM Second Processor unit was one of the last released for the BBC Micro!)

As these are designed to support the ARM they are called co-processors. Up to 16 can be connected and are numbered from 0-15. Instructions such as MCR and MRC can be used to communicate with them and many co-processors add their own instruction sets which are worth investigating.

We have already examined one co-processor in detail: The Vector Floating Point co-processor which provides real number management to the otherwise integer-orientated ARM chip. In fact the VFP occupies two slots, being CP10 and CP11 in the system. CP14 and CP15 are also reserved for system use, but the others are all free for use.

Pipeline

We examined the pipeline in Chapter 14. At that point we looked at the original generic three-stage process and hinted then that ARMv6 has an 8-stage operation. The eight stages are described in Figure 31b. During operation, dependent on the instruction being performed the pipeline will route one of three different ways to process stages 5, 6 and 7 and so will further maximise the instruction process prowess of the chip.

Stage	Name	Description
1	Fe1	This is first stage of the instruction fetch where the address is sent to memory and an instruction returned.
2	Fe2	Second stage of instruction fetch. The ARM will try to predict the destination of any branch at this point.
3	De	Decode instruction.
4	Iss	Read registers and issue instruction action.
5	Sh	Perform shift operations as required.
6	ALU	Perform integer operations
7	Sat	Saturate integer results
5	MAC1	First stage of the multiply-accumulate pipeline.
6	MAC2	Second stage of the multiply-accumulate pipeline.
7	MAC3	Third stage of the multiply-accumulate pipeline.
5	ADD	Address generation stage.
6	DC1	First stage of data cache access.
7	DC2	Second stage of data cache access.
8	WBi	Write back of data from the multiply or main execution pipelines (Load Store Unit).

Figure 31b. The eight-stage pipeline of the ARMv 11 includes sub-pipelines which can be banked in for maximum efficiency.

There are three blocks of operation that can be switched in at stages 5, 6 and 7 depending on the operation taking place. For example, if a multiply instruction is being processed then these stages are induced in place of the other parallel stages. This allows the ARM to deliver just about one instruction for each cycle.

The Fetch stages can hold up to four instructions, while the Execute, Memory, and Write stages can contain a predicted branch, an ALU or multiply instruction, a load/store multiple instruction and a coprocessor instruction in parallel execution.

It would be possible to increase the length of the pipeline but it is impractical to do so as it would increase power consumption and create heat. This would have a devastating effect on small systems such as the Raspberry Pi meaning bigger power supplies and more space between components and perhaps even aided cooling!

Memory & Caches

Depending on what model Raspberry Pi you have it will come with a certain amount of memory. This memory is part of the SoC and this sits on top of the ARM chip in an arrangement called 'package on package'.

The ARM also has a an area of very fast memory called a cache that it can use for its own purposes. These are for instruction and data storage and are respectively known as Icache and Dcache. They are both 16k in size and are collectively known as the L1 cache.

Incidentally these caches are controlled by the System control coprocessor (CP15), as is all memory, thus enabling the ARM to get on with processing instructions.

A second cache called L2 is also onboard. However this is used exclusively by the videocore.

The GPU

The Graphics Processing Unit is the other major component of the SoC configuration. It is a Broadcom VideoCore IV unit that provides 1080 high resolution graphics using a combination of Open software and hardware accelerated computing. Although information on this proprietary system has been thin on the ground, a number of groups have been working at supplying information through GitHub sites. So much so that example files in C can now be downloaded and bindings for other languages such as Python and Java exist.

In Summary

This has been a quick look at the technology that drives your Raspberry Pi, at the core of which is the ARM chip that this book has shown you how to program. It is by no means definitive but it does show that there are exciting new technologies still emerging on your Raspberry Pi that you can investigate and be at the cutting edge of exploring. Check out the book support website at www.brucesmith.info (follow the book link) to find links to many of the websites mentioned in this book and other pages that will be of interest.

Raspberry Pi
ASSEMBLY
LANGUAGE

Appendices

A: ASCII Character Set

Binary	Dec	Hex	ASC	Binary	Dec	Hex	ASC
010 0000	32	20	?	011 1111	63	3F	?
010 0001	33	21	!	100 0000	64	40	@
010 0010	34	22	"	100 0001	65	41	A
010 0011	35	23	#	100 0010	66	42	B
010 0100	36	24	$	100 0011	67	43	C
010 0101	37	25	%	100 0100	68	44	D
010 0110	38	26	&	100 0101	69	45	E
010 0111	39	27	'	100 0110	70	46	F
010 1000	40	28	(	100 0111	71	47	G
010 1001	41	29	)	100 1000	72	48	H
010 1010	42	2A	*	100 1001	73	49	I
010 1011	43	2B	+	100 1010	74	4A	J
010 1100	44	2C	,	100 1011	75	4B	K
010 1101	45	2D	-	100 1100	76	4C	L
010 1110	46	2E	.	100 1101	77	4D	M
010 1111	47	2F	/	100 1110	78	4E	N
011 0000	48	30	0	100 1111	79	4F	O
011 0001	49	31	1	101 0000	80	50	P
011 0010	50	32	2	101 0001	81	51	Q
011 0011	51	33	3	101 0010	82	52	R
011 0100	52	34	4	101 0011	83	53	S
011 0101	53	35	5	101 0100	84	54	T
011 0110	54	36	6	101 0101	85	55	U
011 0111	55	37	7	101 0110	86	56	V
011 1000	56	38	8	101 0111	87	57	W
011 1001	57	39	9	101 1000	88	58	X
011 1010	58	3A	:	101 1001	89	59	Y
011 1011	59	3B	;	101 1010	90	5A	Z
011 1100	60	3C	<	101 1011	91	5B	[
011 1101	61	3D	=	101 1100	92	5C	\
011 1110	62	3E	>	101 1101	93	5D	]

Binary	Dec	Hex	ASC		Binary	Dec	Hex	ASC
101 1110	94	5E	^		110 1111	111	6F	o
101 1111	95	5F	_		111 0000	112	70	p
110 0000	96	60	`		111 0001	113	71	q
110 0001	97	61	a		111 0010	114	72	r
110 0010	98	62	b		111 0011	115	73	s
110 0011	99	63	c		111 0100	116	74	t
110 0100	100	64	d		111 0101	117	75	u
110 0101	101	65	e		111 0110	118	76	v
110 0110	102	66	f		111 0111	119	77	w
110 0111	103	67	g		111 1000	120	78	x
110 1000	104	68	h		111 1001	121	79	y
110 1001	105	69	i		111 1010	122	7A	z
110 1010	106	6A	j		111 1011	123	7B	{
110 1011	107	6B	k		111 1100	124	7C		
110 1100	108	6C	l		111 1101	125	7D	}
110 1101	109	6D	m		111 1110	126	7F	.
110 1110	110	6E	n					

B: Support Information

Companion Website

A companion website exists in support of this book. Go to *www.brucesmith.info* and click on the book cover icon or select RPi Books from the menu to locate additional information and downloads for *Raspberry Pi Assembly Language: RISC OS Beginners*.

The support pages on the website include but are not limited to the following information:

- Source files for all programs in the book

- Additional sample files for you to try and experiment with

- Updates to programs and information in the book

- Errata data, corrections and clarifications

- Links to websites and additional downloads mentioned in the book and instruction reference cards detailing ARM, VFP and Thumb i

- Details of other Raspberry Pi Hands On Guides

Alan Turing Rocks

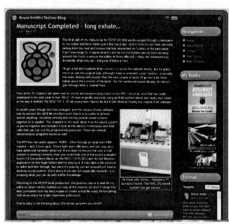

Bruce Smith's occasional blog about computers and technology also includes updates about the projects he is working on. He posts on Facebook and Twitter when he has added a new blog entry.

His blog is named after the *'person he would most liked to have met in the world.'* Alan Turing (23 June 1912 – 7 June 1954) was a British mathematician and cryptographer who is considered to be one of the fathers of modern computer science. He never described himself as a philosopher, but his 1950 paper "Computing Machinery and Intelligence" is one of the most frequently cited in modern philosophical literature. It gave a fresh approach to the traditional mind-body problem, by relating it to the mathematical concept of computability. His work can be regarded as the foundation of computer science and of the artificial intelligence program.

Hands On Guides

Current and forthcoming titles from BSB. Visit www.brucesmith.info for additional details and information about all Bruce Smith Books. Information is subject to change.

Raspberry Pi RISC OS System Programming Revealed

Learn how to get the most from RISC OS on the Raspberry Pi. This book takes the lid off the RISC OS operating system and reveals how to really use it.

Aimed at those wishing to learn how to program RISC OS directly but are struggling with the Programmers Reference Manuals (PRMs) or simply don't know where to start – this book will teach you everything you need to know to get the most from RISC OS and your Raspberry Pi.

Providing lucid descriptions, award winning author Bruce Smith keeps things simple and includes plenty of examples you can try for yourself. Ideas and concepts are introduced in the order required so you should never be left wondering. Just some of the many features include:

- Filing systems including SDFS and FAT32F2
- FileCore and FileSwitch Operation
- The CLI, *Commands and the SWI interface
- Communicating with RISC OS
- Writing and using Modules
- Vectors, Interrupts and Events
- The Window Manager (Desktop) and WIMP Utilities

- The Font Manager
- The Sound System
- SoundDMA and SoundControl
- Floating Point Model
- Programming the GPIO
- Book support pages on authors website.
- 320 pages

Note that the GPIO chapter and some of the information provided in the sections covering VFP and processor modes are duplicates of the information provided in this book.. More information on the website.

NEW: RETRO COMPUTER SERIES

Reviving 8-bit Classic publications for the 6502 for the computer systems that shaped a generation of programmers!

Mastering Interpreters & Compilers

Techniques for the BBC Model B, Master & Electron

RETRO COMPUTING CLASSIC

This clear and comprehensive introduction to compilers and interpreters emphasises the practical side of the art. It moves gradually from the idea of a 'wedge' in the BBC Computer's operating system, to a simple interpreter, a simple graphics language, threaded interpretive languages (including FORTH) and, finally, a stand-alone compiler. Listings of the implementations are given.

This book will give anyone with a good knowledge of assembly language the foundation on which to build an interpreter or compiler of their own."

The above description was taken from the back cover of the original BBC Soft publication, published as a BBC Master Guide in 1987. Now close to 30-years on Bruce Smith is republishing this classic guide in its original form complete with BBC BASIC listings.

Available late first quarter 2014. Further details will appear on the website at www.brucesmith.info nearer the time.

Index

!

*

32-bit

A

B

Want to learn more about RISC OS?
Then...get a copy of:
Raspberry Pi RISC OS System Programming Revealed

Learn how to get the most from RISC OS on the Raspberry Pi. This book takes the lid off the RISC OS operating system and reveals how to really use it.

- Filing systems including SDFS and FAT32F2
- FileCore and FileSwitch Operation
- The CLI, *Commands and the SWI interface
- Communicating with RISC OS
- Writing and using Modules
- The Font Manager
- The Sound System
- SoundDMA and SoundControl

- 320 pages jammed packed with information.

More details at www.bucesmith.info